MW01041650

Enterprise
E-Commerce

Other Books from the Authors

Programming Web Components
Reaz Hoque & Tarun Sharma
McGraw-Hill

The Blueprint for Business Objects
Peter Fingar
Cambridge University Press

Next Generation Computing:
Distributed Objects for Business
Peter Fingar, Dennis Read & Jim Stikeleather
Prentice Hall

The Climb from Chaos:
Reaching CMM Level 2 for E-Commerce
Steven Hagy, Peter Fingar & Michael Fuller
Meghan-Kiffer Press

Enterprise E-Commerce

The Software Component Breakthrough for Business-to-Business Commerce

Peter Fingar
Harsha Kumar
Tarun Sharma

MK Meghan-Kiffer Press Tampa, Florida, USA
Publishers of Advanced Technology Books for Competitive Advantage

Publisher's Cataloging-in-Publication Data

Fingar, Peter.
  Enterprise e-commerce : the software component breakthrough for business-to-business commerce /
Peter Fingar, Harsha Kumar, Tarun Sharma - 1st ed.
        p. cm.
  Includes bibliographic references, appendices and index.
  ISBN 0-929652-11-8 (cloth : alk. paper)

  1. Electronic commerce. 2. Strategic planning. 3. Reengineering (Management) 4. Management
information systems. 5. Information technology. 6. Internet (Computer network) 7. Object-Oriented
methods - Computer science. 8. World Wide Web (Information retrieval system) 9. Computer software -
Development. 10. CORBA (Computer architecture) 11. XML (Document markup language) 12. Information resources management. I. Fingar, Peter. II. Kumar, Harsha. III. Sharma, Tarun. IV. Title.

HF5548.32.F464 2000   99-75765
658.8'00285-dc21   CIP

Published by Meghan-Kiffer Press
310 E. Fern Street – Suite G
Tampa, FL 33604 USA

Any product mentioned in this book may be a trademark of its company.

Cover Art, *E-Commerce: People, Time, Money and Work,* by Lance Sperring.

Meghan-Kiffer books are available at special quantity discounts for corporate
education and training use, promotions and gifts. For more information write
Special Sales, Meghan-Kiffer Press, Suite G, 310 E. Fern Street, Tampa, Florida
33604 or email
mkpress@tampabay.rr.com

MK **Meghan-Kiffer Press** Tampa, Florida, USA
Publishers of Advanced Technology Books for Competitive Advantage

Printed in the United States of America.   SAN 249-7980
  MK Printing 10 9 8 7 6 5 4 3 2 1

Dedicated to the architects and builders
of the 21st century enterprise.

Notes

Table Of Contents

Chapter 1 - Prelude: The E-Commerce Imperative

Chapter 2 - E-Commerce: The Third Wave

Chapter 3 - E-Commerce Applications: I-Markets

Chapter 4 - E-Commerce Applications: Customer Care

Chapter 5 - E-Commerce Applications: Vendor Management Systems

Chapter 6 - E-Commerce Applications: Extended Supply Chain Management

Chapter 7 - Component-Based Development for E-Commerce

Chapter 8 - E-Commerce Business and Technology Strategies

List of Figures

List of Tables

Preface

The Internet is bringing profound change to the business world and has enabled a new way of conducting commerce – *e-Commerce*. To compete in the emerging digital economy, companies will need to change their business models, rethink the way they work and form new relationships with their trading partners and customers. Even though e-Commerce has just arrived on the business scene, this new business framework is changing rapidly. For some forward thinking companies the *third wave* of e-Commerce already has begun. These pioneering companies have come to realize that e-Commerce is neither just a buy-side nor sell-side package. They have learned that mission-critical business opportunities abound. To them, e-Commerce is an infrastructure for a whole new way of doing business and gaining competitive advantage in the Customer Age.

Enterprise E-Commerce takes head-on the challenges, issues and strategies for *enterprise-class* electronic commerce. In this book, we explore the business imperatives, technologies, applications, challenges and strategies of mission-critical, enterprise-class e-Commerce. At the enterprise-level, e-Commerce takes on some very challenging characteristics including scalability, reliability, extensibility, interoperability, adaptability and integration with heterogeneous legacy systems.

From working with the pioneers of e-Commerce on large-scale e-Commerce projects such as GE's TPN Register, GE Capital's Vendor Financial Services, MasterCard's E-Purchasing, Transamerica's Tradex Online and American Express' @Work, we have seen some common patterns and gained valuable insight through observing traits common to companies that have developed sustainable and flexible initiatives. In this book, we recap what we learned and summarize the critical business and technology factors of success.

The book contains in-depth discussions of both business and technology including concepts, jargon and strategy. Anyone can tell you that attempting to include both business and technology audiences for the same book is a big challenge. We, however, believe that e-Commerce is *inseparably* about both business and technology. So we took on the challenge (we now know just how difficult the task is) and hope that if you are a CEO, CIO, COO, CFO, CTO, line-of-business manager, project leader, application developer or shop floor manager you will gain the information and insight you need to think about, act upon and capitalize on the opportunity of e-Commerce. We have strived to provide the information you need to boldly move into your corporation's e-Commerce initiatives.

CEOs will find vocabulary, concepts and notions needed to formulate business strategy – what they need to be thinking about and doing now to prepare themselves and their companies for the digital era. The CIO will find the blend of business and technology discussions useful in developing technology strategy and aligning technology with business. The marketing executive will learn about the shape and nature of emerging digital marketplaces and how to formulate strategies to compete in them. The COO will find breakthrough opportunities to manage total operating resource costs through real-time connections with suppliers and value-chains. The CTO will be able to use the technology discussions to formulate architectural plans that can ensure the scalability, extensibility and reliability demanded of enterprise-class e-Commerce. The Internet generation of developers must command the language of both technology and business. Context is essential to component-based development, and this book provides the business context to which the technologies must be aligned. If you are either a business or technology professional reading this book, we hope you will find information you can use and profit from in your business.

The book does contain jargon from both the business and technology communities. Where either business or technical terms and buzzwords are used, they are not intended to impress or distract – they are there because they are an essential part of a thorough e-Commerce vocabulary. The terms in this book were carefully selected based on their relevance and frequency of use. Both business and technology specialists should understand, for example, the business buzzword, BPR. On the other hand, no business executive should be caught flat footed not knowing the significance, much less the word itself, when Java comes up in conversation. Neither business nor technology people are likely to be familiar with terms like reintermediation, digital non-repudiation and other tongue twisters, but they are included and explained because they are an essential part of e-Commerce vocabulary. Where technical terms are used, they are explained in everyday language, and most technical concepts are illustrated in the more than

70 illustrations presented throughout the book. We have chosen a depth of discussion and language that we hope will serve as a reference guide for managing enterprise-class e-Commerce. We hope you will keep the book on or near your desk to find the sustentative "right stuff" you need to gain competitive advantage, now and in the future.

For this book to reach out to both business and technology professionals, we adopted several writing goals:

- Make the content relevant to *both* business people and technologists.
- Be thorough: produce the best-researched book available on enterprise-class e-Commerce.
- Speak directly to the CIO and his or her immediate colleagues (CEOs, CFOs, CTOs, line-of-business managers and project teams).
- Write from the research, not from the ego or unfounded opinion.
- Respect the reader's limited reading time – business and technology practitioners have very little time to read.
- For each essential topic, make a strong business case as well as a technology case.
- Do not try to trivialize or oversell the content.
- Do not draw conclusions or make assertions that are unsupported.
- Take the reader from current business and technology practice to e-Commerce as an infrastructure for a whole new way of conducting business.
- Tell how to get there.

We'd like to suggest a couple of quick paths for those readers who may not have time to read the entire book in one sitting. The first two chapters offer a complete overview and should be read. Business executives (CEOs, COOs, CFOs and line-of-business managers) should then read one or two of the application chapters (3-6), and proceed to the business strategies and critical success factors of chapter 8. The quick read path for technology managers (CIOs, CTOs and project teams) includes the first two chapters, one or two of the application chapters (3-6), the component-based development overview of chapter 7 and the technology strategies and critical success factors of chapter 8. We hope you will have time to read the entire book and keep it handy for reference.

Over a year of research and preparation went into writing *Enterprise E-Commerce*. Along the way many people including our customers, partners, colleagues and fellow members of the Object Management Group, CommerceNet, WfMC, IEEE Computer Society and the Association of Computing Machinery (ACM) aided us. First, we would like to thank Faisal Hoque and Sathish Reddy for their entrepreneurship, guidance and the inspiration they provided us. For their feedback, fresh ideas and constructive criticisms we would like to give special thanks to our colleagues at EC Cubed: Ephrem Bartolomeos, Dr. Barbara Belon, Garth Bowlby (special thanks for the book layout and the amazing attention to detail), Terrence Curley, Bruce Dorfman, Nikolai Fetissov, Alex Henkin, Naushad Kapasi, Alex Karasulu, Vidyadhar Kareddy, Adel Khan, Andrey Kozhevnikov, Tharak Krishnamurthy, Srivatsa Manjunath, Jim McClafferty, Eric Miller (our OMG architectural representative, thanks for the brain-storming), Shridhar Rangarajan (co-chair of the OMG EC task force and architectural member of CommerceNet's catalog interoperability project), Beatrice Raggio, Pramod Waingankar, Venkat Rao Yadlapalli, Lance Sperring (special thanks for the late nights and "Lancification" of the artwork), Doug Swanson and Jim Upton.

Also helping to influence and shape this book in many ways were: Steven Hagy and Rahul Narain of Perot Systems, Pete Gallo and Demetrious Yannakopoulos of IBM, Jim Clarke of Sun Microsystems, Prof. Roy Young of the University of Tampa, Prof. Ben Shneiderman of the HCI Lab of the University of Maryland, Dr. Thomas Greene of the Lab for Computer Science at MIT, Dave Hollander co-chair of the W3C XML schema workgroup, Mark Ragel for his international perspective as CEO of Al-Gosaibi Information Systems (Mideast), Damien Miller of Kinetoscope, Stephen McConnell of OSM Sarl and Founding Chair of the OMG EC task force, Leslie Heeter Lundquist for her insight from her post of V.P. of Research at CommerceNet, Haim Kilov and his work on information modeling while at IBM's Watson Research Center, and long time mentor, James Odell. Some of the material in this book has been adapted from the recent research and works of Peter Fingar, including reports on Open e-Commerce and *A CEO's Guide to E-Commerce* published as CommerceNet Research Report #98-19 and at Software Engineering Australia; and Harsha Kumar's research conducted with Prof. Ben Shneiderman and published in the *International Journal of Human-Computer Studies*, Volume 46, No. 1, January, 1997.

E-commerce consultant and CPA, Don Blythe of Don Blythe *pc ca* contributed research and writing related to security and Web trust security assurance.

We invite you to read, enjoy and profit from these pages. We look forward to your thoughts and comments as we pursue our vision for the future in the new world of e-Commerce[1].

Peter Fingar
Harsha Kumar
Tarun Sharma
Wilton, Connecticut, Fall 1999

---

[1]The authors can be reached by email at mkpress@tampabay.rr.com by placing their names in the subject line.

Notes

Chapter 1 - Prelude:
The E-Commerce Imperative

Notes

Caveat Venditor

In January, 1999, @Home bought eXcite for $6.7 billion the same month that Ford bought Volvo automotive for $6.5 billion,[1] believe it or not. Meanwhile, Amazon.com's market cap reached $25 billion in December 1998, topping J.C. Penney and Kmart combined. What is actually going on here? Patricia B. Seybold proclaims, "It's the customer, stupid."[2]

Successful customer relationship management is *the* competitive advantage of the Information Age and is the bottom-line for market leadership. As marketing guru Regis McKenna explains, "It's about giving customers what they want, when, where, and how they want it."[3] The power shift from *producer* to *consumer* is well underway, made possible by the capability to use the Internet to learn about individual buying patterns to customize offerings that delight the customer. Customer information is the currency of success in the 21st century marketplace.

Although Amazon.com bills itself as "earth's biggest bookstore," its eyes are on the real prize, "earth's biggest customer database," a database containing not just customer names, addresses, balances and such. The critical information in Amazon.com's database is buying behavior encoded and stored as electronic bits. Amazon.com has already moved into selling music, videos, toys, games and electronics, but the company's potential breakout is its recently acquired Junglee and PlanetAll. "We want to be a leading destination for e-commerce where people can buy almost anything they want to buy on the Net," said spokesman Bill Curry, repeating a goal that Amazon CEO Jeff Bezos outlined when it acquired Junglee.[4] A new Junglee-enabled shopping experience on Amazon.com called *Shop the Web* is intended to be the place to find *anything* customers want to buy online. The new shopping "bot" would make it easy to find and compare products from a number of merchants all at once, turning Amazon.com into a *vortex* on the Web, an electronic market that brings together a fragmented group of buyers with an equally fragmented group of sellers. Of course, merchants may not want such comparison shopping, and it is too early to determine if the service will succeed. The experiment does, however, hint at the new business models emerging on the Web.

Selling products on the Web is not the company's only customer acquisition technique. Amazon.com's PlanetAll provides 1,500,000 members all they need to keep up with important personal and professional contacts. They make it simple, with a self-updating address book, a Web-enabled calendar and individual discussion groups that each member can create. Of course, when PlanetAll electronically reminds a member of a special occasion, any one of the 15 million items in the Junglee Shopping Guide just so happens to be a mouse-click away. Just as department stores aggregated goods for one stop convenience, Amazon.com's aggregation of buyers and sellers could make it "earth's biggest vortex," bringing together all buyers and all sellers of everything, everywhere!

The same kind of prize is the goal of the business-to-business market-space as well. Vertical.net has jumped ahead of the pack in establishing industrial communities-of-interest, and early entrants into the business procurement markets such as Ariba and Commerce One are changing their business models from selling procurement software to establishing multi-seller, multi-buyer procurement marketplaces similar to GE's Trading Process Network (TPN). Thus in both business-to-consumer and business-to-business markets, owning the customer, the whole customer, is the ultimate prize of 21st century business. Instead of owning the product and pushing it to market segments, Internet Age companies will seek to position themselves directly in the path of greatly empowered customers as they pull products and services from a multitude of suppliers to meet their individual needs. As control of markets and economies shifts from the producer to the consumer, the secret is to customize offerings, one customer at a time. Caveat Venditor – seller beware!

There is no magic in owning customers. The new marketing maxim is just give them what they want, when and where they want it. Capturing and analyzing information about buying behavior is the key. Knowing what the customer wants, however, is not enough. Buying processes are complex. Empowered by the Internet, customers demand and will tolerate nothing less than buying experiences that delight. Although the business concept of providing a full spectrum of individualized goods and services, one customer at a time, is simple, its implementation is not. Unless a company starts in a green field as did

Amazon.com, nothing less than business transformation is required. The transformation involves the three pillars of any business: technology, process and people. The initial step in transforming these fundamental assets is to gain a solid understanding of how the Internet changes everything by making it possible to do things that were never before possible.

Business transformation to the world of e-Commerce is not a single event – it is an ongoing journey. Strategy must recognize and navigate the many pitfalls and obstacles. As Tilburg University's Infolab points out, "Although e-Commerce aims at supporting the complete external business process, including the information stage (electronic marketing, networking), the negotiation stage (electronic markets), the fulfillment (order process, electronic payment), and the satisfaction stage (after sales support), currently, e-Commerce is hampered by:

- closed (self-contained) markets that cannot use each other's services
- incompatible frameworks that cannot interoperate or build upon each other
- a bewildering collection of security and payment protocols
- use of inadequate techniques to model business requirements and enterprise policies."[5]

Successful e-Commerce strategy charts a path for optimizing the business return *now* and stays the course as the world of e-Commerce evolves and matures. Strategy is about building bridges to open markets and optimizing value-chains for those markets. Successful e-Commerce strategy must be guided by a solid understanding of how the Internet changes the world of business.

How The Internet Changes Business

The railroad, the automobile and the Interstate highway system all changed the business landscape and the economy. Now, the Internet changes both "what we do," and "how we do it." What does the Internet allow a business to do that was never before possible? How does the Internet fundamentally change the landscape? The answer is simple, yet profound. The Internet enables *business ubiquity,* allowing a company to conduct business everywhere, all the time. E-Commerce eliminates the constraints of time and distance in operating a business.

Just as the computer itself demarcated the end of the Industrial Age and heralded in the Information Age, e-Commerce heralds a new age of ubiquitous business. It moves on from Sun Microsystems' slogan, *"The network is the computer™"* to *"The network is the business."* Not only can the Internet make company information available worldwide, it can distribute an enterprise's business rules and processes in real-time. All the information, business processes and control needed to transact business can flow friction-free anywhere, anytime to customers, suppliers and trading partners. E-Commerce enables a multitude of connections between customers, suppliers and trading partners: process-to-process connections between servers, browser-server connections and a growing number of network-savvy information appliances (e.g. cell phones, pagers, palm tops, WebTV, fax) – all the current and future business touch points. Technology such as Sun Microsystems' Jini™ will extend further the list of information appliances and devices that can plug-and-play on the Internet. Using the Jini "spontaneous networking" architecture, users will be able to plug any kind of device directly into a network and every other computer, device and user on the network will know that the new device has been added and is available.

Business ubiquity is an interesting phenomenon in and of itself, but of immediate interest here is how this phenomenon changes the way businesses operate and what they do. The following brief descriptions provide a glimpse into the major shifts occurring and the business imperatives inherent in these changes.

Power Shift to the Customer

Technology is not neutral. Disruptive technologies tend to cause shifts in power. Information is power. Authoritarian societies rely on one-way, hierarchical information flows where information flows down, from one-to-many. Democracies rely on matrixed forms of communication that provide many-to-many information flows. In the Industrial Age, information flowed one-way, from the producer to customers in a one-to-many fashion. In the Information Age the Internet provides the many-to-many connections among customers. The Internet turns the producer-consumer relationship upside-down with the balance of power going to the customer, enabling the Customer Age.

Enlightened companies are scrambling to shift from being product-centric to customer-centric. Industrial economies were build on the *mass production* business model. Companies built products and "pushed" those products using one-way communication (advertising and mass media) to markets. Enabled by the totally interactive medium of the Internet, consumers can now "pull" the information they want about products and reach out to all sources instantly. This information is power, and fulfills one of the tenets of pure competition, a totally informed consumer. "Fully informed" means access to information from other consumers as well as information in the supply channels.

E-Commerce is about reengineering end-to-end customer processes. Reengineering customer processes means eliminating costs, aggregating all the resources (not just products) needed for a complete solution, reducing time, and eliminating steps where possible. Producers of goods and services must build consumer communities-of-interest and provide full service consumer processes – or someone else will.

Reaching out to the ultimate consumer applies to business-to-business markets as well as business-to-consumer markets. A key dimension of business-to-business e-Commerce is that the consumer of a product is usually not the one who actually does the purchasing. Thus the customer is actually two entities: the one who requisitions, receives and often recommends, and the one who actually places the order, the purchasing agent. Selling strategies in business-to-business markets must take this structure into account. The seller must find ways to reach the ultimate consumer who most likely turns out to be the person who does the recommending. A purchasing agent may be a selling company's customer of record, but the focus of e-Commerce offerings must be targeted at the ultimate consumer, the requisitioner.

E-Commerce Imperative: The price of entry to the digital economy is the fundamental shift from being a product-centric to a customer-centric company. The company that engineers customer processes that delight will win the battles for 21st century markets.

Global Sales Channel

It is the *World Wide* Web. The Internet allows even the smallest of businesses to establish a global presence. The Net levels the playing field for the huge corporation and the sole proprietor alike. As a result, many specialty markets will appear for the first time as even the smallest of businesses now have the ability to reach geographically dispersed markets that would have otherwise been cost prohibitive to consider. Reaching global markets, however, can be a daunting task involving multiple languages, legal systems and business cultures.

On the reverse side of the coin, companies can expect new entrants into their local markets. These new entrants can appear from anywhere, at anytime. Market leaders must never rest as they compete in the global marketplace.

E-Commerce Imperative: The Internet diminishes the importance of geographic market territories because it allows anyone from anywhere to enter any market. Even though a company's current market may be local, regional, or national, strategic planning for e-Commerce must include the global potential and perspective, and consider new entrants into its current market territories.

Reduced Costs of Buying and Selling

Variable costs for online catalogs are near zero, whether a catalog is viewed by one potential customer or millions. Although designing and creating an online catalog can be as costly or even more so than a print catalog, printing and distribution costs are nil. Further, by automating the sales transaction, the high cost of labor can be significantly reduced. A direct sales force, call centers and mail order channels are manpower intensive and expensive. Direct selling online can be simple, "see-buy-get," as in the case of ordering a book with a credit card, or complex, "see-configure-negotiate-contract-fulfill-settle." In both cases, the cost of the sales transaction can be significantly reduced through online automation.

Physical inventories have always been a major cost component of business. If a merchant's business model requires maintaining inventories, the classic goal of "turn" can be dramatically enhanced by directly linking to suppliers. In his new book *Direct from Dell: Strategies That Revolutionized an Industry,* Michael Dell explains, "Inventory velocity has become a passion for us. In 1993, we had $2.9 billion in sales and $220 million in inventory. Four years later, we posted $12.3 billion in sales and had inventory of $233 million. We're now down to less than eight days of inventory and we're starting to measure it in hours instead of days."[6]

In the physical world, Wal-Mart set the example of just-in-time inventories by outsourcing inventory control directly to its major suppliers in real-time. On the Net, companies such as Amazon.com were started with zero or minimal inventories as wholesalers Baker and Taylor and Ingram drop shipped Amazon.com orders directly to the customer (This story, however, is not complete and continues under the Logistics and Physical Distribution section below).

E-Commerce Imperative: The Internet provides a target-rich environment for radically reducing the costs of buying and selling goods and services. A company must take advantage of these opportunities or find itself at a significant competitive disadvantage.

Converging Touch Points

The Internet is much more than the World Wide Web and a browser. For example, Internet protocols are being used to integrate telephony, and leading companies have already integrated their call centers into their e-Commerce offerings. New technologies such as Sun Microsystems' Jini™ promise to put every machine in touch with every machine, opening up a bewildering array of ways of making connections on the Internet.

With the advent of the "road warrior," a growing part of the workforce is mobile and using all sorts of marvelous gadgetry to stay in touch and to transact business. The continuous stream of innovation in electronic devices and gadgets will continue: the palm top, the lap top, the cell phone, the PDA, the fax, the pager, IP telephony, email, digital postal mail, kiosks, and so on. A mobile workforce demands mobile computing and access to e-Commerce resources regardless of the medium used to gain access.

These same touch points equate to new sources of customer information. Increasingly rich customer information, in turn, allows a company to analyze customer buying behavior and customize its offerings to individual customers.

E-Commerce Imperative: E-Commerce applications and systems must be available to all customer, supplier and trading partner touch points (including their computer systems), not just their Web browsers. Access must be made available to the mobile workforce and customers regardless of device or location of the user.

Always Open for Business

Doing business on the Net means never closing up shop. The open sign is displayed 7x24x365, no holidays. A Web site follows the sun, greeting markets as they arise each day in Tokyo, then Hong Kong, and later in Riyadh and Johannesburg, then London, New York and on to San Francisco. The good news is that a "digital sales staff" works around the clock without demanding overtime. The sobering news is that e-Commerce systems require availability and reliability that can be achieved only through much effort and investment. These are lessons learned from Net auctioneer, eBay, as reflected in CNET News.com[7] headlines:

- *eBay outage a one-two punch,* November 3, 1998
- *Auction site eBay hiccups again,* December 9, 1998
- *eBay suffers prolonged outage,* May 3, 1999
- *eBay recovers after outage,* May 21, 1999
- *eBay blacks out yet again,* June 13, 1999
  (the company's stock dropped 9.2% that day)
- *Outages plague eBay again*, June 29, 1999

The company said the outages cut 1999 revenues by $3 million to $5 million in the second quarter.

Not only must an e-Commerce system be technically reliable, it must also be dynamically scalable so that it can withstand the "stampedes" that are frequently associated with breaking news and product announcements. Even without a stampede, speed is important. In a report released in July, 1999, Zona Research reveals that "Slow download times at online shopping sites could place at risk as much as $4.35 billion in U.S. e-Commerce revenues each year. Analysts estimated that online shoppers would wait up to 8 seconds for a site to download. The sales risk crosses all types of sites. For example, an estimated $3 million may be lost monthly due to slow securities-trading sites."[8]

E-Commerce Imperative: The non-stop, mission-critical nature of e-Commerce demands non-stop systems and network assets. Redundancy, scalability and fail safe must be built into all components of e-Commerce systems and the platforms on which they run.

Reduced Time-to-Market

In some cases, lag time from product development to market availability can be reduced to zero. In fact, Microsoft and other software manufacturers reach their markets prior to complete product development. Customers use their products before they are actually released. Beta versions of software products are downloaded free by customers. The result is that the customer actually becomes involved in product development. Because people prefer what they already know, the customer gets hooked on the Beta version of a product, and it takes just one micro-step to convert Beta users to paying customers.

E-Commerce Imperative: Time-to-market is no longer a competitive advantage; it is a competitive necessity. Through collaborative product development and knowledge sharing, time-to-market can and must be successfully managed.

Enriched Buying Experience

Not only can a Web site offer a rich multimedia presentation of a product's attributes and qualities (test drive a new minivan from the comfort of home), but tools also can be made available to assist the customer in the buying process (e.g. calculating monthly payments or configuring a custom PC). In addition, Chat rooms and discussion groups can afford the opportunity for customers to share their product or service experiences with others. In this way, a potential buyer can learn from the experience of others who have been interested in, bought, and used a particular product or service. These interactive capabilities are especially useful for buying specialty goods where purchasing decisions have many dimensions and involve multi-step processes. By providing calculation, configuration and collaboration tools, a Web site can create communities-of-interest where consumers go first to become informed about purchasing decisions.

In business-to-business markets, product configurators, computer-aided design (CAD) systems, and collaborative problem-solving tools can bring dramatic productivity increases to the design, development, and procurement of complex products and services. Large-scale and complex projects can be transformed by sharing product specifications, bills-of-material and production schedules across many suppliers and trading partners in real-time. As bandwidth increases, the use of virtual reality technologies will no doubt be used to further enhance both consumer and business buying experiences.

E-Commerce Imperative: The Internet allows a company to greatly enhance the buying experience through value added services such as collaboration, building communities-of-interest, and multimedia renderings of complex product information. Providing an enhanced buying experience is essential to any e-Commerce strategy.

Customization

When a company interacts electronically with customers, buying behavior can be analyzed so that the company can customize its product and service offerings to the individual customer – this is the essence of the one-to-one marketing revolution. Customization provides value to customers by allowing them to find solutions that better fit their needs and by saving them time in searching for their solutions. Instead of presenting a huge catalog to a given customer to sift through, custom catalogs can be presented, one customer at a time. Not only can a solution be pinpointed for a customer, but also, the greater the relationship grows, the more a business knows about individual buying behavior. This rich customer information opens a multitude of cross-selling and up-selling opportunities – the essence of affinity marketing.

With the Net, the savvy marketer can sense and respond to customer needs in real-time, one-to-one. In addition to demographics, the electronic marketer can track *biographics*: the life passages and temporal and long-term interests of the individual. For example, buying one's first home is a life passage that will lead the marketer to target the consumer for a range of products and services from life insurance to home furnishings.

E-Commerce Imperative: Customization is a cornerstone for building a customer-centric company. The ability to deliver customized goods and services is the basis of the one-to-one marketing revolution and the shift from mass production to mass customization.

Self-Service

The Net can simultaneously cut the costs of customer service while increasing its quality. While customer service is the byword of marketing (what company doesn't give customer service lip service in its sales pitch?) the reality is often a frustrated user who must navigate call center menus that lead to intolerable on-holds or, finally, a human who abruptly tells the customer to call another number in another department. Automating customer service through a single enterprise access point (portal) can put the customer in control of navigating the company's service resources. With the integration of the telephone and the Net, the possibilities of making the company fully accessible increase further. While giving the customer greater control, labor costs can be slashed since the number of customer service representatives can be reduced as a result of outsourcing customer service to the customers themselves. Just as it is with gasoline stations today, an increasing number of customers will go to the self-service lane on the information highway.

E-Commerce Imperative: Self-service allows the customer to do for themselves, potentially yielding a result of greater satisfaction and reduced cost.

Reduced Barriers of Market Entry

Reduced cost of entry into electronic markets is both a benefit and a cause for concern. Just about anyone can enter a market or industry. New entrants can be successful if they can discover and deliver unique value to customers. But they had better not look over their shoulders as once their unique value proposition is discovered by their competitors, replication is sure to follow. A constant stream of innovation is required to sustain competitive advantage.

E-Commerce Imperative: A company cannot rest after introducing an innovative e-Commerce offering. Competitive replication is soon to follow, and the originator must raise the bar if it is to remain out front of its competition.

Demographics of the Internet User

Neilsen Media Research and other organizations research demographics on the Net providing information such as age, income, sex and geography. Early users of the Internet are categorized as young, male and educated. They have a median income about 50% higher than the general U.S. population. On the other hand, as the Net becomes mainstream and access becomes more universal with WebTV, Web enabled telephones and other information appliances, demographics and usage will become more normative. For example, when the Apple iMac was introduced in August 1998 it was snapped up by first time computer users who perceived the device as so simple that they too could join the Information Age.

Understanding shifting demographics is important in electronic marketing since the overall size of electronic retailing has not even come close to critical mass when compared to the total consumer market. Niche companies may enter the market now to ride the tide when it comes in, but they should not expect to make money on the Web the day they open for business. Build it and *maybe* they will come. Because the Net is by no means mainstream in consumer markets, hanging out a retail shingle certainly does not mean they will come. The benefits offered by e-Commerce do not simply accrue by establishing a Web site.

Demographics go hand in hand with bandwidth. The business user of the Internet likely has a high speed connection to the Net. This is not so with the individual consumer. "Bandwidth demographics" will be important until high bandwidth becomes pervasive. Consumer-oriented e-Commerce must be designed to reach the 28.8 modem users who will simply go elsewhere if they have to wait for large multimedia files or Java applets to be downloaded. Keeping it simple and snappy is essential while still using graphic tools to maintain interest. Users should be offered a choice between low and high resolution graphics, or in some cases, text only. In the low bandwidth era of the Net, email will continue to be an important communication tool.

E-Commerce Imperative: Demographics will continue to be very important in business-to-consumer e-Commerce markets. Demographics are changing on the Internet, and smart companies track them closely.

Power Shift to Communities-of-Interest

In the electronic marketplace, marketing push is replaced with customer pull. Electronic communities have been a reality on the Internet since its inception. These are places where people having common interest go to share ideas, information and opinions. Such pools of common interest are powerful agents of change in the marketing equation. The power and influence of these "consumer unions" can be compared to the labor unions that balanced the power of the industrial moguls. In the Industrial Age, industries were largely shaped by the production process. In the Information Age, industries are being shaped by the consumption process. Existing channels of distribution are giving way to global communities-of-interest that eliminate channel components that they do not perceive as adding value. For example, American Airlines' Travelocity was originally designed so that travel agents would still add value by being the means of delivering the ticket. Consumers who represent the travel community perceived little value in this arrangement, and the travel agent was disintermediated from the consumption process.

Nets Inc.'s Industry.net pioneered an electronic marketplace and community-of-interest for industrial goods and manufacturing materials. It is a technical information community enabling one-to-one marketing of industrial products and services. Industry.net offers a wide variety of free and paid editorial and technical information used for specification and sourcing by design and maintenance engineers and procurement professionals around the world. Nets Inc. attracted investments from the likes of Bill Gates and was run by Jim Manzi, founder of Lotus Development Corporation. In 1996 it was recognized by PC Magazine as one of the 100 most important sites on the Web. It had all the right stuff, providing product news and information as well as online industrial catalogs.

At 4:13 p.m., May 9, 1997, Nets Inc. petitioned for Chapter 11 court protection. The company had died. Manzi filed claims for $1.6 million against the company, and hundreds of employees were out of work. Yes, there is a reincarnated Industry.net today. Assets of Nets Inc. were sold to Perot Systems in July 1997 for $9 million after Perot hired 60 former Nets employees. In August that year, Nets creditors sued Manzi, claiming his loans were improperly accorded preferential status for payout. The saga continues. On November 3, Information Handling Services Group Inc., an information database publishing group, acquired Industry.net from Perot Systems who continues to host and develop the Web site under a service contract.

There are many stories about the rise, fall and resurrection of Industry.net. One view is that it was too early, too broad and too shallow. If these observations are correct, VerticalNet, a rising star of business-to-business communities seems to have been a little more lucky with a 1999 market capitalization around $2 billion. The moral of this story for those who would establish communities-of-interest is, "welcome to the *Wild Wild Web*." As rough and tumble as they may be as a business venture, communities-of-interest are the cornerstone of the Customer Age.

E-Commerce Imperative: Communities-of-interest are where customers go first to discover and explore solutions. Successful e-Commerce initiatives require building or directly participating in communities-of-interest.

Cybermediation

Although e-Commerce can eliminate the middleman found in many physical value-chains, customers in both business and consumer markets want complete solutions. For example, buying a home requires many ancillary resources (e.g. a mortgage, title and property insurance and appraisals). By aggregating many and diverse resources around a complete solution, cybermediaries can provide compelling value. Companies wanting to succeed as cybermediaries must change their thinking from the products and services they now provide, and focus on the bundles of solutions their customers need to fulfill their requirements – a plane ticket is not a vacation.

Cybermediation is critical in business-to-business markets. With the diversity of industrial and business goods and services, searching for the right vendor with the right product specifications can be a daunting task. The intermediary that can bring together diverse suppliers and customers and provide them with information unavailable elsewhere will win the game of reintermediation on the Net. GE's TPN Register is an early pioneer in this marketspace and, like its competitors, must keep running hard to stay ahead of the game of adding compelling value and growing business-to-business communities.

E-Commerce Imperative: The middleman is dead, long live the middleman. Middlemen are not dead in cyberspace. Instead, they are reincarnated as the ones who can add value through providing information and aggregating services not previously available. Cybermediaries can aggregate value for buyers and sellers. Traditional wholesalers and brokers pursuing e-Commerce strategies should look for ways to aggregate value, from building an industry portal to participating in open markets.

Logistics and Physical Distribution

Except for products and services that are purely digital (e.g. software, information and music), the other side of the e-Commerce coin is physical distribution. Dennis Jones, V.P. and CIO of FedEx explains, "What often gets lost in discussions about Internet commerce and the digital economy is the physical aspect of doing business. The Internet has engendered a feeling that anyone can start up a Web site to sell widgets, and instantly they're worldwide marketers. To succeed in Internet commerce, we believe a company has to be as effective in the physical world as they are in the electronic arena. The ability to move information around the world at the speed of light is a great enabler of commerce, but it breeds a corresponding need for the physical goods. The information network needs a physical network."[9] Thus the role of the logistics intermediary does not go away, it morphs into the emerging channels of super-distribution that form the *new logistics*.

We have witnessed the opening volleys in a war for owning the total customer relationship through excellence in logistics. The war is all about time. FedEx invented express distribution 25 years ago based on the value proposition of airplanes rather than ships or trains when the time-value of an item is significant in proportion to the overall value of the item. *Time-value* is an essential variable in modern economics and is a critical component of customer service.

Amazon.com Inc., citing the nature of the book business and a belief that customers are better served by the warehouse model, has opened an increasing number of warehouse facilities. "We want to own the whole customer relationship, and part of that is distribution," says Amazon.com spokesman Bill Curry.[10] When Barnes and Noble announced its intention to acquire book wholesaler, the Ingram Book

Group, for $600 million,[11] it certainly must have heightened
Amazon.com's appreciation for wholesalers and the physical distribution channel.

The role of the warehouse itself has changed from being a holding
bin to an assembly plant. Computer distributors such as Tech Data
assemble computers from standard parts to "manufacture" *custom*-IBM,
Apple or Compaq systems in their warehouses. Considering that auto-
mobiles are not "manufactured," but instead "assembled" by their
brand custodians (Ford, GM and DaimlerChrysler), warehouses
become what the *New York Times* calls the "factory of the future."[12] Will
FedEx's "flying warehouses" become flying assembly plants as time continues to be squeezed out of the customer-driven supply chain?

Will Amazon.com stop at regional warehouses, or will they get into
the physical distribution business as well? Will we one day see
Amazon.com trucks driven by Amazon.com employees rushing all
about our city streets delivering books, music and all the millions of
custom goods one can order through their *Shop The Web* service? Will
they even stop at this point, or become book publishers? FedEx may
have other ideas in the battles for the total customer relationship. When
FedEx set up its VirtualOrder™ system in 1997, the logistics company
tiptoed into retailing by hosting their customers' sites, putting FedEx in
between their customers' customers and their suppliers' suppliers. With
all the mega-mergers we have seen in recent years, will we ultimately
see a takeover of FedEx by Amazon.com, or visa versa? It is a battle to
own the total customer relationship through owning the total value-
chain, including logistics and physical distribution. Let the games
begin.

*E-Commerce Imperative: Successful e-Commerce planning must
account for both information and logistics strategies. Physical
distribution is an essential variable in the e-Commerce equation.*

Branding: Loyalty and Acceptance Still Have to be Earned

Branding is dead, long live cyberbranding. Consumers turn to brand
names and pay a premium because of trust. When shopping for a book
on the Internet, cost may be the foremost criterion, but if the best price
is offered by Joe's Book Bin, the consumer may hesitate before entering

a credit card number. Although Joe's Book Bin may use the same secure credit card server as Borders, the consumer may take the price hit to go with a trusted brand name.

The rush in many industries to be first on the Net has a lot to do with establishing a brand name on the Net. But a first-to-market site had better be the most convenient, cost-effective, informative, simple, secure and reliable resource available. These are the ingredients of building loyalty and ultimate trust that result in successful branding. Word travels instantly through electronic communities and reputations can be made or destroyed with the click of a mouse. Without strong branding, a given company will likely be reduced to a commodity provider, competing with ever shrinking price points and margins.

E-Commerce Imperative: Branding on the Net is as essential as branding in the traditional business world. Companies must have an aggressive branding strategy as part of an overall e-Commerce strategy or be reduced to a commodity player. Quality and reliability continue to be critical factors in creating brand awareness.

When Most Markets Behave Like the Stock Market

Fixed pricing is relatively new. When time is eliminated in the supply and demand equation, pricing dynamics change radically. Whether dealing in commodities or premium brands (in either business-to-consumer or business-to-business marketspaces) pricing policy, a core part of business strategy, must adapt to the reality of Internet market mechanisms which are becoming increasingly real-time and global. Coca Cola is already testing a vending machine that sets the price of a can of Coke based on the weather – customers must pay more on a hot, dry day. The fully interactive nature of the Net is moving markets closer to the "perfect information" requirement of pure competition. Ultimately, the result will be the death of fixed pricing. Pricing, however, will not be the only component of the buying decision. Availability, perceived quality, and service still count, but dynamic pricing strategies are vital to successful marketing plans.

E-Commerce Imperative: Whether dealing with a premium brand or commodity, pricing policy, a major component of overall business strategy, must be increasingly dynamic as a result of the market mechanisms of global e-Commerce.

Auctions Everywhere

Following on the notion of the death of fixed pricing, the interactivity of the Internet has led to the growing use of auctions in both business-to-consumer and business-to-business markets. Whether it is selling antiques to consumers or putting surplus inventory on sale, auctions are becoming commonplace in the digital economy.

Generally, auctions are segmented into four major one-sided formats: English, Dutch, first-price sealed-bid, and uniform second-price (Vickrey). In one-sided auctions, only bids are permitted, but not "asks." A double auction is not one-sided because bids and asks take place at the same time (bid/ask trading). The English auction, known also as the open-outcry auction or the ascending-price auction, is the format most familiar to Americans. Here the seller announces reserve price or some low opening bid. Bidding increases progressively until demand falls. The winning bidder pays highest valuation. The bidder may re-assess evaluation during the auction. The item is sold to the highest bidder unless the reserve price is not met, in which case the item may not be sold. Often, the reserve price is not revealed to thwart rings who have banded together and agreed not to outbid each other, thus effectively lowering the winning bid. Competition and enthusiasm is at its highest in the English auction where inexperienced participants sometimes end up paying more for an item than its value – the "winner's curse."

The descending-price auction, commonly known as the Dutch auction, uses an open format wherein the seller announces a very high opening bid. The bid is lowered progressively until demand rises to match supply. When multiple units are auctioned, normally more takers press the button as price declines. In other words, the first winner takes his prize and pays his price and later winners pay less. When the goods are exhausted, the bidding is over. In the Dutch system, a seller tends to receive maximum value since the bidder with the highest interest cannot afford to wait too long to enter his bid.

The third auction type, known as the first-price, sealed bid or discriminatory auction, is common when multiple items are being auctioned. This type of auction has a bidding period in which participants submit one sealed bid in ignorance of all other bids. At the resolution phase bids are opened and the winner, who pays exactly the amount he bid, is determined. Usually, each participant is allowed one bid, which means that bid preparation is especially important. When multiple units are being auctioned, sealed bids are sorted from high to low, and items awarded at highest bid price until the supply is exhausted. The winning bidders can, and usually do, pay different prices.

In the uniform second-price auction, commonly called the Vickrey auction, the bids are sealed, and each bidder is ignorant of other bids. The item is awarded to highest bidder at a price equal to the highest unsuccessful bid. When auctioning multiple units, all winning bidders pay for the items at the same highest losing price. The price that the winning bidder pays is determined by competitors' bids alone and does not depend upon any action the bidder undertakes. Less bid shading occurs because people do not fear winner's curse. Bidders are less inclined to compare notes before an auction.

Online business-to-business auctions are expected to top $7.3 billion in 1999, according to a report released by Forrester Research. They will be a significant portion of all revenue spent in online auctions, which is expected to approach $52.6 billion by 2002. Companies that sell enterprise-capable auction software are focusing on the computer and semiconductor industries because their fast-moving product cycles often cause inventory management problems. The auction market is also touching commodity industries like oil and gas.

For buyers, auctions offer a wide range of goods at competitive prices and low transaction costs. Sellers liquidate surplus goods or use the auction to help set prices on first-run goods. Some companies have turned to customized solutions that account for particular inventory-management needs. Media Auction lets advertisers take advantage of last-minute deals and bargains as they bid for unsold media time on networks and stations around the country. In building an auction site that emulates conventional business practices, a marketer has to be prepared to do a high degree of analysis. Allowing buyers to access lists of available advertising slots – a task that previously required dozens of phone calls – cuts administrative costs considerably. Auctions could end up cutting out the middleman in some types of transactions, and fixed pricing will most likely fade in the digital economy.

E-Commerce Imperative: Even though auctions may not have played a significant role in most industries, auctions now become important due to the interactive nature of the Internet. Auctions should be considered as part of most e-Commerce strategy planning efforts.

Hyper-efficiency

Over the last decade, business process reengineering (BPR) led to new levels of internal efficiencies in Global 2000 corporations. Around the globe, companies networked their internal computers to eliminate duplicate business processes and paper handling. Today, the Internet opens a whole new realm of possibilities for streamlining business processes that cross company boundaries, taking reengineering to new levels. By interconnecting companies with their suppliers and trading partners, inefficiencies can be eliminated in supply chains and total operating costs can be dramatically reduced. Pioneers are creating hyper-efficient supply chains and hyper-efficient companies. They have gone beyond physical supply chains and are using Dave Hollander's notions of "value-chains of information."

E-Commerce Imperative: Companies must take their reengineering efforts to the next level by encompassing what is external as well as their internal operations. They must extend their supply chain management systems and optimize their operating resources using the Net. Competing against hyper-efficient companies and supply chains enabled by the Internet will become increasingly difficult.

The E-Commerce Conclusion

Although we could add to the list of e-Commerce imperatives, the ones we have discussed provide a "look and feel" for the emerging digital economy. These imperatives provide a framework for developing business strategy and should be central to senior management thinking as they prepare their companies for the road ahead. E-Commerce provides a completely new infrastructure for a whole new way of conducting business and competing in the digital economy. Radical new business models and new rules of competition make e-Commerce *the* business imperative of the 21st century.

References

[1] http://cnnfn.com/hotstories/deals/9901/28/deals_wrapup

[2] Patricia B. Seybold and Ronni T. Marshak (Contributor). *Customers.Com: How to Create a Profitable Business Strategy for the Internet and Beyond,* Times Books, 1998.

[3] McKenna, Regis, *Real Time.* Harvard Business School Press, 1997.

[4] http://www.news.com/News/Item/0,4,29589,00.html

[5] http://infolab.kub.nl/general/e-commerce.php3

[6] Michael Dell and Catherine Fredman (Contributor), *Direct from Dell: Strategies That Revolutionized an Industry,* HarperBusiness, 1999.

[7] Scott Ard and Tim Clark, *eBay blacks out yet again,* CNET News.com, June 13, 1999, 11:00 a.m. PT

[8] David Lake, Slow sites cost vendors billions, CNN Interactive, July 9, 1999, from The Industry Standard, http://www.cnn.com/TECH/computing/9907/06/slowsite.ent.idg/

[9] Dennis H. Jones, "The New Logistics," in *Blueprint to the Digital Economy*, McGraw Hill, 1998.

[10] John Dodge, "Forget About Disintermediation: Meet the New Super Middlemen" The Wall Street Journal Interactive Edition, February 9, 1999.

[11] According to the firm's June 2, 1999 press release, protracted litigation related to its application before the Federal Trade Commission (FTC) was cited as the reason for stopping the deal.

[12] Saul Hansell, "Is This the Factory of the Future?" *New York Times,* July 26, 1998. http://www.muhlenberg.edu/depts/abe/business/miller/proddat/tjy25ops.htm

Notes

Chapter 2 - E-Commerce: The Third Wave

Notes

In July, 1997, the White House released a document declaring a revolution, "… a revolution that is just as profound as the change in the economy that came with the Industrial Revolution."[1]

Understanding E-Commerce

The link between technology and business innovation goes back to the very beginning – it was a technology breakthrough that enabled trade and gave birth to commerce. The development of keeled hull ships by the Phoenicians in 2000 BC made it possible to sail against the winds and go beyond the shores to the high seas of the Mediterranean. By doing something never before possible, the Phoenicians broke the bonds of geography and developed a flourishing trade with other peoples. Today, the Internet has broken the bonds of both time and distance and set the stage for profound, global change. Some business observers have given the event little notice, thinking that doing business on the Internet is simply a fad and will fade – after all, who is actually making money selling their wares on the Web? Furthermore, what fool would open up their business systems to the world, especially considering the perceived lack of security of the Internet?

The signs of technology-enabled transformation are not always clear at first. The British parliament scoffed at the invention of the telephone since the Britons already had enough messengers. In the 1940s, Thomas Watson, Chairman of IBM, turned down the offer to buy the patent rights to the electronic digital computer with his prediction, "I think there is a world market for maybe five computers." So much for predicting markets and business impact when disruptive technology first appears. Although the Internet enables a new era of commerce, electronic commerce, the signs of a business revolution are shrouded with the mist and fog of dawn. Some businesses have already recognized the start of a new era of business, the digital era, and have taken decisive action to change their business models. Competing against these transformed companies will become increasingly difficult, and those who wait for the full light of day before they act will find themselves at a distinct disadvantage.

According to the Association for Electronic Commerce, a simple definition of e-Commerce is "doing business electronically."[2] Sound fuzzy and ill-defined? It is. According to this definition, using the telephone to conduct business is e-Commerce. In large corporations e-Commerce is often equated to electronic data interchange (EDI) where structured messages representing standard business forms are exchanged over private networks. Perhaps the most common context in which the term is used as of the writing of this book relates to the use of the Internet and more specifically the World Wide Web as the infrastructure for conducting commerce.

In everyday usage the terms Internet commerce or I-commerce, Web-commerce and e-business are often interchanged with e-Commerce, sometimes leading to academic arguments. In his article, "E-commerce? E-business? Who E-cares?" Walid Mougayar, the founding chairman of CommerceNet Canada explains, "In a nasty little intramural squabble, some analysts and online businesspeople have decided that E-business is infinitely superior as a moniker to E-commerce. That's misleading and distracts us from the business goals at hand. The effort to separate the E-commerce and E-business concepts appears to have been driven by marketing motives [circa 1996] and is dreadfully thin in substance. Here's the important thing: E-commerce, E-business or whatever else you may want to call it is a means to an end. The objectives, as with IT, are to improve or exploit unique business propositions – with the focus now being the online world. Worrying about the definitions of those words, or about which is superior to the other, or about which is a subset of the other, is a silly little inside-the-beltway argument."[3]

So, depending on who is asked, e-Commerce will have a wide variety of definitions and even differing names. This is not bad since vague definitions and various names help to keep our thinking open.

To better capture the spirit of e-Commerce, we can turn to the definition proffered by the industry consortium, CommerceNet, "e-Commerce is the use of inter-networked computers to create and transform business relationships."[4] CommerceNet elaborates, "It is most commonly associated with buying and selling information, products, and services via the Internet, but it is also used to transfer and share information within organizations through intranets to improve decision-making and eliminate duplication of effort. The new paradigm of e-Commerce is built not just on transactions but on building, sustaining and improving relationships, both existing and potential." Figure 2 - 1 provides a structural context for our e-Commerce definition.

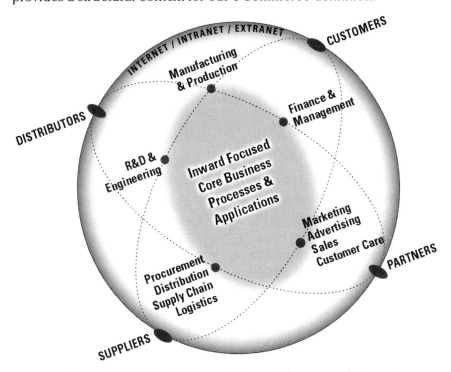

Figure 2 - 1. Extending Inward-Focused Processes Outward

E-Commerce is an infrastructure for extending a company's inward-focused, unique business processes to customers, trade partners, suppliers and distributors with new, outward-facing applications. These new applications are greater than the sum of a company's internal computer applications added to the applications of its partners. The interconnections make it possible to do things in ways not previously possible by eliminating time and distance. Opportunities and challenges permeate the enterprise affecting R&D, engineering, manufacturing and production, supply chains, marketing, sales, and customer care. Because it reaches directly into these core business processes that are the lifeblood of the enterprise, e-Commerce is a mission-critical business issue. From this perspective it becomes clear that e-Commerce is not something a corporation can just go out and buy.

Neither is it based on speculation, but rather on the experience of a handful of companies who already are using it to streamline their business processes, procure materials, sell their products, automate customer service and create new wealth. Electronic commerce is turning industries upside down and forcing enterprises to refocus their information systems from the inside out.

E-Commerce: The Third Wave

In its first wave, e-Commerce was little more than "brochureware." The Web has created a global repository for documents and other forms of multimedia. Everyone can be a publisher of information with as little as an HTML-enabled word processor, a free file transfer program, and a $19 a month account with an Internet service provider (ISP). Product and service information can be displayed easily and accessed anywhere, anytime, giving the smallest of businesses a "Web presence." Forrester Research reported that by the end of 1996 about 80% of Fortune 500 companies had established a Web presence compared to 34% in 1995.[5]

The second wave of e-Commerce is well under way, giving companies the capability to handle transactions electronically. Perceived and real obstacles had to be overcome before electronic transactions became a widespread means of buying and selling on the Internet. According to this same Forrester report mentioned above, only 5% of the Fortune 500 companies with a Web presence handled transactions on the Web in 1996. The major barriers included security on the Internet, lack of accepted standards for authentication and payments, nonrepudiation, and general fear and uncertainty by consumers. Fortunately, several standards and commercial offerings for handling transactions have appeared including SET for credit cards, Open Buying on the Internet (OBI), CyberCash and InternetBill. Attracted by the dramatic cost savings of electronic transactions and the opportunity to exploit new revenue channels, companies have purchased stand-alone procurement packages to streamline purchasing and stand-alone storefront packages to begin selling on the Web.

Most commercially available e-Commerce packages focus on either the buyer model or the seller model of doing business. As a result, e-Commerce applications are usually labeled as either "buy-side" or "sell-side," depending on whether the company hosting the application is buying or selling products or services. A third business model, the broker model, combines buy and sell-side functionality into one site and aggregates both buyers and sellers. These cybermediaries add value for the buyer by reducing the search space for appropriate suppliers, and for the seller by being found more easily by potential customers.

E-Commerce applications are further categorized by the markets they serve, business-to-business or business-to-consumer. The difference is largely that of buying behavior: shopping versus procurement. Consumers do a lot of browsing and price shopping, they are subject to the influence of advertising and merchandising, and many are prone to impulse buying. Purchasing agents, on the other hand, are time constrained to get their tasks done, cannot be distracted with glitzy advertising, do not buy on impulse, and generally order from catalogs where prices have been prenegotiated.

As shown in Figure 2 - 2, e-Commerce applications fall into four major categories: *Vendor Management, Extended Value/Supply Chain, I-Market* and *Customer Care.* In the *vendor management* category, maintenance, repair and operations (MRO) procurement is the most common business-to-business e-Commerce application. MRO procurement is used to reduce costs in the purchasing of office supplies and other non-production materials needed by a business. As an example in the procurement category, GE bought $1 billion worth of supplies through its Trading Process Network (TPN) in 1997 and expects to be procuring over $5 billion over the Internet by 2000. Meanwhile, in the extended *value/supply chain* category, GE Aircraft Engines used its integrated logistics solution to reduce order cycle time by 15 to 30 days and reduced the cost of creating a purchase order from $100 to $5. To be successful, buy-side initiatives will have to deliver such breakthrough efficiencies and achieve dramatic cost reductions. Catalog sales such as Amazon.com's now famous book and music selling site is an example of an *I-Market.* McKesson, a $17 billion pharmaceutical wholesaler, has developed such a comprehensive customer relationship management system on the Web that it has transformed itself from a drug distribution company to a value-added provider in the healthcare industry. In-depth discussions of each of the four categories are available in chapters 3-6.

To be successful, sell-side initiatives have to focus on revenue growth opportunities, holistic customer relationship management, engineering consumer processes that delight the user, and building communities-of-interest. In addition, sell-side initiatives may need to cater to both business-to-business and business-to-consumer markets simultaneously. For example, Office Depot sells to large corporate accounts meeting their procurement needs with prearranged terms and custom catalogs while reaching the retail consumer market as well as those in-between, the small office, home office (SOHO) market-space. Designing their e-Commerce systems specifically for the unique requirements of each of these subtly different customers is absolutely essential for Office Depot.

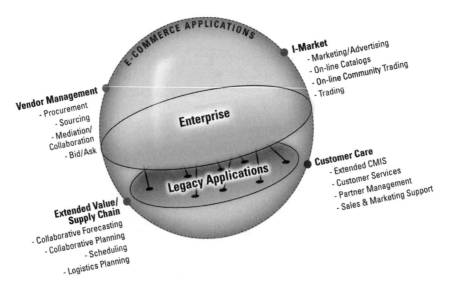

Figure 2 - 2. E-Commerce Application Categories

Most companies, of course, engage in both roles of buyer and seller, sometimes simultaneously in a single commerce transaction. Thus extending a company's existing business processes from the inside out must begin with a thorough analysis and understanding of customers', suppliers' and trading partners' requirements, and designing e-Commerce systems from the outside in.

Whether developing e-Commerce applications in-house or pursuing the package route, a holistic view of e-Commerce initiatives is needed in order to avoid the many pitfalls that result from taking separate and isolated views. Some large corporations already have identified more than 70 e-Commerce initiatives, not just the two buying and selling thrusts. If various lines of business in these large enterprises rushed out to buy their individual point solutions, the compromises of packaged software would be revealed quickly. Trying to realize each of these initiatives individually would mean attempting to tie together and maintain a multitude of business processes and islands of data in the enterprise's new and existing systems. Rather than weaving a tapestry, multiple stand-alone initiatives would tie their systems and their company in knots as illustrated in Figure 2 - 3.

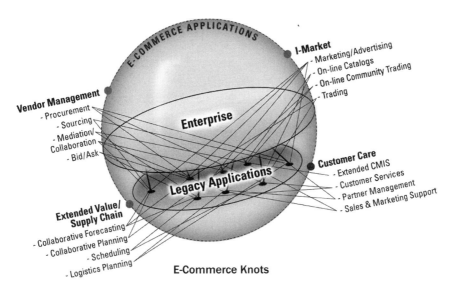

Figure 2 - 3. Without Integration, E-Commerce Could Tie a Company in Knots

Companies experienced with multiple e-Commerce applications have learned that they need a unified, incremental approach capable of supporting and sustaining multiple and continuously evolving e-Commerce initiatives – they need strategies for e-Commerce integration.

Global 2000 companies have a tremendous asset base in their existing computer systems. These systems embody their unique business philosophy, policies, and processes. Smart companies will seek to adapt, not to obliterate, their legacy applications as they embrace e-Commerce initiatives. Much of the functionality needed to implement multiple and diverse e-Commerce applications is identical or similar and thus can be reused – a key to e-Commerce integration. Core e-Commerce functionality includes user authentication and authorization, user profile management, workflow management, event notification, negotiation and collaboration, and data integration with enterprise data. These core e-Commerce components are illustrated in Figure 2 - 4. E-Commerce integration is the key to sustainable business strategy.

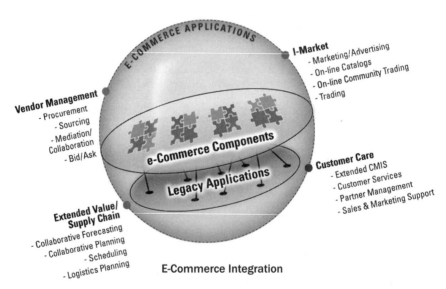

Figure 2 - 4. Untying E-Commerce Knots with Core E-Commerce Components

Figure 2 - 5 summarizes the three waves of e-Commerce. The first wave was about HTML and brochureware. The second wave is about transactions using home grown or packaged software as point solutions for procurement and online catalog selling. Gabriel Gross, President of Centre Internet Europeen, summarizes the current state of electronic commerce applications as "mainly limited to two functionalities: cataloging on one side and payment facilities on the other side. The [current] electronic commerce world is in practice a lot less sophisticated than real world commerce where several levels of interaction can take place between a potential client and vendor, and several levels of intermediaries can act or interfere."[6] Existing packaged applications for e-Commerce fail woefully because they support only simplistic procurement and catalog selling scenarios but have nothing to match the complexity of real world commerce.

For some forward thinking companies, however, a third wave of e-Commerce has begun. With experience as their teacher, these companies have come to realize that e-Commerce is neither just a buy-side nor sell-side package. The third wave companies have learned that mission-critical business opportunities abound. To them, *e-Commerce is an infrastructure for a whole new way of doing business.* They have learned that if they extend their business processes across company boundaries and integrate them with their suppliers' and customers' business processes something totally new starts to happen.

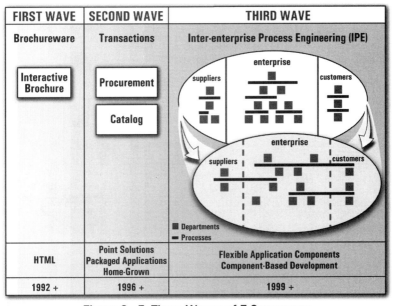

Figure 2 - 5. Three Waves of E-Commerce

Third wave companies are redesigning business processes so that they cross enterprise boundaries to eradicate duplicate processes, ineffective hand-offs and disconnects between and among enterprises. *Virtual corporations* are being created that have shared business goals, common planning, and performance management tools. *Inter-enterprise Process Engineering (IPE)*[SM] is their competitive weapon for designing and implementing hyper-efficient business processes that are integrated in real-time and jointly owned by suppliers and customers. Cheaper, better, and faster takes on a whole new meaning in these 21st century corporations.

Drilling down one level, Figure 2 - 6 illustrates a small sampling of business processes being integrated electronically across corporate boundaries. These processes apply to all kinds of businesses: manufacturing, distribution or services. In any industry, an enterprise is located in a value-chain where it buys goods and services from suppliers, adds value, and sells to customers. Value-chain analysis was pioneered two decades ago by Harvard's competitive strategy authority, Michael Porter. Rather that outdate Porter's work,[7] e-Commerce enables it.

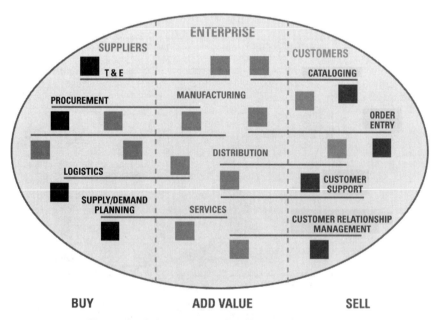

Figure 2 - 6. Inter-enterprise Business Processes

E-Commerce provides the business infrastructure for realizing Porter's visions, and IPE provides the methods for competitive value-chain engineering. Customer-facing processes include cataloging, order entry, customer support and overall customer relationship management. Supplier-facing processes include MRO and supply chain procurement, travel and entertainment procurement and tracking, logistics, and collaborative supply and demand planning.

Figure 2 - 7 shows how clusters of inter-enterprise business processes result in the four major categories of e-Commerce applications. Companies will not attempt to build these applications all at once. Such an effort would overwhelm any enterprise. Instead, e-Commerce initiatives will be launched in the quadrants in an incremental and iterative manner.

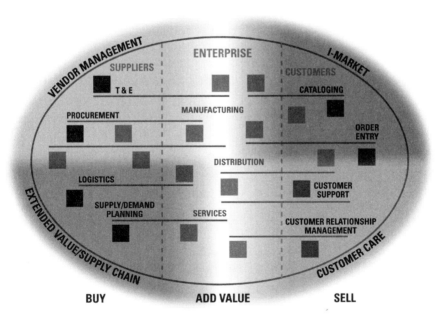

Figure 2 - 7. Inter-enterprise Process Integration with
E-Commerce Applications

For example, key inter-enterprise business processes may be engineered and deployed in the vendor management quadrant. Functionality will be added to these processes iteratively, and additional processes will be engineered and deployed incrementally. It is possible to proceed with work in parallel, but resource restrictions and other constraints will prevent companies from attempting too much at one time. *To maintain the cohesion needed in the ultimate digital business, each e-Commerce initiative must be based on a common business and technology architecture designed for inter-enterprise process engineering.*

Inter-enterprise process engineering, however, does not result in an end state. It is an on-going process that enables virtual corporations to evolve in a continually changing business ecosystem. Organization form and function must be able to sense and respond to change. Agility is the byword of success – an agile business empowered by agile information systems. No longer can software development be on the critical path for organizational and process change. With change being the constant variable, a new software development paradigm – component-based development – is essential to building agile, virtual corporations.

Agile Software for Agile Companies

To achieve coherence and manage the complexity and change inherent in multiple e-Commerce applications, an overarching structure is needed – an application architecture. An application architecture rationalizes, arranges and connects elements for a purpose. Ivar Jacobson explains, "The role of architecture is: to conceptualize the design in a form that developers and stakeholders can understand; to guide construction during the first development cycle, and in the future evolution of the system; and to enable management to structure the project and the organization itself around the architectural elements."[8]

The results of good architecture will be a cost-effective use of legacy assets and commercially available components, and resilience to change. With good architecture business applications will be scalable and extensible. Architecture provides a decision framework for the difficult build or buy dilemma. The structural elements along with their interfaces that comprise the system allow design tradeoffs based on cost and technological constraints. Buy or build decisions and incorporation of new technology can be determined for the structural elements rather than the overall architecture. Likewise, companies can upgrade their applications over time while maintaining integrity and interoperability with other enterprise applications.

Distributed object computing is now recognized as the way forward in building enterprise information architectures that can operate in advanced client/server, intranet and Internet environments. In essence, using objects to build information systems is like building a simulation with *business objects* representing the *people, places, things and events* that are found in the business setting or domain. Business objects reflect the real world and thus greatly enhance understanding and communication among systems developers and business people. And business objects reduce complexity because programmers do not need to know how an object works internally. They only need to know what the object is and the services it provides.

Object technology, however, does have some downsides including a steep learning curve. Business objects, though they represent things in the real world, become unwieldy when they are combined and recombined in large-scale commercial applications. What is needed are ensembles of business objects that provide major chunks of application functionality (e.g. preprogrammed workflow, transaction processing and user event notification) that can be snapped together to create complete business applications. This approach is embodied in the next step in the evolution beyond objects, software *components*.

Components are self-contained packages of functionality that have clearly defined, open interfaces that offer high-level application services. Components can be distributed dynamically for reuse across multiple applications and heterogeneous computing platforms. The later characteristic is why Java™ ("write once, run anywhere") has had such a dramatic impact on enterprise computing and component development, and why the eXtensible Markup Language (XML) is essential for developing a shared Internet file system.

Components take the best features of objects to a higher level of abstraction that is learned more easily by mainstream commercial software developers. Chris Stone, a Novell Vice President and former CEO of the Object Management Group (OMG) explains, "Components promise to be the Lego™ blocks of computing. To accomplish this, components must encapsulate useful, manageable and intuitive solutions to real-world business problems. Components, then, must enable

IT professionals to use object technology at meaningful and relevant levels of abstraction, while the system and service providers worry about the low-level object and system interactions."[9]

A component-based application architecture provides the business benefits of rapid applications development for quick time to market, enterprise-wide consistency of business rules and quick response to changing business requirements. And because major software vendors are committed to a component architecture, applications can mix and match best-of-breed solutions.

In his 1986 landmark book, *Object-Oriented Programming*, Brad Cox forecast a software revolution that would result from taking an engineering approach to programming. Electrical engineers do not design and build hardware from scratch. Instead they create a continuing stream of new and ever more marvelous electronic devices using prefabricated ingredients, integrated chips (hardware ICs). Cox predicted that software factories would fabricate, customize, and assemble software from standard reusable parts – Software ICs. After a decade of advances that took the theory and practice of object technology from a programming construct to a distributed computing infrastructure, Cox's software revolution is now at full fervor. New de facto and open standards have emerged to make it possible to develop large-scale distributed computing systems with "plug and play" components – the Object Management Group's CORBA 3, Sun Microsystems's Enterprise Java-Beans, and Microsoft's DCOM.

The telephone is easy to use while telecommunications technology is very complex. Likewise, a browser is easy to use while Web technology is very complex. Industrial strength server-side components are needed to deal with the complexity of the underlying information systems and distributed computing infrastructures. With components, solution developers can "plug into" standard preprogrammed services such as user authentication, workflow, data interchange, transaction processing, permanent storage of objects, and event handling services. Developers ask for the services without having to know the internal workings of the components that deliver them. The low level systems services call on the actual technology infrastructure that may consist of wrapped legacy systems as well as services provided by native objects.

Components suppress the complexity of the underlying systems technology, meeting Chris Stone's requirement for a clear separation of concerns: component construction versus component assembly. Plug-and-play business application components can be assembled or "glued together" rapidly to develop complex distributed applications needed for e-Commerce. How important is component-based development to large corporations? Research by the META Group revealed that "By 2001, most Global 2000 companies will use a "software factory" model to implement new application systems, requiring developers to move from a "craftsman" approach to a culture of assembly and reuse. These applications will be component-based, message-enabled, and event-driven, using an n-tier design that will leverage enterprises' capacity-on-demand capability." Today components are often thought of as being client-side technology, but the role of server-side component technology will be paramount as companies demand agile software in the face of accelerating business change.

A logical architecture for component-based development of e-Commerce applications can be described in layers as shown in Figure 2 - 8.

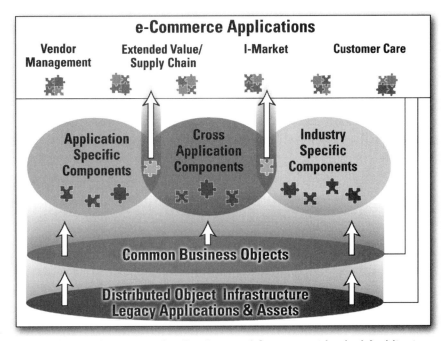

Figure 2 - 8. E-Commerce Applications and Component Logical Architecture

The technology infrastructure consists of combinations of legacy applications that have been wrapped to appear and function as business objects, and services provided directly by a distributed object platform (persistence, transaction processing, event services and the like).

Component-based development for e-Commerce applications is a process of assembly and refinement. The process begins with *cross-application components* that provide functionality common to most types of e-Commerce applications. Typical of such core components are user profile management, authentication, authorization, data management, workflow, negotiation, collaboration, and event notification. These cross-application components can be customized and extended to form *application-specific components*. For example, in a procurement application, a profiling component will contain attributes for identifying a user's role and buying power. When applied to an I-Market application, the profiling component will be extended to hold information that can be used to track customer buying patterns. In addition to the tailored cross-application components, application-specific components will include best-of-breed search engines, shopping carts, catalogs or other elements required for the application. These may be built in-house or purchased.

Cross-application components also can be extended to develop *industry-specific components*. For example, in a manufacturing industry a workflow component can be extended to handle work-in-progress and integrate workflows across enterprises to make "just-in-time" a reality. Additional best-of-breed industry-specific components are added to the framework to provide structure and behavior common to companies in a given industry: for example, cost accounting, warehousing and logistics in manufacturing industries.

The final step in the component-based development process is the configuration of the components to incorporate the organization's unique business rules and user presentation and navigation. It is in this step that a company's competitive advantage is built on top of best-of-breed cross-application, application-specific and industry-specific components, and embedded in its e-Commerce applications. The user may be a human in which case the presentation and navigation layer is browser centric. The user also may be another computer application, perhaps a supplier's order entry application. In this case the presentation and navigation layer concerns program-to-program interactions and data – a process known as web automation. In modern distributed computing architectures both users and applications can be distributed around the globe.

The position of e-Commerce application components within a distributed computing architecture is shown in Figure 2 - 9. Residing on state-of-the-art application servers, application components use standards-based middleware (e.g. CORBA, COM+, EJB) to integrate e-Commerce applications with legacy applications, existing databases, and ERP systems. The distributed component architecture allows the enterprise to leverage its unique business processes and policies embedded in these systems and refocus them from the inside, out.

These brief paragraphs reveal a breakthrough that has been sought since the beginning of software development – true software reuse! Notice that the common, cross-application components will be used throughout the growing portfolio of e-Commerce applications. The architecture is flexible and meant to evolve. Initially, of course, a company has no components.

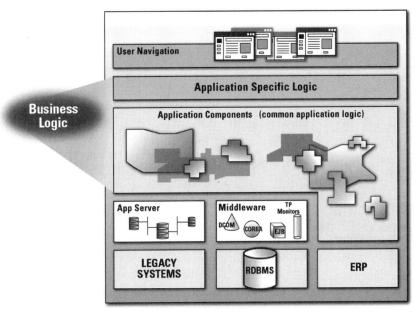

Figure 2 - 9. A Distributed Component Architecture for E-Commerce
Applications

As it proceeds to build its next generation systems it will make or, more likely, buy the components that will populate a growing repository. When necessary, the architecture allows developers to go directly to the underlying business objects that the components encapsulate or directly to the underlying technology infrastructure or legacy systems. Over time the architecture will accommodate robust and adaptive information systems that embrace rather than cringe at business change. Its overarching structure will allow companies to grow the software they need to compete for the future.

Joined electronically, third wave companies must share a common foundation for integrating their unique business processes and embrace the component paradigm as the way forward. Their core business processes are embedded in legacy, enterprise resource planning (ERP) and client/server systems. In order to retarget these internal systems outward, common inter-enterprise application functions are needed. As shown in Figure 2 - 10, information boundaries, workflow/process management, trading services, searching and information filtering, data/process integration, and event notification form the foundation for refocusing information systems from the inside out.

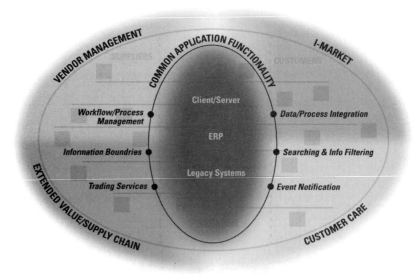

Figure 2 - 10. E-Commerce Common Application Functionality

The leading IT research firms confirm the approach. As shown in Figure 2 - 11, the Meta Group identifies seven fundamental components at the heart of their electronic process interchange model: information boundaries, business rules, messaging, workflow, event/process management, interchange protocols, and trading services.

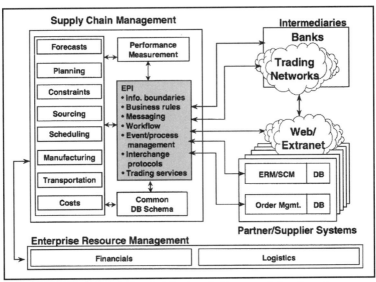

Figure 2 - 11. Meta's Electronic Process Interchange

As shown in Figure 2 - 12, Forrester Research reinforces the message as they advise companies to create object wrappers for their legacy applications and snap in new, outward-facing components to build Internet commerce applications. They advocate an outward-in replacement of legacy functionality over time.

The essence of e-Commerce applications is that they must define "the rules of engagement" needed for process and data integration with trading partners. These are expressed in business logic that is unique and specific to each organization and application scenario. However, what is not specific to each business are the core e-Commerce components underlying the business logic. These common, cross-application components form the foundation for inter-enterprise integration and implementing the third wave of e-Commerce.

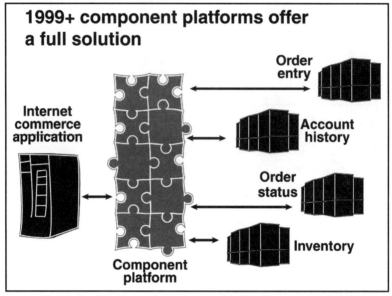

Figure 2 - 12. Forrester's Outward-In Replacement Model

The Way Forward

In the very first line of their classic work, *Reengineering the Corporation*, Hammer and Champy declare "that American corporations must undertake nothing less than a radical reinvention of how they do their work."[10] Their clarion call to management in the early 1990s ushered in a business revolution and reshaped the landscape of business practice. Their message was to tear down the stovepipes of functional management. They dispensed with the wisdom of Adam Smith's specialization of labor and hundreds of years of industrial management "best practice." They tore apart organizations whose specialized departments optimized their individual tasks (often at the expense of the overall customer-facing process) and reunified those tasks into coherent, end-to-end business processes that delivered value to customers. Their prescriptions were not based on magic, they were based on the enabling role of information technology. Herein lies the wisdom of their message. They recast the way a company must think about technology. They assert that a company that equates technology with automation cannot reengineer. A company that looks at and seeks to automate what they are doing cannot innovate, they simply reinforce and speed up old ways of doing things. Hammer and Champy rephrased the technology question: "How can we use technology to allow us to do things we are not already doing?" The reengineering revolution was underway. The focus of the business reengineering revolution was internal, on how the company must reorganize and streamline work.

As the '90s draw to a close it is once again time to ask, "What if you could do something that has never before been possible? What if that something fundamentally alters what it is you do?" The result would be a paradigm shift. The Internet makes it possible to do things that were never before possible. The Internet's distinguishing characteristic is ubiquity (existing or apparently existing everywhere at the same time), an attribute that can transform the very fabric of society and commerce. Déjà vu – it's reengineering all over again, only this time it's on steroids. The Internet calls to us to reengineer not just our business, but to reengineer complete industries. It calls to us to extend our internal business processes to the world outside the corporation: customers, suppliers, and trading partners. And it turns the producer-consumer relationship upside down, placing the consumer in control. It calls to us to reengineer our corporation and shift the focus of business engineering from the inside, out.

Today's forward thinking business leaders recognize the challenge of e-Commerce as a strategic business issue, not just one more technical issue to be delegated to the IS department, perhaps the existing EDI group. They already have looked below the surface of the daily press hype about the Internet. What they have seen is nothing short of a business revolution. They recognize the Net not as just another technology, information medium or distribution channel, but as the infrastructure that will cause profound change in the way companies organize work and conduct business, and ultimately in the structure of the economy itself. It's the death of distance and the eradication of time between participants in markets. Pioneers are making mistakes. They are chalking up wins and losses, but they recognize that the winners and losers of the future will be determined by those who are able to capitalize on the Net's capability to inter-network suppliers, customers and trading partners in a way never before possible – in real-time.

Although a company may already have reengineered its internal business processes and perhaps painfully installed an enterprise resource planning (ERP) system to bring efficiencies to the back office, e-Commerce is about engineering *outward-facing* processes – inter-enterprise process engineering versus business process reengineering (IPE vs. BPR). It's about redefining industry boundaries, inventing new industries, repositioning, disintermediation (cannibalizing distribution channels), and reintermediation (establishing portals to the Web). It's about 1-to-1 marketing, segmenting the needs of a single customer instead of segmenting mass markets. Its about outsourcing customer service to the customers themselves. It's about relationship marketing and building communities. It's about honoring the customer not as king, but as dictator who is but one mouse click away from turning his back on you. This is the stuff with which CEOs, not just programmers, must grapple.

Bob Metcalfe, Inventor of Ethernet and Founder of 3COM, explains, "The Internet is the Information Age. Business people know that, even if they don't have a clear idea of what the business model is."[11] What is a business model? It provides an architecture for the product, service and information flows across various business actors who play specific roles and add value along the way. BPR is a tool for analyzing a company's internal business model, disassembling the actors and roles contained in the departmental stovepipes of traditional companies and reassembling them around end-to-end business processes that are seen by and add value to customers. In their classic BPR book, *Improving Performance,* Rummler and Brache use "managing the white space on the organization chart" as the book's subtitle and metaphor for this process. Just as the BPR movement eradicated duplicate processes, ineffective hand-offs and disconnects between departments within a company, the new, real-time interconnections enabled by e-Commerce allows a business to tear down process barriers between its customers, suppliers and trading partners. While BPR crosses departmental boundaries, IPE crosses enterprise boundaries and is about "managing the white space in the value-chain."

Boeing provides a world class example of third wave value-chain management. Boeing designed its 777 in cyberspace by bringing together engineers, customers, maintenance people, project managers, and component suppliers electronically. No physical model. No paper blueprints. The result is the slogan that "the 777 is a bunch of parts flying together in close formation."

Business and Technology Architecture: The Key to E-Commerce Development

Competing for the future with e-Commerce is not just about technology. It is not just about business. It is inseparably about both, and architecture is the key to fusing the two. In his book *Systems Architecting*,[12] Eberhardt Rechtin paints the picture, "Both architects and business managers live in ill-structured, unbounded worlds where analytic rationality is insufficient and optimum solutions are rare. Both have perspectives that are strategic and top-down. Top managers, like chief architects, must architect strategies that will handle the unforeseeable, avoid disaster and produce results satisfactory to multiple clients – to boards of directors, customers, employees and the general public. Their common modus operandi is one of fit, balance and compromise in the overall interest of the system and its purposes."

The key components of a business architecture are organization, processes and technology. The arrangement and connections of these components make up the business architecture. When a business is simple and small, its architecture is implicit. Without explicit business architecture, however, large complex organizations would move rapidly to a state of chaos. The profound and discontinuous change that is being wrought by the emergence of e-Commerce demands a fresh approach to business design. No longer can a company sit comfortably in its niche in its industry and carry out business planning by extrapolating yesterday's assumptions. And it cannot plan alone since forging new electronic relationships with suppliers, distributors, partners and customers requires direct participation by these stakeholders. A new approach is needed to design a sustainable, changeable business architecture and to build the essential components that must cross company and industry boundaries, forming a new business ecosystem. An effective approach to business architecture must include an integrated and seamless method of business engineering and software development. What is needed are end-to-end, strategy-to-code methods for designing and deploying e-Commerce initiatives as illustrated in Figure 2 - 13.

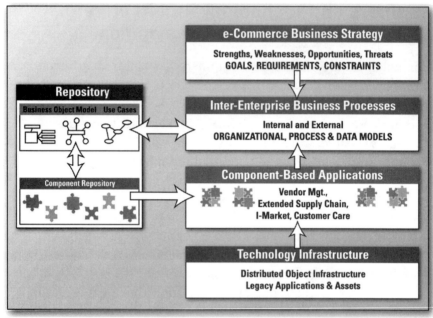

Figure 2 - 13. E-Commerce Development Method

Business strategy is not strategy-as-usual when it comes to e-Commerce. Working directly with the stakeholders inside and outside the business, a shared vision must be developed that allows the players to invent their shared future. Perhaps the greatest challenge is to achieve out-of-the-box, lateral thinking. Vince Barabba of General Motors describes GM's envisioning process, "Dealing with uncertainty requires that we adopt a "learning" rather than a "knowing" attitude toward the future."[13] Alternative futures are many for today's corporation, and building e-Commerce scenarios useful for the decision making process requires a multidisciplinary effort and participation by all stakeholders involved.

This envisioning process centers on asking the right questions. What are our customers' Internet expectations? How does the Internet allow us to change our value proposition for our customers? How does the Internet as a communication medium affect our value-chain? Should we cannibalize our supply chain? If we do not, who will? If we do, what will happen to our existing supply chain relationships? Which business model do we use to reintermediate: aggregator, open market, or value-chain integrator? How can our internal business processes be remapped and integrated with our business partners, customers, and suppliers? What is their readiness for process integration? How does the Internet blur the boundaries of our existing industry? What new goods and services can we aggregate to more fully serve our customers? If we do cross industry boundaries, what is the competitive landscape and how will we differentiate our offerings? If we use the Internet to reach global markets, how do we internationalize our logistics, language and legal frameworks?

The business strategy phase of e-Commerce development identifies "what" to do. The business process engineering phase addresses the "how." The task at hand is the mapping and engineering of the inter-enterprise business processes. Work activities, steps and hand-offs are redesigned using the methods and tools of business process reengineering, only this time the mappings are inter-enterprise. Inter-organizational processes may be loosely coupled as in the case of open markets where pass-throughs are made from the I-Market to individual organizations. Or they may be tightly coupled as in the case of a supply chain where process hand-offs are made electronically.

Best practice BPR methods, such as Rummler and Brache[14] or IDEF, are suitable for extending process definitions across organizational boundaries. There is no need for a company to change the methods and tools it already uses. What is different, however, are the external actors and resources that will result from modeling inter-enterprise business processes. Also new is the incorporation of emerging standards such as SWAP. The interoperation of workflow systems is embodied in the W3C's Simplified Workflow Access Protocol (SWAP), a standard that allows the execution of external workflow systems rather than the migration of process definitions from one system to another.

Process engineering is a model-based approach to problem-solving. As functional requirements are passed through to the process engineering phase, a *repository* of previously developed models can be searched for processes that match the requirements. A shared repository of the artifacts produced by business and systems modeling serves as a reference architecture. The repository also contains a standard representation of requirements, *use cases*. Use cases not only serve as a way of capturing the requirements of a system, they also trigger later development steps from analysis through design, implementation and testing. Each step provides further elaboration of previous steps. The use cases bind the steps together providing traceability and thus permit the management of inevitable change. Use cases are a part of the Unified Modeling Language (UML) which has become the standard for modeling business systems. UML is designed to model components and guide in their construction, assembly and reuse. New and existing components are held in the component repository for reuse.

In summary, a strategy-to-code method of developing e-Commerce systems fuses business architecture with technology architecture. Business strategy involves domain experts who define the initiatives to be pursued based on an analysis of the company's strengths, weaknesses, opportunities and threats. Business strategy determines what problem is to be solved, generating requirements, goals and constraints. Interenterprise process engineering defines how the requirements are to be satisfied through new or modified organizations, processes and data shared among the company's partners, suppliers and customers. Component-based applications implement the newly designed business processes, leveraging the technology infrastructure. The entire process is guided by an architectural approach that enables rapid development of business solutions through reuse of all elements in a growing repository of models and software components.

Mission-Critical E-Commerce

As e-Commerce becomes the preferred way of doing business it becomes mission-critical; by lowering costs or increasing revenues it directly affects the bottom line. Investments in e-Commerce require the same ROI analysis, risk assessments and solid management as other strategic investments. Understanding the new critical success factors is essential. New opportunities and threats will become routine affairs among the players in this brave new world, and thus *agility* is *the* critical success factor. When new opportunities are discovered, rapid response is essential. The ability to change is now more important than the ability to create information systems that underlie e-Commerce. *Change* becomes a first class design goal and requires business and technology architecture whose components can be added, modified, replaced and reconfigured. Software solutions must be agile, capable of rapid bundling, unbundling, and rebundling.

Formulating e-Commerce strategy should be at the top of management's priorities. Today's successful businesses have developed their unique style, form and ways of doing business. Their legacy assets are the basis of their success and should be leveraged, not obliterated, in the process of developing e-Commerce strategy. A firm's competitive advantage is embedded in its unique business processes and its communal knowledge. By leveraging existing mission-critical processes and extending them to its customers, suppliers and partners, a corporation can build bridges to the digital economy.

Something new happens when a company extends its inward facing business processes outward. New value-chains can be created and customer processes can be integrated with the company's internal processes. Likewise with suppliers and trading partners. It is the engineering of these inter-organizational processes that allows costs to be cut, revenues to be increased, time to market to be decreased, and supply chains to be converted to dynamic supply grids – a whole new level of business engineering for competitive advantage. A new class of holistic computer applications emerge that are greater than the sum of the parts of the participants' individual business processes. This new class of computer applications, e-Commerce applications, enables not only the next level of efficiency but also a whole new realm of possibility for the corporation to make something where once there was nothing. Management's ultimate challenge is organizational design that not only aligns technology with the business, but fuses the two with inductive, out-of-the-box thinking. Moving forward, e-Commerce should be the centerpiece not only of technical strategy, but, first and foremost, of business strategy. For in the third wave of e-Commerce, the business is its system.

This chapter opened with a brief reference to the difficulty of predicting the business impact of radical technology breakthroughs. Returning to these thoughts, Peter Drucker summarizes and prescribes,

"It is not so very difficult to predict the future. It is only pointless. But equally important, one cannot make a decision for the future. Decisions are commitments to action. And actions are always in the present, and in the present only. But actions in the present are also the one and only way to make the future."[15] Using the first principles of business and technology architecture, now is the time to act.

References

1 President William J. Clinton and Vice President Albert Gore, Jr., *A Framework For Global Electronic Commerce,* July 1, 1997.

2 http://www.eca.org.uk/

3 Walid Mougayar, "E-commerce? E-business? Who E-cares?" *Computerworld,* 11/02/98.

4 http://www.commerce.net/resources/pw/chap1-9/pg2.html

5 *Economist,* May 10, 1997.

6 Stephen McConnell, Editor, *The OMG/CommerceNet Joint Electronic Commerce White Paper,* July 27, 1997.

7 Porter, Michael E. *Competitive Strategy: techniques for analyzing industries and competitors,* Free Press, 1980; ISBN: 0029253608, *Competitive Advantage: creating and sustaining superior performance,* Free Press, 1985. ISBN: 0029250900. 1998. ISBN: 0684841460, and *On Competition.* Harvard Business School Press. 1998. ISBN: 0875847951.

8 Ivar Jacobson, "Use Cases & Architecture in Objectory," *Component Solutions* magazine, August, 1998.

9 http://www.sigs.com/cso/frompages/9807/sidebar.kara.html

10 Michael Hammer and James Champy, *Reengineering the Corporation,* HPF HarperBusiness, 1993.

11 http://computer.org/internet/v1/metcalfe9702.htm

12 Eberhardt Rechtin, *Systems Architecting: Creating and Building Complex Systems,* Prentice-Hall. 1991.

13 Vincent P. Barabba, "Revisiting Plato's Cave," in *Blueprint to the Digital Economy,* McGraw Hill, 1998.

14 Geary A. Rummler and Alan P. Brache, *Improving Performance: How to Manage the White Space on the Organizational Chart,* Jossey-Bass Publishers, 1995.

15 Peter F. Drucker, *Managing in a Time of Great Change,* Truman Talley Books, 1995.

Notes

Chapter 3 - E-Commerce Applications: I-Markets

Notes

The Marketplace of the 21st Century

"The marketplace is the place of exchange between buyer and seller. Once one rode a mule to get there; now one rides the Internet. An electronic marketplace can span two rooms in the same building or two continents. How individuals, firms and organizations will approach and define the electronic marketplace depends on people's ability to ask the right questions now and to take advantage of the opportunities that will arise over the next few years." – Derek Leebaert.[1]

"It's not hyperbole to say that the 'network' is quickly emerging as the largest, most dynamic, restless, sleepless marketplace of goods, services, and ideas the world has ever seen." IBM CEO Lou Gerstner, speaking at CeBIT 98 in Hanover, Germany, predicted that the global e-Commerce will reach US $200 billion by 2000, an estimate that he considers conservative.[2]

"No company is an island, and industry boundaries are becoming blurred into new and evolving business ecosystems."[3] Component Strategies magazine, February, 1999.

As EDS' former CEO, Les Alberthal, explains, *"By now we know the revolution will never abate. In the next 10 years we will witness one of history's greatest technological transformations, in which the world's geographic markets morph into one dynamic, complex organism."*[4] Such transformations do not occur with one big bang, nor are they a matter for tomorrow. Several industries have already been turned upside down and chaos hangs above other industries since, as Derek Leebaert writes, *"Anyone with access to electricity can make a market at will."*

Throughout history, markets have always *re-created* themselves, shifting the economic fortunes of those present at the creation. The dam on the Amstel river bears witness to the Dutch trading power that was driven by ships and trade winds as the medium of commerce.[5] In the 17th Century, the Netherlands was the leading maritime nation in the world. This 'Golden Century,' as it is known in Dutch history, was a period not only of great prosperity, but extended the wealth of its nation to art, architecture and culture that can be enjoyed to this day in the city built around the Amstel dam, Amsterdam. Today's *market re-creations* are not paced by the speed of the winds moving merchant ships, they are happening *at Internet speed.* Rather than taking centuries to evolve, now the very notion of what a market is can change by the day – after all it is the "e-Commerce Century." How does a company build a "dam on the Internet" and create its Golden Century?

An I-market is the place of exchange between buyer and seller in cyberspace using the Internet. An I-Market is a virtual, *digital* marketplace where buyers and sellers congregate to buy and sell products and services. The "virtual" part eliminates the market-friction caused by the barriers of *time* (a customer can buy products 24 hours a day 365 day a year), *space* (from anywhere in the world), and *form* (for a growing list, atoms can be replaced by bits in delivering goods and services). No longer does a company need to have a physical presence to enter a new market. No longer are customers required to do business during normal business hours. And products can often make the leap from atoms (a compact disk, a software program, a bank statement, a check, or an airline ticket) to bits (MP3 audio, downloadable software programs, online financial statements and payments, or e-tickets). In one fell swoop, a Virtual I-Market can give a company an immediate, 24x365 presence in the global marketplace. More importantly, it allows a company to more effectively meet the needs of its customers. Executed correctly, the results are new customers, increased loyalty from customers, increased sales, and reduced costs. If executed poorly however, the results can be disastrous.

Figure 3 - 1 provides a top view of an I-Market that provides a channel of communication between an enterprise and its customers. To be successful, an enterprise's I-Market initiatives must *attract customers*, *handle customer transactions*, and *retain customers* through excellent customer care. The entire framework must be carefully managed to bring about reliability, cost reductions and continuing process improvement – all judged from the customer's perspective. The benefits provided by e-Commerce must flow throughout the entire supply chain, from manufacturers, wholesalers and resellers to the ultimate customer. An I-Market serves *communities of customers* that, because they can collaborate, have the power to demand the best possible value. Anything less will not be tolerated.

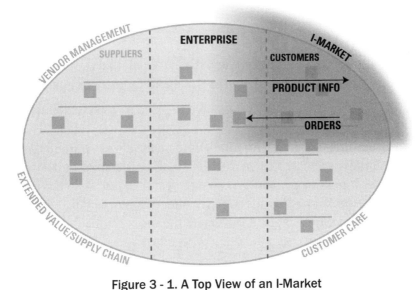

Figure 3 - 1. A Top View of an I-Market

Business and Consumer Markets

There are two major types of virtual I-Markets: business-to-business and business-to-consumer. Business-to-consumer I-Markets such as Amazon.com or eBay tend to command the lion's share of press attention, but the volumes of transactions in business-to-business I-Markets are orders of magnitude greater than that of the consumer I-Market. With all the hype over the Net startups like Amazon.com, eBay and iVillage, the real business action of e-Commerce gets lost. In 1998, business-to-business e-Commerce was five times as large as the consumer sector. General Electric alone, for example, plans to purchase goods and services worth $5 billion over the internet in the year 2000. By 2003, Forrester Research calculates that the marketspace will grow to $1.3 trillion (that's $1,300,000,000,000.00) making up 9% of U.S. business trade – more than the GNP of the U.K. or Italy. From there, Forrester predicts that up to 40% of all U.S. business will be conducted electronically by 2006.

Although business-to-business and business-to-consumer models differ in many ways, they share core functionality. Whether a customer is a business or a consumer, I-Market applications need to manage customer profile information to customize the user experience and deliver personalized information (one-to-one marketing and service). Customers require easy-to-use capabilities to search catalogs and view products, to place orders, to review orders and to be notified when relevant events occur. These are some of the fundamental pieces of a virtual I-Market that cross all market types and industry segments.

Cybermediaries – Digital Brokers

The digital broker is a cybermediary who adds value to and mediates between buyers and sellers. In the business-to-consumer market-space, the broker functions primarily as an aggregator of disparate buyers and sellers. The broker aggregates supplier offerings, simplifying matching and searching for the buyer. Conversely, the broker brings an aggregation of potential buyers to the seller whose tasks of getting buyer attention is reduced. The broker model requires the functionality of both buy-side and sell-side forms of commerce plus sophisticated market processes for mediation between buyers and sellers.

The broker's role in business-to-business markets often requires a high degree of sophistication as dynamic trading networks go beyond content aggregation to process integration. Web sites built to support this domain are process-centric. They must align, integrate and automate business processes and rules. For example, a seller must cross company boundaries and integrate with the buyer's requisition approval processes in order to provide complete procurement solutions. In business-to-business markets the focus is usually on supply chain management where critical processes include forecasting, materials requirements planning, scheduling, manufacturing, logistics, and cost accounting. Information boundaries among participants must be carefully managed to preserve the unique business rules of each participant and provide one-to-one customization. Real-time event notification and workflow must cross disparate information systems and messaging protocols. Within industries such as manufacturing or institutional brokerage, cybermediaries such as GE's Trading Process Network (TPN) will give rise to what Forrester Research calls "Internet commerce power grids," the backbone for dynamic trading processes. Currently, TPN provides the real-time connections among buyers, sellers and intermediaries through which catalog content, payments, bid/ask offers and digital goods flow. With systems such as TPN, flat supply chains become multidimensional matrices or power grids driving markets toward hyper-efficient means of production.

Multiple, Simultaneous Market Models

Portals, niche portals, vortices, interoperating I-Markets, and supply chain integrators are some of the terms that will soon be taught in graduate and undergraduate marketing courses. They are the new realities of classical channels of distribution. Because of the ubiquity of the Internet, a given company may need to support all these market models simultaneously.

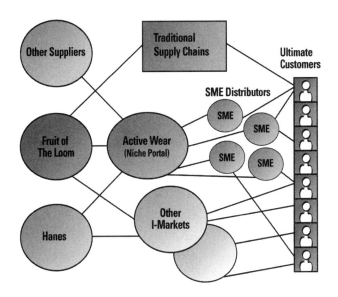

Figure 3 - 2. A Multi-Market Scenario for Fruit of the Loom™

Figure 3 - 2 shows a scenario most companies will need to embrace as I-Markets emerge and mature. The figure shows how a company like Fruit of the Loom may likely evolve its many I-Markets. Fruit of the Loom's Activewear division is a leading manufacturer of T-shirts, fleecewear and knit sport shirts in the Imprinted Sportswear market. The Activewear division offers a wide selection of apparel products for garment decoration, screen printing, embroidery, appliques, heat transfers and more. When FOL pioneered its Activewear Web site it became a "niche portal" for this particular industry segment. By providing hosting services for its small and medium enterprise (SME) Activewear distributors, it wisely locked in its position as an industry portal, even at the expense of allowing its distributors to carry competing brands at the site.

So, what is the best model for creating I-Markets? All of the above! Successful companies in the Information Age will deploy stand-alone corporate Web sites, establish brokerage sites, and participate in multiple marketspaces. Sub-forms of these marketspaces have already emerged. In a *governed maketspace,* interactions occur with the market, not the participants directly. In an *open market* or trading network, interactions occur directly between participants with the market only playing the role of mediation. In a *closed marketspace,* typical of supply chains, trading partners are tightly integrated and work from contracts, prenegotiated pricing and rules of engagement.

Again, what is the best model for creating I-Markets? In actuality, the best model is an *agile* model. Agility is the key to riding the waves of e-Commerce. Amazon.com began as a simple I-Market, an online bookstore. As CEO, Jeff Bezos, remarked, "We had a world class site the day we launched – but it is only a tenth as good as the site we have now."[6] He went on to say that they have only 2% of what they will need in the coming years. Not only has the site itself grown in robustness, it has positioned itself at portals such as ABCNEWS, Netscape and eXcite. With its "Shop the Web," PlanetAll, and auction services, it aspires to be a *vortex,* a Web-based market-maker that brings together a fragmented group of buyers with an equally fragmented group of sellers.

Positioning and rapid evolution are essential to success in I-Markets. It is not enough to establish a transaction enabled Web site. The I-Market pioneers have been nimble, innovative, experimental and brave. They have learned that their business models will change in concert with rapidly changing marketspaces and opportunities. The secret is to build a business *metamodel* that is agile enough to support new and changing I-Market models as the infant world of digital markets matures to become the digital economy.

In the 17th century, Amsterdam became the vortex of the new merchant class. Societies were transformed. The building of the 'Interdam' will be a feat of historical proportions.

The Business Case for I-Markets

I-Markets make for interesting investment propositions in that they provide double leverage. They can increase revenue and decrease costs, simultaneously. This fact alone deserves a "wow," for not many business resources can do that.

A well-designed I-Market can deliver multiple revenue opportunities:

- As a new, global distribution channel, an I-Market allows a company to reach new customers.
- Better customer access to a company's products and services. In the form of 1-to-1 marketing, each customer can have personalized access.
- Convenient access can enable a company to obtain significantly more information about customers and their buying behavior. This information represents a new way to learn which customers actually contribute to the bottom line. By allowing a company to concentrate on the needs of its best customers, new profit opportunities become visible.
- Up-selling and cross-selling opportunities can empower a company to expand its product lines and offer more goods and services to the customer. In complex purchases such as buying real estate, the many ancillary processes (insurance, moving and storage, financing and so on) can be aggregated to provide the customer with "total solutions." A company can expand its product and service lines to offer complete solutions, changing the very nature of the business: what and to whom it sells.
- By focusing on customer behavior, one customer at a time, ever-changing needs can be met through offering new, personalized products and services. One-to-one marketing is the new frontier for competitive advantage.
- With ongoing, instant access to supply and demand information, an I-Market provides marketers new opportunities for managing pricing policy as a marketing strategy, in real-time. As I-Markets continue to grow, fixed pricing will be an artifact of history. "Fixed

pricing" is a recent phenomenon and the case for "dynamic pricing" is compelling to both buyers and sellers.

■ In concert with the previous bullet point, companies can use their I-Markets to conduct auctions. This capability offers a new channel for moving surplus goods and one day may lead to most markets operating much like a stock market. Further, as automated buying software becomes applied to auctions, they will no longer be auctions. They will morph into dynamic pricing mechanisms needed to support almost "perfect competition" and market equilibrium. That is, of course, a long-range possibility. In the meantime, auctions are already a powerful means to draw both consumer and business traffic.

■ An I-Market, in conjunction with complete customer care offerings, can build customer loyalty through personalized service. For example, in the business-to-business market, a seller can build customer loyalty by tying into and supporting the buyer's internal business processes such as requisitioning and purchasing approvals. (This subject is explored more fully in Chapter 4). Loyal customers sell themselves and can be counted as part of a company's sales force as they spread the word.

New and radical cost saving opportunities are many:

■ An I-Market can significantly reduce the costs associated with processing sales transactions, fully automating the transaction life cycle.

■ An I-Market can significantly reduce marketing costs. While the cost of developing quality marketing materials does not change, their distribution is essentially free via the Web. Electronic brochures, catalogs, and other forms of company and product information can be disseminated without incremental cost. A brochure can be read by millions as readily as by one – no printing, mailing or distribution required.

■ I-Markets with real-time connection to their supply chains, can significantly reduce or even eliminate warehousing, shipping and inventory costs.

■ An I-Market can significantly reduce customer care costs, while increasing quality and fostering loyalty

■ When bits can replace physical media, an I-Market can eliminate the manufacturing costs of burning information onto paper and plastic and moving it from the manufacturer through the supply chain to the customer. In an I-Market, just the information moves and its highway is essentially free. Software, music(MP3), research services, electronic tickets (eTickets) and magazines (eZines) are but a few of the growing lists of products and services being delivered through digital channels of distribution.

- When complex products or services are being sold, costs can be significantly reduced by supplying customers with digital planning, specification and configuration facilities. Such "self-selling" can reduce errors, costs of shipping and returns processing, and costs associated with maintaining a staff of sales engineers and other highly trained knowledge workers.

Several I-Market pioneers have already changed their business models and offer lessons learned along the way. Their stories are summarized in Figure 3 - 3.

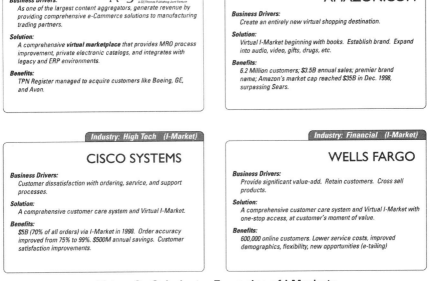

Figure 3 - 3. Industry Examples of I-Markets

A premier example of an open business-to-business I-Market is TPN Register. TPN Register, LLC is a 50/50 joint venture between GE Information Services, a global leader in electronic commerce services, and Thomas Publishing Company, publishers of the Thomas Register of

American Manufacturers. These parent organizations have been using both technology and information to facilitate sourcing and enhance inter-enterprise relationships between buyers and sellers for decades. TPN Register applies this expertise to provide comprehensive Internet commerce solutions for industrial buyers to procure MRO (Maintenance, Repair and Operation) and other indirect goods and services. TPN Register provides services that enable corporations and their trading partners to streamline the procurement of MRO suppliers. TPN Register creates, customizes and hosts secure, private electronic catalogs that contain accurate, searchable and comprehensive product data that integrates with legacy and ERP environments. TPN Register works with both buyers and sellers to build electronic trading communities that benefit all participants.

As previously mentioned, Amazon.com is probably the most widely referenced example of a business-to-consumer I-Market. Beginning with books and tools to establish a collaborative community-of-interest, the eTailer is an outstanding example of a new market entrant that was first-to-market in the digital world. Being first-to-market with a high quality site resulted in an eBranding coup d'état. While selling books and establishing its brand, Amazon.com keeps running hard. They have expanded their product line to include audio, video, gifts, toys, electronics and drugs. If "Shop the Web" gains acceptance by merchants who, frankly, are afraid of being reduced to commodity vendors, Amazon.com will likely become "earth's largest everything store," offering just about anything a consumer could want to buy. Backing this ambition, Amazon.com's growing customer database positions the company with the greatest business asset in the 21st century: broad and deep information about customers and their buying behavior. To add even more substance to its customer database, Amazon.com's PlanetAll offers free self-updating address books, calendars, and ad-hoc groups for personal information management. The company is an exemplar of a totally customer-driven enterprise.

In making the Business On The Internet (BOTI) awards,[7] Brian Walsh commented, "It's not much fun to nominate a large, well-known company as the best business-to-business electronic-commerce site. It would have made better copy to nominate a small bootstrap operation – one that pursued the Internet dream on a shoestring, using it as a way to steal marketshare from a large competitor. However, it's hard to argue with success – Cisco's site is an example of a complete, effective approach to the challenges of delivering E-commerce solutions to the widest possible audience." As of December 1998, Cisco conducted almost 70% of its commerce transactions via the Web, and anticipates over $6 billion of its $10 billion run rate for Fiscal Year 1999.[8]

In the financial sector, Wells Fargo first offered online banking in 1989 and Internet services in May 1995. Wells Fargo customers can bank online through the Internet using Quicken and Microsoft Money. Consumers can pay bills to anyone in the U.S. using each of these channels. They may also view their account information and transfer money between their checking, savings, credit card, line of credit and money market mutual fund accounts. Customers using the Internet can apply for new accounts and download account history into personal financial management software. Customers who apply online for home equity credit receive instant decisions, without waiting several days for a response. Other services, such as check reorder, address changes and travelers checks are also available over the Internet.

I-Market Application Framework

Having defined what they are and why they are so important to the bottom line of a business, we can gain a deeper understanding of I-Markets by examining the business processes that an I-Market must support and the application drivers needed to implement these processes in software.

Key Business Processes for an I-Market

Although each type of I-Market has it's own set of activities, many are common to all market types and can be represented by looking at the life cycle of a selling/buying transaction. Table 3 - 1 shows several marketplace life cycle models differing in levels of complexity and the number of steps involved: buying a book is a short and simple process (see-buy-get), while contracting for components to build a commercial airliner is a long-lived, complex proposition.

Table 3 - 1. Various Marketplace Life Cycles

See-Buy-Get
Information stage (electronic marketing, networking), Negotiation stage (electronic markets), Fulfillment stage (order process, electronic payment) and Satisfaction stage (after sales support).
Discovery, Evaluation, Negotiation, Order Placement, Scheduling & Fulfillment, Receiving, Billing, Payment, Customer Service/Support

The functions and capabilities underlying most transaction life cycles in an I-Market are listed in Table 3 - 2.

Table 3 - 2. Typical Components in I-Markets

Business-to-Consumer	Business-to-Business
Content publishing tools	Content publishing tools
Storefronts	Access management, authentication
Auctions	Bid/ask trading
Access management, authentication	Auctions, on-sale
Merchandising: promotions, coupons	Catalogs, Custom catalogs
E-mail, Chat	Parametric Search
Catalogs	Product Configurators
Classification search	Aggregation
Product Configurators	Supplier Management
Profiling and personalization	Order Processing
Aggregation	Invoicing
Order Processing	EDI integration
Credit Authorization	Event notification
Payment Facilities	Fulfillment
Fulfillment	Business Rules facility
Business Rules Facility	Payment facility
Order Tracking	Workflow
Customer Service	Reporting
Reporting	Integration to Back Office
Integration to Back Office: product data management and ERP systems	

Although the overall life cycles are roughly the same, business-to-business I-Markets must have an emphasis on custom catalogs that reflect prenegotiated pricing, different forms of payment (credit cards are seldom used in business-to-business transactions), integration with existing EDI systems, and workflow engines that are generally needed by both buyers and sellers in business-to-business trade.

A simplified life cycle (Marketing, Catalog Management, Order Processing, Fulfillment, and Settlement) is sufficient to describe the key inter-enterprise business processes common to all forms of I-Markets. These core business processes appear at the center of Figure 3 - 4.

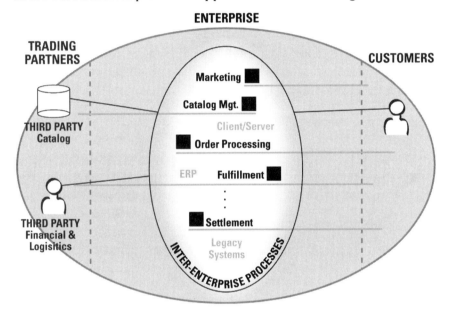

Figure 3 - 4. I-Market Application Framework

Going further, Figure 3 - 5 peels back another layer of the I-Market model to reveal some of the activities and tasks of the key business processes. To explore these processes, each is first discussed in context of business-to-consumer I-Markets, followed by a discussion from the perspective of business-to-business I-Markets.

Marketing

Customization is the byword of the 21st century marketing revolution. By interacting with customers electronically, their buying behavior can be evaluated and responses to their needs can be tailored. Customization provides value to customers by allowing them to find solutions that better fit their needs and saves them time in searching for their solutions. Instead of presenting a huge catalog to a given customer to sift through, custom catalogs can be presented, one customer at a time. Not only can a solution be pinpointed for a customer, but also as the relationship grows, the more a business knows about individual buying behavior. As a natural result of the growing relationship, cross-selling opportunities will abound. With the Net, the savvy marketer can sense and respond to customer needs in real-time, one-to-one. In addition to demographics, the electronic marketer can track *biographics*: the life passages and temporal events that shift the interests of the individual. For instance, buying one's first home is a life passage event that can lead the marketer to target the consumer for a range of products and services from life insurance to home furnishings.

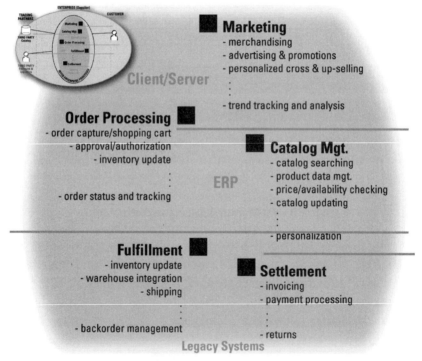

Figure 3 - 5. I-Market Business Processes

In the world of electronic consumer markets the success factor mantra is: relationship, relationship, and relationship. Successful marketers have shifted their focus from products to the customer – the whole customer. The goal is to build an ever-deepening relationship with a customer to meet as wide a variety of the customer's needs as possible.

The business that owns the primary customer relationship is the business that excels at electronic commerce – they will be the first place a consumer will go to meet their shopping needs. Considering that it is 5 to 8 times more expensive to gain a new customer than it is to sell to an existing customer, the stakes are high indeed. Companies that are able to capture substantial information about their customers' buying behavior can anticipate needs for goods and services of all kinds – this is the essence of one-to-one marketing where each customer is treated as a market segment of one.

The Internet provides two-way information opportunities and benefits not available through traditional retail channels. Initial success in the business-to-consumer market-space can produce new sources of revenues and cuts costs of marketing and delivery of goods and services.

What is involved in a robust business-to-consumer system that draws customers and promotes return visits? A well-designed consumer oriented system will mimic the way people shop. When Intuit, Inc. introduced its home bookkeeping system for the personal computer, Quicken, it was a smashing success. People already knew how to write a check. Intuit capitalized on what people already knew and gave them direct manipulation of a checkbook as the user interface to their system. The computer per se disappeared from the mind's eye of the user; they were simply using their checkbook digitally – no training required. In addition to the intuitiveness, the software added value by taking care of the tedious work of calculating balances, reconciling to the bank statement, and maintaining the budget.

People already know how to shop. A well-designed business-to-consumer application will capitalize on what they already know. Understanding and modeling the consumption process is key to designing a system that is not only simple to use, but can *add significant value for the shopper.* It is not enough to take a company's catalog and place it on a web site with an order form. Consumer-oriented systems need to be designed from the customer's perspective, from the outside, in.

Getting noticed and attracting customers is just as important in consumer-oriented e-Commerce as it is in the physical world of retailing. Thus, advertising on the Web is essential as the retailer still must compete for the attention of potential customers. Web advertising takes on many forms including placing *banner ads* on popular sites (CNN, local or regional newspapers, industry niche portals, trade associations, or general Internet portals like eXcite or Netscape). Another major shotgun form of advertising is registering Web sites with the major *search engines* (e.g. Hotbot, Yahoo, and Alta Vista). According to the eAdvertising Report by eMarketer, American companies spent $1.5 billion on Internet advertising in 1998. The research firm estimates that the figure will increase by 73 percent to $2.6 billion by the end of 1999, and to $8.9 billion by 2002.[9] In the international markets where Web advertising is even less developed, including Europe, Asia, and Latin America, less money is spent on Web advertising. eMarketer found that only $132 million was spent on Web advertising in Europe in 1998.

Advertising must go beyond the Internet itself. The "www.company.com" hallmark is already standard fare for magazine ads, billboards, and broadcast media. "In the mad race to build awareness, establish online brands and drive site traffic, Web marketers will continue to divert the majority of their advertising and marketing budgets to offline media and their own corporate Web site development," said eMarketer's Geoffrey Ramsey. "The brand battle for Web marketers will be waged, not so much on banner ads, but on television sets, radios, and in magazines, as well as on company Web sites where real consumer interaction takes place."

Merchandising is a marketing tool of long standing and applies to business-to-consumer e-Commerce as well. Consumer-oriented systems need to include the digital counterparts for coupons, promotions and sales. Shoppers like to browse and bargain shop. A retail web site must have an attractive storefront that entices the browser inside. Giving away useful information or digital coupons for entering are two such techniques.

Catalog Management

Once inside an I-Market, the potential customer must be free to browse. The catalog of goods and services must be extremely easy to navigate, letting the shopper browse just the aisles of greatest interest without having to go through an entire catalog. The buying process, however, may not be as straightforward as a simple catalog search. The customer's buying process may involve many steps and decision points (for example, vacation planning) and require information from multiple sources. When there are many sources in the search space, the buyer can be overwhelmed by search engines. In this case the seller may take on the role of broker or aggregator in order to add value by bringing together the needed resources.

When entering a consumer-oriented site, the user may be offered the option to register with the site to better serve him or her, but this should not be a prerequisite. Access control is important to all forms of e-Commerce, but in the consumer space, browsing a catalog should be open to anyone. Even if users do not register interests and preferences, the click streams they create while browsing can be used to personalize the experience. High end or specialty goods and services require much more information than commodities. For such items, chat rooms, collaborative filtering, e-mail, electronic newsletters and similar technologies can add great value to the consumer experience. These technologies allow the seller to build communities-of-interest at their site. Should the browsing consumer or community participant decide to buy, then the purchase becomes the trigger point for obtaining initial customer information.

Order Processing

The move from providing electronic information and building electronic relationships with the shopper to conducting the electronic transaction must be seamless. While browsing, but not yet taking the decision to buy, the site will likely provide a shopping cart where the consumer can place tentative selections. Once browsing is complete, the shopper should be able to review the cart and discard those items he or she decides against as they proceed to the "check-out" lane. As the shopping process enters the electronic transaction stage, the first step with a new customer is gathering essential customer information:

name, primary address, billing address, shipping address, and payment method for the transaction. The first step with an existing customer is authentication. Once the identity is verified, much of the information in the customer's files can be reused to complete the current transaction. Completing an order requires payment authorization, usually from links to credit card services on the network where the payment funds are committed. Additionally, taxes and shipping costs must be calculated. Finally customer confirmation of the order with details of any back ordered items must be produced as a customer receipt, and typically emailed to the customer.

Fulfillment

Completed orders progress to a fulfillment stage that may be as simple as preparing picking and packing slips for the warehouse, or initiating the process of aggregating the items from many sources, or as complex as triggering workflows in a supply chain for made-to-order goods. In addition, fulfillment may be completely digital when the product or service being sold is information. Digital fulfillment means granting access to the information, such as a subscription to the New York Times, or downloading software from Egghead.com. With fulfillment completed, the transaction moves on to settlement where funds actually transfer to the seller. Throughout the process, customer service facilities are needed to allow the customer to inquire about the status of the order and handle exceptions.

Settlement

Credit cards play a central role in business-to-consumer I-Markets. SET (Secure Electronic Transactions) is a system for ensuring the security of financial transactions on the Internet. With SET, a transaction is conducted and verified using a combination of digital certificates and digital signatures among the purchaser, a merchant, and the purchaser's bank in a way that ensures privacy and confidentiality. In business-to-business I-Markets, procurement cards (P-cards) from companies like MasterCard provide functionality comparable to consumer credit cards. With recent P-card initiatives, line item detail can be tracked for reconciliation back to general ledger accounting records. Further, high volume transactions in trading networks are settled with existing EDI facilities. Standards for payment gateways are being developed and will ultimately simplify the connections made from any given I-Market to all forms of secure electronic payments.

The inter-enterprise processes described for I-Markets are, of course, more elaborate than highlighted in the paragraphs above. These summaries, however, do provide a high-level view of the major activities common to I-Markets. Reflecting on these five business process areas and their multiple options, it can be readily seen that no pre-packaged point solution can possibly hope to meet the unique needs of all companies and provide the *agility* companies need to compete in dynamic markets.

Business markets. The key shift in focus from addressing the business-to-consumer market to the business-to-business market is one from *shopping* to *procurement*. Currently, the business-to-business market is about 100 times greater in transaction volume than the business-to-consumer market-space. Much of the future growth is expected to involve small and medium sized firms that were not able to participate in e-Commerce prior to the availability of the low cost, highly accessible Internet.

Procurement differs from shopping in several ways. Purchasing departments are under pressure to get orders placed quickly and efficiently. Almost by definition, the professional buyer or purchasing agent is a repeat customer. In order to complete their work within time constraints, reuse of data and authorized access information must be available from buying session to buying session. Purchasing agents do not engage in impulse buying. Often they buy from suppliers where the terms and condition of trade are prenegotiated. While merchandising, coupons, and up-selling are essential in the business-to-consumer market, they are largely irrelevant to the business-to-business market.

In the online business-to-business marketplace, the seller's first concern when a potential purchaser connects to do business is authentication so that custom pricing and custom catalogs can be presented to the purchasing agent. Not all transactions, however, are based on simple catalog selections. Configuration processes may have to be designed and implemented, or the seller may be participating in bid-ask procurement scenarios. In addition, features must be available in the seller's systems to be able to conduct auctions and promote items put on sale to move discontinued inventory. On the buyer side of transactions, a purchase request may need to be routed to a designated purchasing agent who in turn must obtain approval before committing to placing an order.

One of the most widely used business-to-business applications of e-Commerce addresses Maintenance Repair and Operations (MRO) where businesses buy non-production goods and services from custom catalogs: office supplies, repair parts, cleaning supplies and facility maintenance items and services. As much as 30% of the total cost of doing business falls into this category. That fact alone makes it obvious why companies have rushed to use the Internet to reduce costs. These are high volume, low value purchases that are repeated routinely. They involve high order processing costs for the buyer and supplier, relative to the item costs of each order. As an example, it may take $10 in purchasing costs to order a $1 box of paper clips.

Although MRO is the initial killer application of business-to-business I-Markets, integrating business processes between and among players in value-chains will earmark future development. In short, business-to-business e-Commerce is about dynamic process integration. *Inter-enterprise Process Engineering (IPE)^{SM}* provides the foundation for competitive advantage. Process integration is possible at three levels: intra-company via intranets; between tightly aligned partners via extranets; and in an ecosystem of trading processes established dynamically, possibly in real-time, via the Internet. Open business I-Markets such as TPN Register are pursuing this progression to the future. As a prime example of a double-edged sword, the amount of complexity and the potential for competitive advantage increase at each level of process integration.

Key Application Drivers for an I-Market

A core set of application drivers is needed to implement I-market business processes in software. These include Information Boundaries, Workflow/Process Management, Data/Process Integration, Searching and Information Filtering, Event Notification, and Trading Services facilities, as shown in Figure 3 - 6.

Information Boundaries

Profile management application facilities are needed to manage information boundaries between the selling company, its customers, suppliers and third party entities such as shipping and payment services. User authentication, authorization and access controls are maintained by profile management software and facilities.

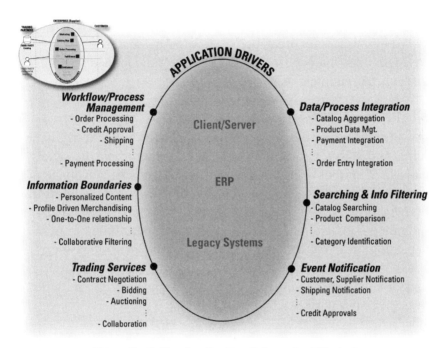

Figure 3 - 6. Key Application Drivers for I-Markets

Dynamic profiling is essential to customization, the key to one-to-one marketing. Customer privacy, however, is critical throughout the profiling process. The Open Profiling Standard (OPS) is a proposed standard for how World Wide Web users can control the personal information they share with Web sites and I-Markets. Standards that protect the privacy of the customer are absolutely necessary for the widespread acceptance of e-Commerce. Companies must design their information boundaries to comply with appropriate profiling standards.

Workflow/Process Management

Workflow facilities are needed for processing credit authorizations and driving ordering, fulfillment, shipping and settlement processes. Workflows between the seller and its suppliers must be tightly integrated so that customers can be fully informed throughout the ordering and fulfillment processes. In business-to-business I-Markets, workflow is also essential to the approval processes within the buying organization as well as the selling company and its trading partners. In governed markets, workflow facilities are a major part of what the market makers provide. In open markets, workflow facilities of the individual participants play a principle role.

Data/Process Integration

Data integration is essential to catalog aggregation and management, pricing, and inventory management – in real-time, across the supply chain. I-Markets must be integrated with existing resource management and accounting systems of the selling enterprise – the same holds true for buying organizations in business-to-business markets. Of special importance is integration with a product data management system so that catalogs in all media (paper, CD-ROM and online) are synchronized. When build-to-order marketing is employed, product data integration must extend into the realms of engineering and shop-floor production support systems.

Event Notification

Event notification facilities are essential for providing sellers, customers and suppliers with notifications of exceptions, changes and other situations requiring their attention. As the Web reaches out to more and more devices (pagers, PDAs, telephones, and faxes) to support a growing mobile workforce, event notification facilities must accommodate each of these customer touch points. Event notification facilities are also essential for application-to-application interoperation. For example, when a back ordered item is received, the receiving event triggers the shipping and payment processes of fulfillment and settlement. Applications subscribe to and are notified of events that affect them – such messaging is at the heart of robust I-Markets which, by their very nature, are event-driven systems.

Trading Services

Robust I-Markets include dynamic trading services facilities. Going beyond simple catalog sales, trading services are needed to provide discovery, mediation, matchmaking, negotiation and collaboration environments. Trading services facilities underlie auctions and are the foundation for building communities-of-interest. Trading services facilities will become very sophisticated as I-Markets become more advanced in response to growing demands from customers.

Searching and Information filtering

Searching and information filtering facilities are needed by all I-Market participants. Business-to-consumer search requirements may be simple and basic key word or hierarchical search may suffice to allow users to browse through various categories in a catalog.

At the heart of 1-to-1 personalization and community building is a technology known as "collaborative filtering." The technology can be used to collect ratings about items available in an I-Market. By making the sales rankings available as a customer browses an item, customers can see similar items with high rankings by other customers. For example, a customer browsing a particular book title can see what other customers bought who also bought the book being browsed. Once an I-Market has collected a critical mass of ratings, it can respond to customer inquiries with recommendations that are tuned to customers' preference patterns. Customer-driven collaborations and buying patterns tracked by collaborative filtering facilities also can be used to achieve advertising precision never before possible – the ultimate tool for up-selling and cross-selling.

I-Market Business Strategies

In their often-documented success, Cisco Systems' executives reflect on lessons they learned and offer their prescription for success.[10] "1. If you're not adding value for the customer, don't bother. 2. Know who your target audience is. 3. Listen to your customers. 4. Start small. 5. Focus on quick payoffs first. 6. Combine traditional marketing and new media to promote the site. 7. Expect Success: plan to expand infrastructure quickly. 8. Market the applications both internally and externally."[11]

The starting point for any successful I-Market initiative is a deep understanding of a company's customers. What are their e-Commerce expectations? What is their Internet readiness? How can the I-Market add value? Whether in business-to-consumer or business-to-business environments, the "consumption process" must be engineered to provide total solutions to customers. Channel conflict is a part of the equation of providing total solutions to customers. Should an enterprise disintermediate or support its existing distribution channels? Answers to these questions are determined by how the customer perceives the value-add of each entity in the overall value/supply chain. For example, if the customer sees no value in keeping travel agents in the supply chain when their role would be reduced to distributing the physical ticket, disintermediation makes sense. When customer service and support are key ingredients, the value-add is usually such that distributors and other intermediaries in the value/supply chain are critical, and reinforcement of existing channel partners makes sense. In short, evaluation of the customer-centered value/supply chain comes first in determining the appropriate business model. I-Market strategy is about new business models – simply setting up a Web site to display a company's existing products and take orders is the least likely road to success.

For all but simple catalog commodities where the sales transaction is "see-buy-get," customers want help. They want their buying experience to be intuitive and the information they access to be robust. Lands End's "Your Personal Model" offers an interactive shopping experience where the customer supplies information about their hair color, height, shoulders, hips, waist, waist placement … and a name for the personal model. Then clothes are checked out to a dressing room where they can be tried on the model. Adding visual and sensory aspects to the buying process, Garden.com lets customers download its interactive garden planner software where plants can be selected and dropped onto a planning grid or an existing garden template can be used to jump start the design. Once design is complete, a click of the mouse adds the plants to the shopping "wheel barrow" and proceeds to the check out lane. In business-to-business consumption processes, equally intuitive and useful tools are needed, and the process must cater to internal approval cycles of the buying company.

A common mistake an enterprise can make is to view the development of an I-Market as a singular event, resulting in a single Web site I-Market. This perception is short-sighted and has strategic consequences in the emerging worlds of open markets and digital business ecosystems. A given enterprise will participate in multiple I-Markets simultaneously. For example, Hilton Hotels Web site replicates itself and lives inside I-Markets formed by travel agents, tourism promoters and airlines. Corporate strategists need to think in the plural form, "I-Markets," and adopt an approach that can sustain the building of multiple, simultaneous business initiatives. To be practical, the approach must rely on a core set of reusable software components.

Putting It All Together

Enterprise-class I-Markets harness the Internet to automate the business processes of selling a company's products and services. An I-Market can deliver a double impact, reducing costs while increasing revenues. A sustainable approach to implementing multiple I-Markets levers legacy enterprise systems and extends them to customers and the enterprise's trading partners. Howard Anderson, Founder of The Yankee Group and Battery Ventures confirms, "Every company has built order entry systems, customer support systems, and sales automation systems. What the smartest are doing is turning that embedded cost into "customer-facing" systems. By putting a user-friendly front end on top of a tried and true internal solution a company can build a strategic advantage. A company has achieved double leverage."[12] Of course the tasks at hand are more than just putting a pretty face on top of existing enterprise management systems. Putting it all together for next generation I-Markets means extending core business processes with e-Commerce application drivers as shown in Figure 3 - 7.

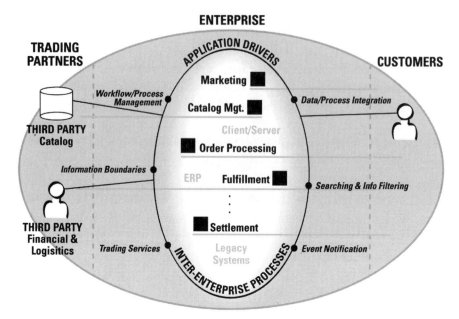

Figure 3 - 7. Putting It All Together

Companies that have mastered I-Markets have already turned complete industries upside down. Competing against them will be increasingly difficult. The pioneers show no sign of slowing their pace of new developments. To win in 21st century markets, a company should start by identifying its unique requirements and issues – independent of the packages available on the market – then select low hanging fruit for initial implementation projects. Central to this approach is the reuse of a common core of e-Commerce application components to incrementally develop new applications and grow their capabilities as new market opportunities are discovered. By adopting a component-based development approach for agile software development, companies can implement breakthrough I-Markets today and take advantage of new opportunities that will appear tomorrow.

References

1 Derek Leebaert (Editor), *The Future of the Electronic Marketplace*, MIT Press, 1998.

2 "IBM's Gerstner Speaks On E-Commerce," Newsbytes News Network, March 19, 1998.

3 Peter Fingar, "Blueprint for Open eCommerce," Component Strategies magazine, February, 1999.

4 Les Alberthal, "The Once and Future Craftsman Culture," in *The Future of the Electronic Marketplace*, MIT Press, 1998.

5 A Report *"The Marketspace: eCommerce in the Digital Economy,"* Tampa Regional Technology Council meeting, April 19, 1998.

6 "Jeff Bezos: selling books, running hard!" *Forbes ASAP*, April 6, 1998.

7 http://www.internetwk.com/BOTI/boti2.htm

8 http://customers.com/cases/cisco.html

9 http://www.cyberatlas.com/segments/advertising/emark.html

10 http://www.datamation.com/PlugIn/workbench/ecom/stories/08ecom.html

11 Kate Maddox, *Web Commerce,* John Wiley, 1998, p. 42.

12 http://www.battery.com/yankee.html

Notes

Chapter 4 - E-Commerce Applications: Customer Care

Notes

One Customer at a Time

"The central economic imperative of the Industrial Age was to increase productivity. The central economic imperative of the network economy is to amplify relationships. Since a relationship involves two members investing in it, its value increases twice as fast as one's investment. Outsiders act as employees, employees as outsiders. New relationships blur the role of employees and customers to the point of unity. They reveal the customer and the company as one. In the network economy, producing and consuming fuse into a single verb: prosuming. And whoever has the smartest customers wins. The world's best experts on your product or service don't work for your company. They are your customers, or a hobby tribe. The network economy is founded on technology, but can only be built on relationships. It starts with chips and ends with trust."[1] – Kevin Kelly, Executive editor, Wired Magazine and author of *Out of Control* and the *New Rules for the New Economy*.

"We had a simple goal. Find the right customers, learn what they want, sell it to them, and service all their needs." – Gabrielle Battista, President of Cable & Wireless.[2]

As this decade comes to a close, businesses are being buffeted by a silent revolution and a power shift in global markets. Armed with networked information technology, the customer has grabbed power from producers. It is now the fully informed, never satisfied customer that holds absolute power in the marketplace, determining what is to be made, when, where and at what cost. And, they want it all, not just the buying transaction. Whether it is buying a PC, spare-parts, engineering services or life insurance, customers want complete care throughout the consumption life cycle, from discovery all the way through support after the sale or contract. Today, customers demand the best deal, the best service and solution-centered support. The Industrial Age was about mass production. The Customer Age is about mass customization. It is about turning a company, and its entire value-chain, over to the command and control of the customer – wow. Because it is about gaining customers for life, it is about a conversation, an interactive dialog and shared know-how, not a transaction.

In his keynote at Neosphere 98, Bob McCashin, EDS Corporate VP, summed up the power shift to the customer and the need for enterprise customer management, "We are entering a new era – or perhaps it is the rebirth of an older one – in which the individual customer is central. It is an era of understanding, or intimacy, with the people we serve – even when they live on the other side of the world. It's a time when we can know hundreds of thousands of customers well – particularly our best customers. And we can show them that we appreciate their business in meaningful ways. It's called "enterprise" because market leaders today realize that all forms of interactions with their customers – whether through sales, service, or delivery – affect their customer relationships. These interactions can help you acquire the right customers – retain them by meeting their individual needs – and maximize the lifetime value of the most profitable customer relationships."[3]

Throughout the customer cycle, from customer acquisition to building loyalty, *Customer Care* is the cornerstone of the customer-driven company. Customer Care applications meet several strategic business objectives including:

- Improve customer service while reducing costs
- Put the customer in control by providing self-service and solution-centered support
- Segment customer behavior 1-to-1 to individualize goods and services, and
- Earn customer loyalty to gain a lifetime of business.

Customer care has many definitions. Historically customer care has meant responding to customer questions and problems via a company's toll-free number – the call center. Customers also use call centers to find out the status of their orders or accounts. But now there is another channel for customer care. Virtually every area of customer service (information, support, maintenance, warranties, upgrades and status) can be handled via the Internet. Customers can ask questions via email, search support databases for similar problems or questions and get product information via the Web.

For some companies, their customer care offerings go beyond simply problem-solving to moving the center of their relationships with customers to the Web. While the Web cannot totally replace the phone and face-to-face communication with customers, it can strengthen these and all customer touch points. Web-based customer care can become the focal point of customer relationship management and provide breakthrough benefits for both the enterprise and its customers – substantially reducing costs while improving service.

In the Customer Age, customers become first class business assets, to be managed with the same care as traditional assets such as capital and labor. Like other business assets a company must *invest* in its productive customers to achieve maximum value. Classifying customers by their lifetime value to the enterprise can guide the investment in building relationships. Cambridge Technology Partners explains, "Customer relationships are assets that require investment in order to reach full potential. The enterprise must determine which relationships are worth the investment and how to get the highest return from each one. Since building relationships is not a cost-free proposition, customers with the highest potential to perform should receive the most attention. For one-time customers as well as "churners," who display little loyalty despite all attempts to retain them, close relationships may represent losing investments. Personalized customer care makes sense if the customer's lifetime value sufficiently exceeds the cost of building the relationship."[4]

Like any other business asset, the management of the customer asset requires information, and customer care applications provide the information platform for the enterprise to manage life-long customer relationships. "Calculating 'lifetime value (LTV) of customers' will be a key trend for valuing commerce sites. One of the ways in which the virtual world will converge with reality in 1999 will be in a growing demand for rational ways to measure the value of online sites. Today, just over 40% of the leading Web sites surveyed by IDC attempt to measure LTVs, and many do so quite informally."[5]

The domain of Customer Care applications is shown in Figure 4 - 1. The basic elements are simple to picture: an enterprise provides its best service and support in return for customer loyalty. Notice in the figure that both I-Markets and Customer Care applications are customer-facing. A useful distinction between I-Market and Customer Care applications is *"buying* versus *using."* The processes of the I-Market focus on a customer *buying* a product or service while the Customer Care processes focus on *using* the product or service. The two sets of applications overlap and intermesh, of course, because excellent service naturally leads to increased sales: cross-selling and up-selling in the process of rendering service. Often, the Customer Care applications are the ones first encountered by a customer, perhaps in researching or shopping for solutions to their problems. In fact, Customer Care can be *the* e-Commerce anchor – the enterprise portal.

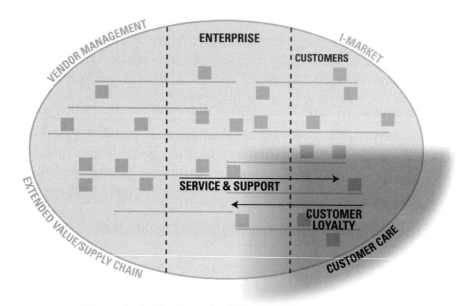

Figure 4 - 1. The Domain of Customer Care Applications

By providing a rich and ongoing dialog, Customer Care applications help companies acquire and retain customers. Customer Care applications can deliver double benefits: increased customer satisfaction through better quality service, and reduced costs through customer self-service. Loyal customers increase repeat business. Studies report that over 60% of a company's total business is repeat business. Self-service customer support can contribute millions to the bottom line in large corporations. Customer Care applications put the customer in control and are used by companies to integrate new kinds of behavioral and tacit information about customers. Understanding customer behavior and preferences gives a company the ability to better segment the market (1-to-many), but more strategically, it allows the company to segment the ever changing needs of an individual customer and deliver customized product and service offerings, one customer at a time (1-to-1). Failure to provide these services will result in lost customers – smart companies understand that a dissatisfied customer is one click away from doing business with the competition.

While, as Gabrielle Battista writes, the goals of customer care applications are simple, designing and implementing them can be another matter – three central problems must be solved:

- enterprise information and customer information must be integrated into a unified whole,
- new kinds of customer behavioral information must be captured and processed, and
- customers and employees must share a common knowledge base.

Typically, as shown in Figure 4 - 2, customers have a fractured view of an enterprise. Like the parable of the blind men and the elephant, a company is defined by an individual customer by that part of the company that it sees and interacts with – the enterprise's touch points. As shown in the left side of Figure 4 - 2, customer information can be, and usually is, scattered around and locked away in many departmental silos.

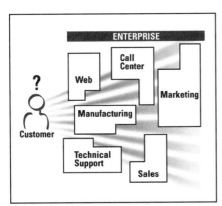
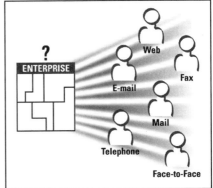

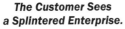

The Customer Sees   **The Enterprise Sees**
a Splintered Enterprise.   **a Splintered Customer.**

**Figure 4 - 2. Neither the Customer Nor the Enterprise
Have Complete Views of the Other**

Today, the customer navigating these silos to solve a problem must run the gauntlet of "touch tone hell" to piece together the relevant information. Life-long customer relationships require a much more holistic view of both the enterprise and the currently disjoint customer information dispersed throughout the enterprise.

Conversely, the enterprise has only a splintered view of the customer, again determined by touch points. To better serve a given customer, the enterprise must gain a window into wide-ranging and ever-changing customer attributes and behavior. It needs to piece together the splintered views of customers as shown in the right side of Figure 4 - 2. To build and maintain life-long relationships, customers and the enterprise must share common and holistic views of each other, as shown in Figure 4 - 3 and as confirmed by the Gartner Group, "As enterprises make the transition to customer-centric business models, all organizational functions must have access to a consistent picture of the customer relationship."[6]

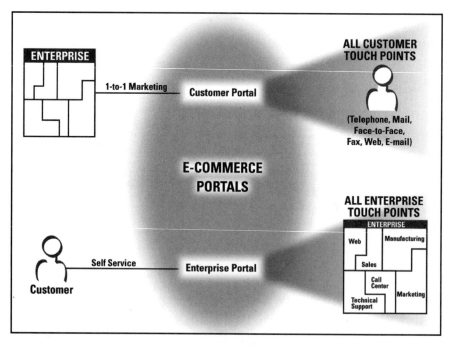

Figure 4 - 3. Holistic Views Needed for Life-Long Customer Relationships

With all the talk, press and rush to establish e-Commerce "portals," the ultimate portal is overlooked. In the Customer Age, the customer is the portal, a doorway to a broad and ever-changing world of needs. It is marketing in reverse – instead of making a product and finding customers for it, we repeat Gabrielle Battista's formula, "Find the right customers, learn what they want, sell it to them, and service all their needs." Ditto, from the customer perspective: find the right company, learn what they can provide to meet my individual needs, buy it from them, and demand excellent service.

How does a company really get close and stay close to customers in the world of automation? It must overcome the second problem, capturing and processing new kinds of information. An enterprise needs to make a quantum leap in its information systems – from handling *transactions* to handling *conversations* – collecting and processing behavioral data.

Click-streams through a company's Web site, buttons pushed on a touch-tone phone, email, postal mail and faxes are all parts of conversations with customers. Yet this wealth of information is not captured in meaningful ways to maintain a complete view of the attributes and behavior of customers. Forrester Research interviewed 50 Fortune 1,000 companies and learned that less than half use any customer data collected from the Web and email in their other sales, marketing, and customer service applications. Of the customer information they do capture in their various systems, 66% of the companies feel they do an adequate job by synchronizing customer data via batch interfaces and manual re-keying of printed reports.[7] Such care and feeding of these batch information processes can hardly be the basis for a real-time customer dialog. The Forrester Report reveals that although the respondents expect the Web to be the dominant approach to customer service by 2001, few firms today integrate on-line customer behavioral data with other contact channels.

Cambridge Technology Partners elaborates, "Enterprises tend to think of customer information in terms of transactions. This customer placed 32 orders worth $617,000. We made 119 shipments to four different addresses. That customer signed up for a contract valued at two million dollars over a three year period. While this information is certainly customer data, it is not the stuff that relationships are made of – it doesn't address what is really important to the customer. For instance, are they enjoying the product? Are they getting the most out of the service? Do they show productivity increases in their business? What features do they like, dislike, or want to see added? Has this purchase helped further their goals? This type of so-called "fat" [tacit] information is valuable for relationship building because it turns an account number into a living customer. Many companies, however, are not set up to manage relationship information, which often remains invisible or unavailable to the greater enterprise. Information simply stays with those to whom it was given because there is no mechanism for properly recording and disseminating it. When this happens, information is not only underutilized, it is at risk. If employees leave the company, their information leaves, too. Personalized customer care on a large scale is only as good as the enterprise's ability to capture, store, integrate, and disseminate customer information. Every employee should be able to learn from the collective knowledge of the enterprise."[8] This "fat" information also has a limited life span of usefulness. Because of the temporal nature of the information, the emphasis must be on *real-time* collection and dissemination.

Rich Melmon, Partner in The McKenna Group, explains the essential elements of the right kind of customer dialog, "If these [customer] dialogues are designed properly, they will allow a wide range of people with varying needs to find their way through the system easily to get what they come for. From the user's point of view, the dialogues will integrate four basic elements:

- *Personalization:* I want it my way, with my particular needs driving the system's responses to me
- *Self-Service:* I want to explore on my own, select on my own, and troubleshoot on my own
- *Immediacy:* I want the information now; I want the product now
- *Intimacy:* I want it to feel like a two-way process; I want to know that my actions are being used by the company to learn what I want; I want my feedback to register with the company; and I want tangible evidence that I'm in the loop.[9]

Excellent self-service, also means providing the "know-how" to gain maximum benefit and marginalize problems from using a product or service. This leads to the third major problem, providing know-how, not just data. Building Customer Care applications does not mean integrating all the information in a company and unleashing it on the customer. A company should not throw its entire catalogs of goods and services at the customer. Instead, the company should find ways to learn of the customers' needs and summon individualized options and alternatives. This requires more than "data", more than "information" – it requires "knowledge."

Sure, customer care means providing transactional data like order and account tracking and customer history information. Transactional data and information are, however, no longer sufficient. Holistic customer care requires that customers gain access to more than data and information – they need access to the company's knowledge base. A company's "know-how" is typically contained in the communal knowledge of employees. This knowledge, including common solutions to common problems, needs to be captured in computer systems if it is to be shared by customers. Solution-centered customer services can be simple, requiring little more than maintaining a "frequently asked questions" (FAQ) Web site, or may require advanced knowledge-based technologies such as case-based reasoning.

To sustain life-long relationships, customers and companies must share holistic views of each other, gain intimacy through capturing behavioral information, and have access to a common pool of "know-how," provided not just by the enterprise but also by customer communities. A robust e-Commerce platform for Customer Care applications can enable new kinds of interactions, new kinds of information, and comprehensive access to all customer and enterprise touch points. The ever growing customer care initiatives can foster joint problem-solving, convenient self-service and self-selling. Given the information they need in the consumption process, customers will sell to themselves (customers can be a company's best sales force) and service their own information needs.

The Business Case for Customer Care Applications

What differentiates one company from another in the same market? Several years ago, quality was the key. Then quality and low cost together became the winning combination. But now, quality and cost are givens. Returning to the Forrester survey, "large companies risk poor customer service daily due to the grab bag of independent applications they use to support their customers. While this problem has existed for years, it will soon end as the Web becomes an ever-stronger force and high-quality self-service becomes a competitive differentiator. In the Internet economy, high quality customer service is an absolute requirement. And the current haphazard approaches to customer management will destroy a company's future."

Forrester defines the new standard for customer service as "consistent, high-quality customer support across all communication channels and business functions, based on common, complete information shared by employees, their customers, and business partners."[10] A robust e-Commerce infrastructure is essential to realizing the new customer care standard and the Web becomes central to customer care strategy. The Web will not replace call centers, face-to-face meetings and other forms of communication. Instead it will transform, support and integrate them. The Web will be the first place a customer will choose go among the many enterprise touch points. All touch points are vital to what Cambridge Technology Partners (CTP) calls "zero-loss learning."

According to CTP, "Collecting customer-specific information begins with the practice of zero-loss learning. Zero-loss learning views every point of contact with the customer as a potential learning experience. Every customer interaction – whether it be with a sales person, clerk, or customer support representative – yields insight into the customer relationship that can be captured and stored in a knowledge base. As a relationship matures, the knowledge base becomes more comprehensive and more accurate. Ultimately, the entire enterprise can benefit from this growing library of customer data, which is leveraged to provide customers with personalized and consistent service."[11]

Transamerica Leasing recognized that electronic commerce offered the opportunity to reduce operating costs, while providing expanded services to its customers. Moving from ship, to rail, to truck, and back again, each container in Transamerica Leasing's fleet must be tracked as shipping lines lease and return equipment throughout the world. To meet its customers' requirements, Transamerica must supply not only first rate equipment but also up-to-date information about leasing agreements, equipment status, licensing and inspection records, and physical and technical specifications. Transamerica developed the Tradexonline tracking system to allow customers and vendors to track their shipping containers and respective lease accounts via the Web. "Much of our business has been conducted over the telephone," says George Reilly, Director of Business Systems at Transamerica Leasing. "Customers call our service representatives to place equipment on lease or to make arrangements to return it. They can also ask how many units they have on lease, how many they have returned, or how many are slated for return. Our regional offices operate over an extended business day, but some customers now have centralized logistics offices operating around the clock; they're inconvenienced if they need information in order to respond to their customers, but our local regional office is closed for the night. While on the telephone, our service representatives access their computers to get answers," Reilly continues. "We recognized that electronic commerce could provide a way for customers to look up information and initiate transactions 24 hours a day, seven days a week, making it easier for them and for us. We decided to use our e-commerce initiative to redesign our whole business model, away from requiring person-to-person contact to delivering more information electronically."[12]

Transamerica's system does much more than track containers and lease accounts; it provides a new marketing vehicle. Considering that the worldwide shipping industry spends $20 billion per year to move empty containers from one port to another, Transamerica saw a market opportunity. "One in five containers in transit is filled mainly with fresh air," said Paul Crinks, a vice president at Greybox Logistics Services, Inc., a subsidiary of Transamerica. So a business service called "Greybox" was launched to serve as an electronic stock exchange to match carriers that have extra containers with those lacking containers. For example, under the service, which is supported by Tradexonline, a shipping company planning to move 40 empty containers from Los Angeles to Hong Kong can check to see if other carriers want to "rent" those containers for that leg of the journey. Greybox charges $50 for each container that changes hands, and the shipping companies save between $250 and $400 per container by having another company move it for them, Crinks said. The service has been a hit: Greybox is interchanging 1,200 containers per month for 150 customers, and the interchange rate is growing 30% per month, Crinks said. Crinks and his team are evaluating incentive options, such as a frequent-usage program or Internet pricing models.

In addition to Transamerica, three other industry examples of customer care applications are shown in Figure 4 - 4. HP Customer Care is the single-branded name that the Hewlett-Packard Company has given to all of its support programs and technologies keeping commercial customers, small businesses and consumers up and running. HP Customer Care offers full-service support through a broad range of services including trouble-shooting tools; setup and installation; warranty upgrades, repair, and exchange services; phone and Web support; software updates; and self-maintenance services. In May 1998, HP announced an improved HP Customer Care Web site as well as enhancements to the HP Customer Care call center.

The Customer Care Web support site provides customers with free, one-stop access to technical support for more than 600 HP personal computer, printer and imaging products. HP Customer Care call centers also provide technical support from numerous locations worldwide.

"This improved site plays an important role in increasing customer satisfaction by making support easier to access and understand," said Doug Moore, worldwide manager of online services for HP's Product Support Division. "Increasingly, customers prefer the control and convenience they get with around-the-clock online support, and this site will be our key platform for providing future enhancements."[13]

Features of the HP Customer Care Web site include:

- *proactive notification* – customers now can request e-mail notification of the availability of new software and drivers, and solutions to frequently asked questions. Customers can create their own profile with multiple HP products, creating an integrated, personalized, proactive tool for their HP solution.

Industry: Transportation (Customer Care)

TRANSAMERICA

Business Drivers:
20% of all shipping containers were being returned to their home destinations empty, costing the industry $20B annually.

Solution:
***Customer care** application that allows shippers to 'rent' empty containers that return 'home'.*

Benefits:
Shippers have reduced container handling costs by $400 per unit (potential $36 million savings for TAL customers in 1999).

Industry: High Tech (Customer Care)

HEWLETT PACKARD

Business Drivers:
Inefficient support infrastructure costly and time-intensive

Solution:
Online Customer Care Web provides FAQ, automated email response, personalized configuration.

Benefits:
Number of customer inquiries increases 10% each month, 80% handled over the Web

Industry: Manufacturing (Customer Care)

MICHELIN

Business Drivers:
Phone based interaction with dealers demanded high personnel costs

Solution:
Extranet for 280 dealers that lets them look up inventory, place orders, check order status, and get answers to questions

Benefits:
Allowed Michelin to reduce customer service staff from 240 to 175 while maintaining quality of care.

Industry: Shipping/Transportation (Customer Care)

UPS

Business Drivers:
Conventional customer service practices expensive and inefficient.

Solution:
An Internet system to track shipments, provide service information, calculate rates, find transit times, etc.

Benefits:
System fields over 4.7 million customer inquiries per month resulting in savings of millions, improved customer retention, and repeat business.

Figure 4 - 4. Customer Care Industry Examples

- *trouble-shooting tools* – includes many new problem-solving tools, print-quality diagnostics and trouble-shooting trees that provide step-by-step solutions for common problems.
- *improved software download tools* – printer drivers can be downloaded more accurately, and Oil Change, a software tool that automates the locating and updating of printer drivers, is provided free of charge for commercial HP LaserJet printer products.
- *support guides* – new guides include repair-path advice and a reseller locator, complete with maps, to find the nearest HP authorized support provider. These tools help customers find convenient repair locations whether at home or on the road.
- *moderated online forums* – customers can post support questions, and receive advice from HP in a community-forum format. Other forum members also can share advice and their collective knowledge. The forum is open to observers and sales prospects who can benefit from reading the online dialog without actually having to participate.

United Parcel Service of America, Inc. launched a project in 1997 that distributed vital customer service functions, making some of its electronic services less visible. UPS is integrating its package-tracking capabilities directly with corporate customers' sites. Puzzled by the initiative, Computerworld's Sharon Machlis asked,[14] "Why, when conventional Web strategy is to create more links to your site and increase public traffic, is UPS moving the other way?"

Ross McCullough, electronic-commerce group manager explained, "We want to enable the merchants to speak directly to their customers." By helping retailers offer more services to consumers, he said, those retailers might generate more repeat sales – and thus more shipping business for UPS. By linking the confirmation number with a shipping number when an order is first entered, customers get the information they need to track the package immediately – there is no need to check in another time for the shipping number. And the tracking information is integrated with the retailer's site, so a user would get status information from the site where the order was placed, not from the separate UPS page where 4.7 million tracking requests were logged in December 1997. UPS's strategy cements its place in the value-chain by way of Customer Care applications.

Not long ago, Michelin North America Inc.'s report card from its 1,700 independent tire dealers was dismal – their overall grade was a "D," for "Difficult to do business with." They just had to do better. So, Michelin put together a cross-functional team from its marketing, sales, customer service and information technology departments to develop its Michelin's Bib Net Web site – named for the 100-year-old inflated "Bibendum" Michelin man. The team also enlisted their independent tire dealers, visiting 55 of them and bringing 15 to 20 to South Carolina to brainstorm a technical wish list and help design the user interfaces. Computerworld's Carol Sliwa reports that, as a result of the team's work, "dealers now can access Michelin's Bib Net site to order products, schedule deliveries, check order status, make real-time inventory inquiries, receive advance shipment notices, create claims, scan pricing and see a national account directory."

"We didn't really go into this to save money," Lynn Melvin, manager of electronic commerce application development at Michelin said. "Basically, we wanted to create close partnerships."[15] Thanks to the simplicity and ubiquity of Web browsers, Michelin does not have to worry about dealers' disparate hardware and software platforms and their widely varying technological savvy.

These industry examples reveal that Customer Care is not a single application, but a growing and changing family of applications. Some of the applications represent small incremental steps while others can be completely new, large and complex initiatives. The latter is often the case when competitive threats are discovered, which, in turn, create severe time-to-market challenges. Success will depend on a company's ability to establish and maintain an *agile* e-Commerce platform for industrial-strength rapid application development and management of its growing Customer Care applications portfolio. This approach must be based on the first principles of business and technology architecture.

Customer Care Application Framework

Having defined what Customer Care systems are and why they are so important to the bottom line of a business, we can gain a deeper understanding by examining elements of an underlying business and technology architecture – business processes and application drivers or enablers. Some of the key business processes that a Customer Care system must support are illustrated in Figure 4 - 5.

Key Business Processes for Customer Care Applications

Figure 4 - 6 drills down to reveal the major elements of some of the key business processes that Customer Care applications must embody, including Account Management, Customer Self-service, Customer Support and Marketing.

Account Management. As business conversations turn into engagements and contracts, records are established and maintained in multiple, often disparate, information systems across an enterprise. These systems must be integrated and secure, and extended to the Web for convenient customer access. Customer Care applications must provide the facilities for order tracking; maintaining personalized account information; and maintaining contracts, billing and other business processes of account management. Employees and customers need real-time access to accurate and secure account information in order to participate in self-service, support or marketing processes and interactions.

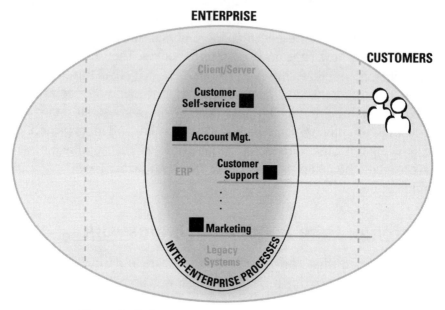

Figure 4 - 5. Customer Care Application Framework

Customer Self-service. Today's enterprise portal for customer service is the call center – a place where a customer, if honestly greeted, would hear, "Welcome to Touch-tone hell. Please listen to all 23 options before making your selection. Your call is important to us: please continue to hold, and hold, and hold." Businesses and consumers are worn out with traditional customer service. Analysts cited in a recent Silknet report estimate that "a straightforward request, handled on the phone costs a company between $25 and $30. By comparison, resolving the same problem through a Web-based self-service application costs between $2 and $3. Costs are compounded by the fact that call center operations offer little opportunity for economies of scale. Customers tend to ask the same questions over and over again. And service representatives answer them one customer at a time. Analysts estimate that repeat rates run as high as the 50 to 70 percent range. No company can afford to keep supporting customers this way."[16]

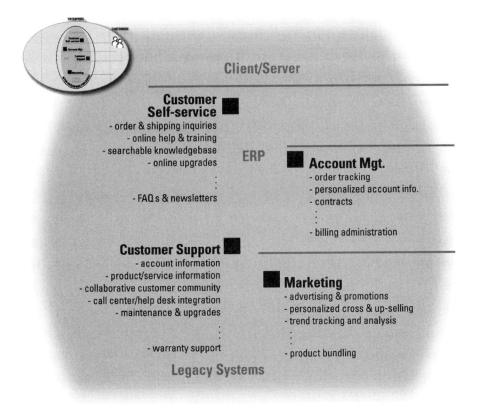

Figure 4 - 6. Customer Care Business Processes

The call center is really little more than using the customer service representative as a customer's browser. The CSR is the customer's remote eyes and hands. What's wrong with this picture? Why not let the customer use their own browser to get what they want? Customers know best what they want. Anything that gives power to the customer to conveniently (repeat, *conveniently*) serve themselves is going to be a winner; to wit, the automatic teller machine (ATM) that eradicated the lines of customers on hold in bank lobbies.

The fully interactive nature of the Internet changes everything in the world of self-service. Relevant information and intelligent support processes all can be marshaled in real-time, anywhere, anytime – here and now. From tracking orders or shipments, to searching a knowledge base to solve a problem, customer service processes will support an increasing array of useful and intelligent services. Online help, education and training, FAQs and newsletters, and product and service upgrades can be just a click away.

Customer Support. Maintenance, upgrades, warranty, product, service and account information make up but a small part of a next generation customer support offering which may include collaborative customer communities, call center and help desk integration, and knowledge-based support systems. As defined by the Customer Support Consortium, "Solution-Centered Support is a vision for leveraging support transactions by creating knowledge that empowers the business. Solutions represent both what is needed by the customer, and what is gained by the support organization as support requests are handled. Leverage is obtained through a system that can capture the solutions generated by the customer support process, and make them available for reuse throughout the support organization. This allows support to harness the knowledge power of its employees and customers to improve both quality and efficiency, and to scale the business, while effectively managing costs and resources."[17] Solution-centered customer support plus customer self-service go together to form the centerpiece of next generation customer care. Further, companies that connect their customers to each other can create a community-of-interest that becomes part of the company's support resources (customers become virtual support staff employees!).

Marketing

What does "customer care" have to do with "marketing?" In a word, it is "loyalty." Cambridge Technology Partners' Joe Giffler explains, "We've all heard the statistics about customer loyalty:

- "...the average company loses half its customers over a five year period..."
- "...reducing defections 5% can boost profits from 25% to 85%..."
- "...yet companies typically spend five times more on customer acquisition than on retention..."
- "...65% to 85% of customers who defect say they were satisfied with their former supplier..."
- "...totally satisfied customers are six times more likely to repurchase than satisfied customers"
- "...a happy customer will tell five people about their experience, while each dissatisfied customer will tell nine..."[18]

Michael Meltzer, NCR Corporation's director for financial services consulting, has made some interesting observations about Pareto's Law. "Pareto's Law, also called the 80/20 rule, makes the observation that 80% of the profit is derived from 20% of the customers. While Pareto's Law is considered by some to be naive and overly simplistic, this 80/20 relationship appears too often to be ignored. In the past, it was always easier to attempt to "poach" your competitors' customers. However, studies have shown that companies spend five times more money on acquiring new customers as they do on retaining those they already have. Further studies demonstrated that: 'As a customer relationship with a company lengthens, profits rise.'[19] – And not just a little. Companies can boost profits by 100% by retaining just 5% more of their customers."[20]

The winning strategy is to segment customers with the 80/20 rule, and then invest in real-time 1-to-1 marketing and lifetime customer care with the 20%, most productive market segment – create communities-of-interest and provide solution-centered knowledge resources. Companies must listen and learn what these customers want and find ways to meet those needs, now and in the future. The 20% club is not static. In both B-to-B and B-to-C marketspaces, customer needs change over time. By blending sales force automation (SFA) with customer self-service a new generation of marketing strategy can be implemented for competitive advantage. And since the customer and the sales force can have a 360° view of each other, true customer partnerships can be forged. Marketing guru, Regis "Real-time" McKenna describes customer partnerships, "Ultimately, marketing should involve the customer as a partner in development and production. It won't be easy to do, because most companies today have focused their processes on improving time to market and, by inclination and culture, see the customer as an end target rather than a partner."[21]

Investing in the top 20% of customers does not mean closing doors. Cambridge Technology Partners' Paul McNabb and Mike Steinbaum explain, "Of course, the door for new customers is always open, but the less glamorous areas of customer care often pay higher returns. The effort required to further develop existing relationships is often quite small compared to the potential payoff. Existing customers represent the "low-hanging fruit" because a relationship has already begun. And loyal customers are an enterprise's best customers. Each year a customer remains with the company, his or her value increases – spending tends to go up. Also, existing customers are often the best source of referrals.[22]

Key Application Drivers for Customer Care Applications

A core set of application drivers is needed to implement customer care business processes in software. These include Information Boundaries, Searching and Information Filtering, Workflow/Process Management, Trading Services, Event Notification and Data/Process Integration facilities, as shown in Figure 4 - 7.

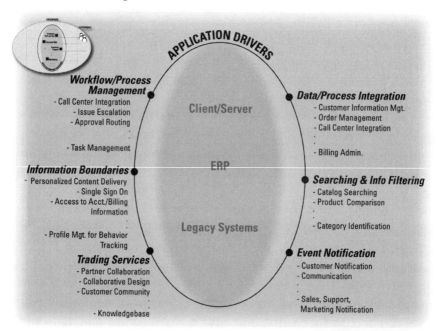

Figure 4 - 7. Key Application Drivers for a Customer Care System

Information Boundaries

Profile management application facilities are needed to manage information boundaries among all participants in Customer Care systems – security is essential to all parties involved. User authentication, authorization and access controls are maintained by profile management software and facilities. Dynamic profiling capabilities are needed to enable cross-enterprise application access and resource allocation. Personalized content delivery, single sign-on, access to account and billing information, and profile management for behavior tracking are all essential to delivering personalized service.

Workflow/Process Management

Workflow facilities underpin collaborative customer care. Existing workflow systems of participants in the chain may be triggered by events as they occur. Workflow plays an integral role in call center integration, issue escalation, approval routing and task management.

Data/Process Integration

Data and process integration is required to link together multiple systems of suppliers, trading partners and customer touch points. Internally, existing ERP and legacy accounting systems must be integrated with outward-facing Customer Care applications. Key legacy systems include customer information systems, order management, call center integration, billing administration and knowledge-based support systems. Data and process integration is an ongoing activity. Over time customers and trading partners may come and go, making it essential that data and process integration facilities are easy to understand, use and administer.

Event Notification

Event notification facilities are essential for providing customer service personnel and customers with notifications of exceptions, changes and other situations requiring their attention. These include customer notification communication, sales, support and marketing communication.

Trading Services

Trading services provide essential application facilities needed for collaboration: trading partner collaboration, collaborative design and building customer communities-of-interest. With trading services facilities a company can create and maintain online collaboration boards where buyers, sellers and brokers can share information and conduct business. Trading services components are the key to connecting customers to customers and connecting customers to the fabric of support resources contained in the value-chain.

Searching and Information Filtering

Searching and information filtering facilities are needed by all users of customer care systems. Catalog and document search are most common. While catalog searching, product comparison and category identification are essential, Customer Care applications also require knowledge-based techniques such as collaborative information filtering and case-based reasoning to provide customer support for using complex goods and services.

These six application drivers are key not only to Customer Care systems but can be reused for all e-Commerce applications. By establishing a common core of these e-Commerce application drivers, a company's unique business processes, rules and policies can be extended outward to trading partners and customers.

Customer Care Strategies

Wired magazine's Kevin Kelly has done a magnificent job of netting out the strategic goals of customer care:

- "Make customers as smart as you are.
- Connect customers to customers.
- All things being equal, choose technology that connects.
- Imagine your customers as your employees.
- Don't just solve problems; pursue opportunities."[23]

"We don't think of technology as a cost center. It's a strategic weapon. It contributes to service, so cost is not the only or even the primary consideration," [24] states Robert F. McDermott, chairman emeritus and former CEO of USAA. USAA wants all customer information to be integrated into its Customer Care systems. The moment a piece of correspondence reaches its San Antonio or Tampa offices, it is scanned, indexed and made available to any agent across the company.

In succeeding with Customer Care applications, metrics count. Companies must measure the right things, and measure them right. Traditional measures such as how fast customer service representatives can get a customer off the phone, how many calls the agent can handle in an eight hour shift, or a salesman's meeting of a quota simply do not measure relationship building. Retention and growth of sales to existing customers are far better indicators of success. Getting the customer's problem solved in one call, cross-selling and up-selling, or gaining valuable customer feedback (complaints included) can generate metrics that count when it comes to measuring success in relationship management. Customer care initiatives cannot be evaluated unless they can be measured and companies wanting to succeed must design and implement appropriate measurement strategies.

Personalized customer care opens the door to new opportunities to offer value-add services, especially in the business-to-business marketspace. Thus, customer care should be thought of as not just another cost center, but as a potential revenue opportunity. Such opportunities will, of course, vary by industry and by the sophistication of the knowledge base associated with particular goods and services.

As we have explored in this book, Customer Care applications have many dimensions and specific applications. Point solutions do not get the job done. Instead a Customer Care platform is needed to provide the foundation for growing a portfolio of solutions. For such an approach to work, the Customer Care platform must support incremental growth, allowing the enterprise to continuously improve customer care offerings and take advantage customer service opportunities as they arise.

By constructing solutions from best-of-breed e-Commerce application components, an enterprise can arrange, rearrange, and reuse the components as customer care requirements dictate. Returning to Transamerica's Reiley, "We didn't consider buying a pre-packaged solution, because there wasn't one that offered the kinds of e-commerce applications we needed," says Reilly. "We knew the applications we were planning to offer were unique to our business, so we would have to develop them ourselves. However, we also knew we would need some common Web-site management facilities that were not unique to our business." As Transamerica began to implement its e-Commerce solution, it realized that there were two aspects to the work. "We needed to build business-specific applications to provide our customers with electronic access to the information they required, and we had to put an infrastructure in place in order to deliver our enhanced services in a controlled and effective manner," says Reilly. Like most companies, Transamerica had limited IS resources to spare for application development. "Our challenge was to make sure that we were working on the right things ourselves, while identifying those things that could be provided by somebody else," Reilly added. "The component architecture enabled us to strengthen our e-Commerce infrastructure while protecting our investment in existing applications; by using application components we avoided internal infrastructure development, allowing our developers to focus on new business applications."

By leveraging common components an enterprise can reduce costs and complexity for building, managing, and delivering customer relationship management, obviating the need to buy specific packages for every customer care process. These common components can be purchased and modified for specific Customer Care applications, while requiring minimal incremental skills from the IT department. This permits reduced time and capital investment when creating future customer care solutions or evolving existing solutions to support changing customer demands.

Putting It All Together

Customer Care applications harness the Internet to automate the business processes of customer service and support. They can provide a company with extraordinary customer service advantages not possible before the advent of e-Commerce. A sustainable approach to implementing Customer Care systems leverages legacy enterprise systems (including traditional call centers) and extends them to customers in a convenient and robust self-service format, as shown in Figure 4 - 8.

A company should start by identifying its unique requirements and issues – independent of the packages available on the market – then select low hanging fruit for initial implementation projects. Central to this approach is the reuse of a common core of e-Commerce application components to incrementally develop new Customer Care applications and grow their capabilities. By adopting a component-based development approach for agile software development, companies can implement breakthrough Customer Care systems today and grow ever more rich service and support systems for tomorrow.

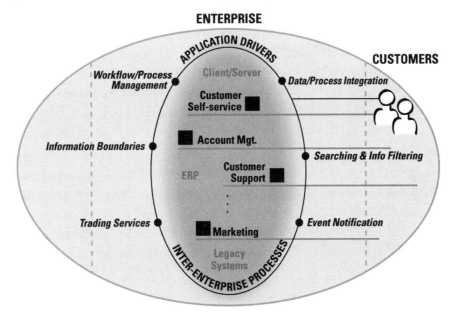

Figure 4 - 8. Putting It All Together

References

[1] Kevin Kelly, *New Rules for the New Economy: 10 Radical Strategies for a Connected World,* Viking Press, November, 1998.

[2] Fred Wiersema. *Customer Intimacy: Pick Your Partners, Shape Your Culture, Win Together,* Knowledge Exchange, 1996.

[3] http://www.centrobe.com/news/keynotes/neosphere98.asp

[4] Paul McNabb and Mike Steinbaum, "Reclaiming Customer Care: The Milkman Returns," Cambridge Information Network, 1999.

[5] Frank Gens, Sr. VP, Internet Research, "IDC Predictions '99: The 'Real' Internet Emerges, "International Data Corporation, Online. 1999.

[6] http://gartner12.gartnerweb.com/public/static/home/home.html

[7] J. Thomas Gormley, III, "Web-Centric Customer Service," *The Forrester Report,* February, 1999.

[8] Paul McNabb and Mike Steinbaum, "Reclaiming Customer Care: The Milkman Returns," Cambridge Information Network, 1999.

[9] Rich Melmon, Partner, The McKenna Group, "Real-time Marketing versus One-to-One Marketing," http://www.mckenna-group.com/realtime/rt/index.html

[10] J. Thomas Gormley, III, "Web-Centric Customer Service," *The Forrester Report,* February, 1999.

[11] Paul McNabb and Mike Steinbaum, "Reclaiming Customer Care: The Milkman Returns," Cambridge Information Network, 1999.

[12] Thomas Hoffman, "Broker keeps containers from shipping empty," *Computerworld,* 09/14/98.

[13] http://www.hp.com/pressrel/may98/28may98c.htm

[14] Sharon Machlis, "Integrated tracking," *Computerworld,* 11/24/97. http://www.computerworld.com/home/print9497.nsf/all/SL47UPS16F5E

[15] Carol Sliwa, "Michelin links dealers Web site frees access to accounts, orders," *Computerworld,* 11/30/98 http://www.computerworld.com/home/print.nsf/all/9811307E6A

[16] http://www.silknet.com/resource/whatitmeans.asp

[17] *"Getting Started with Solution-Centered Support^SM: A Framework for Leveraging Knowledge,"* White Paper Overview, 1997. http://www.customersupport.org/inits/scs/scsprog.htm

[18] Joe Giffler, "Capturing Customers For Life," *Decision Magazine,* May 1998.

[19] Reichfield and Sasser, *Harvard Business Review,* 1990.

[20] Michael Meltzer, NCR Corporation, *"Using the Data Warehouse to Drive Customer Retention, Development and Profit,"* http://www.crm-forum.com/crm_forum_white_papers/crpr/ppr.htm

[21] Regis McKenna, "Real-Time Marketing," *Harvard Business Review,* July-August 1995, p. 92.

[22] Paul McNabb and Mike Steinbaum, "Reclaiming Customer Care: The Milkman Returns," *Cambridge Information Network,* 1999.

[23] Kevin Kelly, *New Rules for the New Economy: 10 Radical Strategies for a Connected World,* Viking Press, November, 1998.

[24] Thomas Teal, "Service Comes First: An Interview with USAA's Robert F. McDermott," *Harvard Business Review,* September-October 1991, p. 127.

Notes

Chapter 5 - E-Commerce Applications:
Vendor Management Systems

Notes

Integrating the Value-chain: the Next Frontier

Companies are struggling with fundamental shifts in the business environment. Power has shifted from producer to customer. Using the Net, fully-informed customers demand made-to-order, high quality, just-in-time goods and services. No longer can a company compete along one dimension: price, quality or first-to-market. Today, all three are required for value leadership. In response, businesses are integrating their value-chains to provide complete, custom solutions to meet customers' demands.

Companies cannot operate alone. To become a value-chain integrator, a company must forge new, real-time alliances to provide seamless, end-to-end value streams to the customer. Key to this new customer-driven world of business is the need to develop a single, shared information system that appears to the customer as a single, end-to-end value-chain. The virtual value-chain serves as the backbone of the virtual corporation, and customers operate the controls!

As part of the new business ecosystems demanded by customer-driven value-chains, companies are designing and implementing inter-enterprise processes with their suppliers and trading partners. These initiatives are not individual "projects." They are a new platform for managing all of today's and tomorrow's value-chain partnerships and relationships. This new class of value-chain computer applications, known collectively as a vendor management system (VMS), is the basis of sustaining a growing portfolio of supplier-facing information systems. *Vendor management systems are e-Commerce applications that streamline enterprise buying processes by automating the procurement of production and non-production goods and services. A VMS provides the building blocks needed to establish ad hoc and permanent supply-side trading relationships in dynamic value-chains.* A top view of a vendor management system (VMS) appears in Figure 5 - 1, showing the high level enterprise processes of vendor sourcing and purchase order processing followed by the provisioning of goods and services by suppliers.

In Global 2000 companies, 35% of expenditures go to non-production goods and services needed to operate the business. Although these numbers represent a large outflow of corporate cash, surprisingly, indirect procurement has been largely unmanaged from an enterprise-level, and has relied on manual, paper-intensive buying processes.

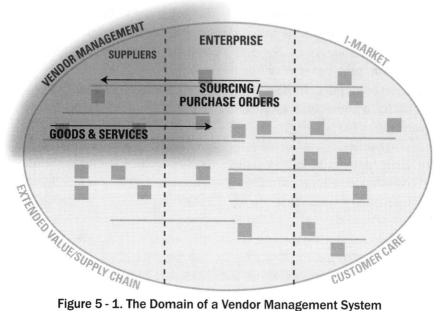

Figure 5 - 1. The Domain of a Vendor Management System

Available figures on corporate procurement typically combine both production and non-production goods and services, as shown in Table 5 - 1. By adding production materials to the equation, 57% of Global 2000 companies' expenditures go to outside procurement – a potential gold mine of cost savings if there were ways to streamline the processes between a company and its vendors of these goods and services.[1]

In today's downsized companies, the total spent for indirect goods and services alone is the single largest cost item of a business, surpassing the combined expenses for salaries, taxes and depreciation, according to the Center for Advanced Purchasing Studies (CAPS), a non-profit independent research organization affiliated with the National Association of Purchasing Management and the Arizona State University College of Business.[2] The benchmarks vary by industry as expected.

According to the CAPS studies, the average manufacturer spends 57% of revenues on outside purchases, 39% of which goes to raw materials and resale items, while a surprising 61% goes to indirect purchases.

In the petroleum industry, combined direct and indirect purchases can amount to 85% of revenues. Although state and local governments spend only 14% of revenue on purchases, fully 95% of that spending goes to operating resources.[3] What is even more surprising is that expenditures for non-production procurement typically receive little scrutiny and management control compared to production goods and services.

Table 5 - 1. Procurement Categories

Procurement of Goods	Procurement of Services
Non-Production Goods	**Non-Production Services**
-Office Equipment and Supplies	-Cleaning
-Spare and Replacement Parts	-Advertising
-Computer Hardware and Software	-Consulting
-Publications	-Courier Services
-Real Estate	-Insurance Plans
-Capital Equipment	-Payroll Processing
-Vehicle Fleets	-Payment Services
Production Goods	-Telephone and Data Communications
-Raw Materials	-Travel and Entertainment
-Goods for Resale	-Recruiting
	-Temporary Help
	-Security Services
	-Cafeteria Services
	-Property management
	-Maintenance and Repair
	-Shipping Services
	Production Services
	-Contract Labor
	-Design Services
	-Inbound and Outbound Logistics

CAPS' research found that, for the typical Fortune 500 company, a majority of outside purchases (54%) are spent on services, not goods.[4] Today, business travel services are moving online with travel agencies extending their booking systems directly to the desktops of the companies they serve: transaction costs can be cut in half. Staffing firms such as Manpower, Olsten and Kelly Services are moving to the Net. Forrester expects that $220 billion in services will be traded over the Internet in the United States in 2003.[5] Their analysis reveals that "if a $2 billion company achieves a 50% reduction in the processing costs of service buying, it will save $20 million annually, increasing net profits dollar for dollar."[6]

Because such costs are a major component of the income statement and balance sheet, they deserve full attention of management. To do this, they must rise to the level of importance given to enterprise resource planning (ERP) and human resource planning (HRP) systems. Forward thinking companies have already begun their journey to gain external, hyper-efficiencies and are designing and implementing Vendor Management Systems (VMS). These pioneers are going after the next competitive advantage frontier in streamlining business operations.

Professional buyers play a strategic role in supply chain management by overseeing the purchase of raw materials and resale items. This is not the case with procurement of operating resources as illustrated in Figure 5 - 2. Non-production expenditures for goods and services make their way into income statements through expense accounts and P-cards. Where professional buyers do get involved in this realm, unfortunately, is in the supporting paperwork. Purchasing agents report that 67% of their staffs' time is devoted to clerical paperwork.[7]

Automating and controlling indirect procurement processes was not economically feasible until the advent of the Internet. Today, however, the rush to harness the ubiquitous, low cost capabilities of the Internet has led to one of the killer business-to-business e-Commerce applications, procurement of indirect operating resources. At the center of this rush to automate non-production sourcing and purchasing, several first generation maintenance, repair and operations (MRO) procurement application packages and home-grown systems have appeared on the scene. The Aberdeen Group explains, "MRO procurement automation is a "slam dunk" opportunity for many organizations – with ROI payback likely in less than one year."[8] As we have seen in the Table 5 - 1 above, however, the opportunities are far greater than MRO alone, and each company will have its unique needs and opportunities for savings. They require comprehensive and flexible vendor management systems.

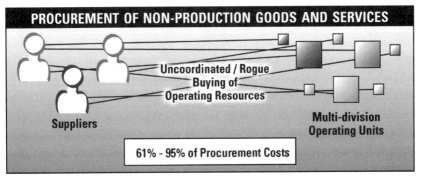

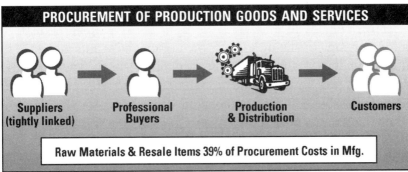

Figure 5 - 2. Production and Non-production Procurement

Vendor management systems bring order to the uncoordinated buying of operating resources. If the knowledge and work of professional buyers is automated and applied to outside spending enterprise-wide, it is possible to consolidate and optimize sources of supply, improve purchasing power, streamline any process requiring internal approvals, control rogue purchasing, and provide self-service and decision support at the point-of-use. A VMS extends the expertise of a company's best buyers beyond the supply chain to the desktops of business users throughout the many divisions and operating units of an entire enterprise.

The Business Case for Vendor Management Systems

Using the Internet as a backbone, a vendor management system makes it possible to capture efficiencies and volume discounts for all purchases of goods and services by every employee in a company. At the same time, it reduces the internal administrative costs of requisitioning and purchasing processes. Unlike a dollar increase in revenue where sales costs and cost-of-goods sold must be subtracted before reaching the bottom line, every dollar saved through operating resource management goes directly to the bottom line. A dollar saved has a multiplier effect of 5-to-6 times that of a dollar increase in sales. Thus, a 5% cost savings results in a 25% to 30% gain in profits when measured against the same impact of sales dollars.[9]

Many operating resource purchases such as real estate, capital equipment and consulting services are not repetitive and subject to the automation benefits inherent in supply chain systems. However, procurement of even these unique, non-standard, and often one-off resources can be facilitated and enhanced if a VMS provides access to trading communities and brings them under the umbrella of managed procurement policies. For example, the growing number of industrial Internet auctions and industry buying consortiums can be incorporated into a VMS, bringing them under the purview of enterprise-wide procurement management.

According to a study by Forrester Research, early adopters of Internet procurement have reported costs savings of up to 15% of MRO spending alone.[10] Properly designed and implemented, a VMS can:

- Reduce requisitioning, internal approving and order processing costs
- Reduce suppliers' costs enabling them to pass along savings
- Reduce cycle time from requisition to fulfillment, thus reducing stocking requirements
- Reduce inventory costs and enable vendor managed inventories
- Provide accountability and control
- Track usage and order frequency data to optimize economic order quantities

- Consolidate purchasing power for volume discounts
- Allow resources to be redirected
- Reduce theft, loss and rogue buying

Split between the buyer and supplier, a typical purchase order in some industries can cost $50 to $300[11] to generate and process. Considering the many thousands of purchase orders processed by large corporations, the costs can be staggering. A study of a $2 billion semiconductor equipment manufacturer revealed that the transaction cost of each purchase transaction was $222, $139 attributed to the purchase transaction and $83 associated with the requisitioning and approval cycle.[12] The company processes over 31,000 purchase transactions annually. Reducing these transaction costs through automation is, perhaps, the easiest ROI calculation a company can make.

Moving to the Internet for procurement does not mean replacing existing suppliers. Over 86% of the suppliers companies use on the Net are existing supply sources.[13] What is new, however, is that by consolidating enterprise-wide purchasing and integrating processes with a few key suppliers, scale and processing economies accrue to both buyer and supplier. Through negotiation, these savings can be passed along to the entire buying organization. For example, by creating friction-free inter-enterprise processes with preferred suppliers, staffing levels of "clerical" purchasing agent staff in the buying company and order processing staff of the supplying company can be significantly reduced. This shift empowers purchasing agents to work strategically. Forrester Research concludes, "Gone will be the paper pushers. In their place will arise a three-pronged [professional purchasing] staff of: relationship specialists for predictable demands, spot market and surplus gurus, and RFP teams."[14] They predict that by 2002, 70% of a professional purchaser's work will be relationship management.

Figure 5 - 3 highlights the experience gained by some companies that have pioneered vendor management systems. Systems integrator, AMPeMerce Internet Solutions successfully implemented an online bid/ask (RFQ) system for iBattery, an Internet portal for batteries and battery-related products. The system provides a unique opportunity where like-minded individuals can seek information on batteries and related products. The benefits include surplus inventory management for suppliers, and leveraged purchasing for buyers. Using component technology, the system was implemented in four weeks, giving iBattery first-to-market advantages.

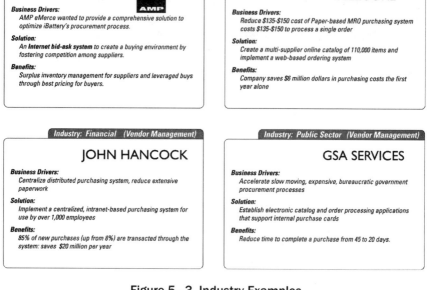

Figure 5 - 3. Industry Examples

Bellcore,[15] the telecommunications research company based in Morristown, New Jersey, automated the internal purchasing process. The system is used each time one of its 6,000 employees shuffles through his or her desk looking for pens, paper or floppy disks and comes up empty-handed. Bellcore's initial 11 suppliers have posted over 110,000 items in Belcore's online catalogue that is hosted safely behind the company's firewall. Bellcore saved $6 million in the first year alone, where in their industry, the average purchase order costs $135 to $150 using paper-based processes.

John Hancock Mutual Life Insurance Co. ran the numbers and intends to save $20 million per year using its new Internet-based corporate purchasing system.[16] The insurer spent $337 million in 1997 on supplies needed to run the business, but a mere $28 million (just 8%) went through the central purchasing department. Hancock expects to boost that figure to 85% without any increase in staffing, said Roy Anderson, the company's director of corporate purchasing. Not only does the system reduce the paperwork and increase the speed and accuracy of processing orders, it leverages its position with suppliers by aggregating its buying power for just about anything it buys. Of Hancock's 7,000 employees, 1,000 are potential users of the system. These sheer numbers mean that Hancock needs the ability to manage the privileges and approval processes of business users of the system. By 2000, Hancock's target is to have $200 - $300 million of its $375 total spending managed by the system and professional buyers.

In the government sector, the General Services Administration's *GSA Advantage* ordering system contained 220,000 items and was handling $1 million a month in 1997, allowing federal agencies to buy "smart." The system is a world-wide Federal link supporting supply and procurement, fleet management, excess property disposal, and travel and transportation services. The GSA's Federal Supply Service provides other Federal agencies billions of dollars worth of supplies and services each year with savings going to both the agencies as well as to the taxpayer. Requisitioners can choose from items in stock or request overnight ordering for slightly higher prices – requisitioners are able to see their options on the Web and make their choices based on price and delivery. In addition, suppliers can see competitors' prices online and may feel compelled to edge down their own, says Theresa Sorrenti, director of the Acquisitions Operations and Electronic Commerce Center of the General Services Administration's Federal Supply Service. "Vendors look at their competitors [on the agency's GSA Advantage service], and if they see that someone is beating their price, they can submit a price change to us immediately," says Sorrenti. "They stay competitive, and the government benefits."[17]

Vendor Management Application Framework

Having defined what vendor management systems are and why they are
so important to the bottom line of a business, we can gain a deeper
understanding by examining the business processes that a VMS must
support (Sourcing, Catalog Management, Requisitioning, Purchasing,
Receiving and Payment) and the application drivers needed to implement these processes in software (Information Boundaries, Searching
and Information Filtering, Workflow/Process Management, Trading Services, Event Notification, Data/Process Integration and Payment
Processing). The key inter-enterprise processes are illustrated in Figure
5 - 4 along with their relationship to an enterprise's suppliers and trading partners.

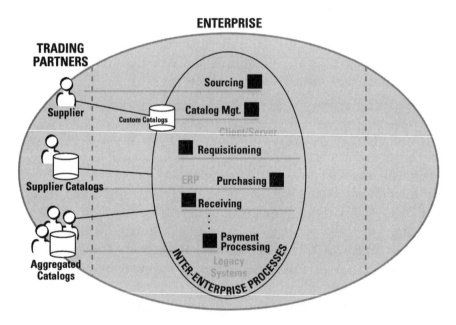

Figure 5 - 4. Vendor Management Application Framework

Key Business Processes for Vendor Management Systems

Figure 5 - 5 drills down to show the major elements of the key business
processes that a vendor management system must support.

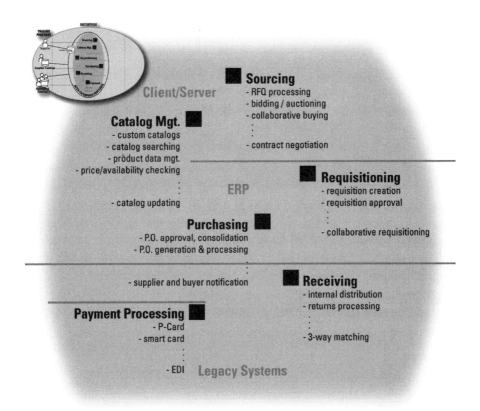

Figure 5 - 5. Vendor Management Business Processes

Sourcing. Purchasing agents and professional buyers want to consolidate company purchases so that they can negotiate volume discounts and service level agreements. Over time, the purchasing agent wants to be able to research actual supplier performance as sourcing contracts are renewed.

All this supplier information must be maintained in the VMS to assist the buyer by presenting short lists of qualified, preferred vendors during the contract negotiating process. In addition, the VMS must assist the buyer in discovering new sources of supply through advanced searching, matching, and mediating facilities.

Supply contracts typically are not static and may involve performance-based criteria. Pricing, for example, may be multi-tiered and depend on actual volumes to trigger higher discount levels. In addition to pricing, buyers evaluate the total *value-add* of suppliers including lead times, returns policies, support and service. Ultimately, agreements on these variables translate into sets of business rules that need to be realized in software and must persist over the duration of the contract agreement. At contract renewal time, the purchasing agent requires decision support to facilitate the next round of contract negotiation.

Capital assets and infrequently ordered items are usually out-of-catalog purchases. The professional buyer requires tools and facilities to streamline Request for Quotation (RFQ) preparation, distribution, negotiation and award processes. Buyers may want to pre-qualify and solicit quotes from around the globe, distribute product specifications to these selected suppliers, and manage bids and supplier communications in near real-time. Electronic communication of RFQ and bid information dramatically reduces cycle time, reduces human error, and extends the reach to suppliers that could not be considered through traditional communications media. In addition to bid/ask RFQs, buyers need access to the auction and surplus sales sites that are rapidly growing in number on the Internet.

Buyers want access to online trading communities where they can collaborate and share best practices and information. Such communities are emerging in several industries; community building can ensure that a company stays in the mainstream of all available information and resources. In addition to community, trading process networks offer access to supply grids where transactions can be consummated. The Meta Group predicts that "By 2002, accelerated business cycles and channel alignment strategies will transform "closed" supply chain relationships to dynamic trading networks. Web-based operations resource planning (ORP) systems (managing non-production procurement) will act as catalysts, transforming EDI to adaptive "EPI" (electronic process interchange) relationships."[18] Now is the time for buying professionals to participate in trading communities and the evolution of their profession.

Catalog Management. At the heart of an automated procurement system is the *virtual custom catalog*. The catalog is *virtual* because it can be hosted by the buying enterprise, the supplier(s) or trading networks (such as GE's TPN), or all three as shown in Figure 5 - 4. Catalog replication and integration can be very involved and complex. Wherever it is hosted, the *virtual catalog* integrates the information from multiple suppliers into a custom catalog with prenegotiated prices and delivers it to the desktop of individual business users. To them it is just "the catalog" where they can find the goods and services they need to get their work done.

Catalog content can be simple or, in some industries, extremely complex. To be useful, complex catalogs must be accompanied by advanced searching, collaborative filtering and product configuration tools that guide the business user through intricate content including sub-assemblies, superceded and substitute parts. In order to permit comparison shopping and integration of multiple suppliers' catalogs, industry standard information schemes, taxonomies and semantics need to be contained in a metadata facility. The extensible markup language (XML) provides a new technical standard that various industries are using to define the needed information interchange standards. We discuss XML at length in chapter 8. Some traditional metadata structures such as Universal Product Codes (UPC), D&B's SPSC, the Thomas Registry product headings, and SIC codes provide a basis for some of the work of creating metadata facilities. In 1999, CommerceNet, the e-Commerce consortium, launched a member-supported program to establish standards and architectures for catalog interoperability.

Bandwidth, proprietary product configurators, and readiness of suppliers to share information all go into the mix of variables that can determine where catalogs are hosted and replicated. The virtual catalogs seen by business users in some large enterprises may be populated with information coming from catalogs hosted by the buying enterprise, suppliers and trading process networks, simultaneously. Each company will have to carefully define its unique catalog requirements. Most likely, a combination of best-of-breed catalog management services will be mixed-and-matched to provide complete solutions. For example, a company may need the services of an industry consortium, commercial catalog aggregators and internally hosted catalogs. The VMS must be flexible and allow a company to add, drop, and reconfigure catalog resources over time as new sourcing opportunities become available in a rapidly growing market of catalog content providers.

Although the procurement of services is not traditionally suited to a catalog format, more and more services are being structured into catalogs. For example, the U.S. General Services Administration's procurement catalog contains a growing number of professional service categories and items: graphic designers, architects and IT consultants along with their skills, experience and compensation requirements. Still, not all procurement is suited to a catalog format. Thus, a complete vendor management system includes *out-of-catalog* facilities to procure services, post requests for quotations (RFQs), discover new suppliers, negotiate sourcing agreements and allow buyers to participate in Internet auctions. The process of purchasing, using, and managing services is extremely communications intensive. A VMS should have capabilities to facilitate collaboration and interaction: discussing project plans, brainstorming ideas, comparing prices, sending documents and referencing data.

Requisitioning. As a desktop business user decides on items in a procurement catalog, he or she places the items in a requisition – a shopping cart for business users. Once a requisition is complete, the requisitioner triggers a series of processes. First, the requisition goes through internal approval processes. Internal approval cycles are critical to the overall procurement process. Thus, along with bringing the purchasing function to the desktop, requisition approval processes, rules and policies must be brought to the desktop as well.

Requisitioners require convenient and efficient access to catalogs and non-catalog sources to purchase goods and services. While this requirement sounds simple, complex catalogs must be customized for each user and should be accompanied with advanced searching and decision support tools as needed. For example, at Sylvania Lighting, if a customer selects 1,000 6-packs of bulbs, the system has to be smart enough to suggest 2,000 3-packs if the original selection is not available. Requisitioners want help in getting their procurement tasks done quickly and efficiently. When catalog content is derived from multiple suppliers, the business user wants a seamless, consistent look and feel of the information.

For repetitively ordered items like office supplies, templates can be populated with up-to-the-minute item availability and cost for the requisitioner to select. For items with which a user may not be familiar, collaborative filtering can assist the requisitioner by presenting information about what others have ordered in a particular product category.

For non-catalog goods and services, requisitioners need access to trading communities and networks as described above in the discussion of professional buyer requirements.

To aid business users of the procurement system, purchasing agents require the ability to create, maintain and distribute Reorder Lists or Templates of commonly ordered sets of items. For example, a company may provide a specific set of items to a new employee. The new hire order template simplifies the task of the new employee's manager who can "point and click" to get the job done.

Automated requisitioning processes not only assist the business user in the procurement process, they embed the business controls that reduce errors and inhibit rogue buying. Business rules and authorization limits may be unique to different divisions, operating units, individual employees and roles (e.g. buyer, administrator and manager). Thus, the VMS must include user administration facilities to maintain these many and diverse profiles and spending limits of its users in order to provide the business controls needed throughout the full requisitioning process.

After a requisitions have been submitted for processing, the users want the ability to track them all the way through the procurement process. They also want to be notified of events that affect their requisition including approvals, items back ordered or cancelled, and notification of receipts. Requisition approvers need automated decision support so that they do not waste time on trivial purchases, but do get involved when true decisions must be made. In addition, they need routine access to budget and variance reports to manage the purchasing activities for which they are accountable.

Purchasing. Approved requisitions flow into the purchasing process. Requisitions are consolidated, suppliers are selected, and purchase orders created. The VMS should be capable of automatically issuing purchase order releases by supplier or by product, based on stocking requirements, item reorder points and economic order quantities. The purchasing processes cross enterprise boundaries and may take place through traditional EDI messages or, in advanced systems, through real-time interaction with suppliers' order management systems. At this stage in the procurement process, workflows are hybrid internal-external processes. Some may be embedded in the legacy systems of buyers and suppliers and others are new, jointly designed and owned inter-enterprise processes.

If suppliers fall behind in meeting the required shipments, the system must provide expediting reports to assist in determining which P.O.s are outstanding and for how long. Supplier reports are also needed to provide statistical analyses of the suppliers' performance. Histories of inquiries for past purchases and receipts assist the buyer in future contact negotiations with suppliers.

Up-to-date information is critical to the effectiveness of all participants in the procurement process. At the same time, they want the process of updating content to be automated – outsourcing the work to the suppliers – within the constraints of the negotiated business rules. Purchasing agents need to be notified of supplier updates. At the same time, automated business rules must prevent the supplier from making unauthorized changes.

Receiving. Fulfillment by the supplier culminates in the receiving process where goods are placed into stock at the buying company. Throughout the procurement life cycle, all parties must be able to inquire and track activities by vendor, product and purchase order number. The VMS must automatically notify each party of events which affect an order, such as exceptions. In addition the VMS must provide multiple receiving options: at the dock, in the mail room or by electronic delivery. Services typically have a different fulfillment and receiving cycle than goods (for example an email of a confirmation number for an airline eTicket). The VMS must provide a comprehensive facility for three-way matching of receipts, purchase orders and supplier invoices.

Payment. Suppliers' fulfillment systems, in turn, can trigger processes contracted with third party providers of logistics and payment services. In response to the problems of handling ad hoc and low volume purchasing, the procurement card (P-card) was introduced around 10 years ago, but with mixed results. Although the P-card relieved purchasing departments of huge amounts of paperwork for ordering items under $2,500 (good results), it did not provide the business controls, reconciliation, and auditing mechanisms needed to manage spending (bad results). Companies that used the card to reduce the cost of going through a central purchasing processes for trivial buying were surprised to see how nontrivial the total spending could be. It did not take long before many companies dropped their use of P-cards. With an automated requisitioning process, on the other hand, P-cards can provide their benefits without their number one pitfall – uncontrolled spending.

Along with P-cards, payment processes often include gateways to smart cards and EDI processing. Smart cards have been deployed for the last 15 years in Europe. The cards hold "cash" that can be used wherever smart cards are accepted. They are protected by a number of means: personal identification numbers (PIN numbers), digital signatures and, soon, fingerprints and retinal scans. Inexpensive smart card readers may soon be standard equipment for personal computers and network devices.

In addition to supporting the six key business processes of sourcing, catalog management, requisitioning, purchasing, receiving and payment processing, a vendor management system must be integrated with ERP and other legacy systems. Throughout the procurement life cycle, the vendor management system must interoperate with accounting systems and leverage the functionality of existing enterprise management systems where possible. The VMS must provide accounting with extensive reporting to identify variances between order cost and invoice cost, and quantities ordered and received. The VMS should be capable of analyzing expected receipts using delivery dates to determine the cash requirements for cash flow projections.

Existing purchasing and receiving systems can be leveraged and extended outward to provide much of the functionality needed in new online procurement systems. Because existing systems are already integrated with Inventory Control, Accounts Payable and the General Ledger, many benefits accrue and new development is reduced. For example, if a company's existing ERP systems support internal requisition approval workflows, this functionality can be integrated into the VMS to avoid redundancy of business rules and processes. Every business has its own unique purchasing processes, policies, business rules and requirements that change over time. On the other hand, new internal-external hybrid workflows are needed across corporate information boundaries if enterprises and their suppliers are to interoperate in real-time.

Feedback of results is the secret to procurement optimization. Professionals responsible for the management of purchasing services need reporting and decision support systems equal to the sophistication of the buying process. Analytical processing allows purchasing management to determine which suppliers get most of the company's business, which divisions do the most rogue buying, what items are most in demand and so on. While decision support can help the purchasing staff work smart, automating reporting requirements lets the staff work more efficiently. Summary reports for management, exception reports for expeditors, and tax reporting to the government are all needed by purchasing management.

Accounting and financial management requires information throughout the procurement life cycle for cash flow planning, accounts payable, and management control. They need the new online procurements systems to interoperate with their existing asset management, inventory and general ledger systems. Human resource systems are another point of integration needed for managing user profiles and roles in the organization.

Supplier requirements of an e-Commerce enabled procurement system can vary widely, depending on the complexity of the trading arrangement and the nature of the goods and services involved. The foremost issue is the degree of integration, which may vary from arms-length message passing to real-time process integration. At higher levels of integration, workflows and data are integrated electronically and can yield greater efficiency on the part of both buyer and supplier organizations. When business transactions take place electronically, the supplier requires facilities to ensure nonrepudiation. Typically, this is achieved by using digital signatures and third party authentication services.

In conclusion, a VMS should leverage existing systems and business resources, extend them outward, and provide the agility that businesses will require as the new market for Internet procurement evolves and matures – no small order. Cookie-cutter approaches and point solutions will not serve the enterprise that requires a dynamic solution to optimize its spending over the long term.

Key Application Drivers for Vendor Management Systems

A core set of application drivers is needed to implement vendor management business processes in software. These include Information Boundaries, Workflow/Process Management, Data/Process Integration, Event Notification, Trading Services, Searching and Information Filtering, and Payment Processing facilities as shown in Figure 5 - 6.

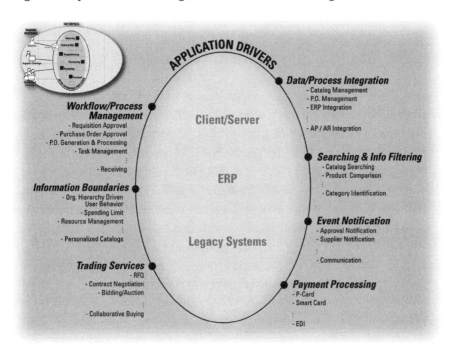

Figure 5 - 6. Key Application Drivers for a Vendor Management System

Information Boundaries. Profile management application facilities are needed to manage information boundaries between the buying company, its suppliers and third party entities such as logistics and payment services – security is essential to inter-enterprise integration. User authentication, authorization and access controls are maintained by profile management software and facilities. Further, dynamic profiling capabilities are needed to enable customizing and individualization – the keys to user productivity.

Internally, purchasing agents need the ability to control and manage the access, authorizations and privileges of requisitioners from within the system. This does not mean, however, that purchasing agents need to control each individual user. Instead, organizational hierarchies need to be maintained so that individual operating units can maintain their own controls over access and authorizations. With this approach, access and authorizations can be assigned to individuals, groups or roles and the administration of these vital business controls can be delegated to the appropriate managers and organizational units. In most automated procurement systems, the purchasing agent needs to be able to suspend accounts of policy violators, establish new supplier accounts and otherwise administer the profiles in the system without having to go to the IT department for reprogramming.

The purchasing agent needs to produce customized subsets of the master catalog for organizational units and individuals. There is, for example, no need for a clerk who orders office supplies to sift through the details of control and instrumentation spare parts in, let's say, a pharmaceutical manufacturing company. Those responsible for these spare parts, on the other hand, need fast and efficient access to them. The access controls are maintained in the profile management facility.

The profiles of the users of the system must be dynamic as well as able to provide more static access controls: users want the system to start where they left off as they suspend and reinitiate work sessions. Dynamic profiles also can be used to individualize catalog content by tracking and analyzing individual usage of the system.

Workflow/Process Management. Workflow facilities are need by all the participants in procurement systems. Workflow underpins requisition approval routing, catalog updates, purchase order processing, supplier fulfillment, receiving, and accounting reconciliation.

Although a VMS should leverage existing workflow systems within supplier and buyer organizations, their interoperation requires inter-enterprise workflow mechanisms. Standards such as W3C's Simplified Workflow Access Protocol (SWAP) and the Workflow Management Coalition (WfMC) workflow interoperation standards are increasingly vital as new, shared workflows are jointly designed and owned.

In the current climate where business processes, policies, organizational hierarchies and business rules change often, purchasing agents need to reflect these updated business rules and workflows accordingly and immediately. They must be the linchpin in the decision-chain for approving and making changes to established terms and rules contained in the automated system.

Data/Process Integration. Data integration with all the participants is required throughout the procurement process. Catalog aggregation and management, real-time pricing, and purchase order management as well as accounting require data integration within and outside the buying organization. Unfortunately, each supplier likely will have differing data formats and content that must be transformed for use. Standards for data interchange are very important. A number of general and industry specific e-Commerce standards have emerged and are evolving. These standards will make the job of integration much easier, but the VMS will continue to require facilities to interchange data and other information resources. Integration facilities must be robust as the integration job is not a one-shot affair. Instead data integration is an ongoing activity needed when supply sources are added, changed or removed.

Event Notification. Business event notification facilities are essential for providing requisitioners, approvers and suppliers with notifications of exceptions, changes and other situations requiring their attention. Notification facilities must be dynamic and capable of transmitting critical information to the users of the VMS. In highly integrated Web-based systems event notification goes beyond human user notification to application-to-application event messages. Applications subscribe to be notified of events that affect them – such messaging lies at the heart of component-based information systems.

Trading Services. Trading services application facilities are integral to meeting the needs of professional buyers and desktop business users who need to access non-catalog procurement resources. Negotiations, requests for quotations, access to auctions and trading communities all depend on robust trading services. Trading services applications must provide facilities for maintaining negotiation/collaboration boards, creating resources within the boards, defining user privileges and managing resource sharing among users. With these facilities, companies can develop buy-side RFQ applications, sell-side auctioning platforms, and partner collaboration environments.

Searching and Information Filtering. Searching and information filtering facilities are needed by all users of a VMS. If requirements are simple, then basic key word or hierarchical searching may suffice to allow users to browse through various categories in a catalog. On the other hand, most business-to-business catalogs require parametric search facilities where a search is specified by a set of parameters, and their desired values, or range of values. Such search techniques also provide the capability to make comparisons among attributes of like products. To compliment direct user searching methods, collaborative filtering can be used to compare the purchasing selections and buying patterns among all buyers to uncover trends and obtain indirect information on buyer preferences. In addition, collaborative filtering can be used as a mediation technique for matching buyers and suppliers in an open supply network. In short, searching in the business-to-business world is much more that a key word lookup.

Payment Processing. Depending on the selected payment mechanisms and payment terms, accounts are settled and payments made to respective suppliers or credit issuing banks. Two of the most common billing and payment mechanisms are EDI (e.g. an invoice and payment order/remittance advice) and P-cards. P-cards, offered by the major credit card companies and associations, are becoming a preferred way of making payments for high volume, low dollar procurement. By going through the VMS, business rules and constraints can be built into the system to prevent rogue-buying. By providing reconciliation and settlement features within reporting applications (provided by issuing banks or credit card corporations) P-cards can offer simplicity and business control. A VMS should provide services that allow procurement applications to be linked with payment networks, accounts payable and general ledger systems, thus providing more context and line item data required for efficient reconciliation and settlement.

These seven application drivers are key not only to a VMS but also can be reused for all e-Commerce applications. By establishing a common core of these e-Commerce engines, a company's unique business processes, rules and policies can be distributed to every desktop in the enterprise, and extended outward to suppliers, trading partners and customers. Getting it right with a company's vendor management systems means getting it right with its I-Market and Customer Care applications as well.

Vendor Management Systems Strategies

The decision to automate procurement may be what the Aberdeen Group calls a "slam dunk," but the development of implementation strategies is daunting. Formulating a VMS strategy must account for two major dimensions: 1) "make, buy or both" and 2) degrees of process integration.

With such a compelling business case, companies can be eager to begin reaping the savings from Internet procurement as soon as possible. How might a company proceed? To some the knee jerk reaction is "buy a package, of course." A careful analysis of package solutions, however, reveals a number of show-stopping shortfalls for meeting enterprise-class procurement requirements. In its 1999 report, *EC Architecture Approaches,* the Meta Group explains, "Single-purpose, highly integrated (without easy disintegration capabilities) applications will do little to make organizations and supply chains flexible, rapidly adaptable and dynamically changeable." The report continues, "Companies must be aware that highly specialized packages (e.g., Ariba, Open Market) are often expensive, require customization and generally are not precisely fit to specific business needs, process rules, or trading partner requirements."

"Applications that are highly functional within their own solution packs are often difficult to integrate with other solutions/packages, as evidenced by the explosive growth of the systems integrator/middleware markets and the realistic expectation that professional services will often exceed the cost of software by 200% - 400%. Packaged solutions may also have extra features (e.g., workflow functionality, reporting tools) that, while not required/desired by the purchaser, are included in the price. Because every business has unique processes, trading partner relationships, and strategies, EC packages must often be modified at considerable expense (e.g., the fees for Andersen Consulting's change management, business processing re-engineering services, as well as technical consulting to configure, integrate, implement, and deploy an Ariba procurement package, can run 50% - 100%+ of Ariba's average $2 million purchase price). Also, custom modifications are often difficult to maintain as packages evolve through version releases."

Building vendor management systems from scratch also has major pitfalls. An obvious one is the lack of technical and business domain knowledge and skill to design and implement robust, agile, Web-based, standards compliant, secure, real-time procurement systems. Existing development staff would have to have the capability to design and build each of the application drivers (profile management, workflow, event notification, data integration, trading services and search engines) from scratch. This is a tall order considering that IS staffs already have their plates full with ERP conversions and Y2K modifications.

Much of what is happening in corporations today is that various operating units obtain funding and launch business-driven e-Commerce initiatives to take on a pressing problem or market opportunity. They have a very specific need and the IS department is assigned the task of developing the system. To do this, most large corporations use outside contractors and services for software development. Whether the development of a VMS is carried out in-house or contracted, the scope of operating unit initiatives often do not include enterprise-wide architecture. The result, assuming that the isolated project is a success, is that the point solution cannot interoperate with existing enterprise management systems or other present or planned e-Commerce systems.

Considering that some large companies already have identified over seventy e-Commerce initiatives and that the state of electronic procurement is in its young and formative stage, *point solutions* are simply the most obvious mistake an enterprise can make in investing in any e-Commerce initiative. Point solutions also represent the biggest obstacle to building the fully digital business needed to compete in the digital age. They will create major integration and interoperation problems that will need massive fixing as companies realize that they cannot participate in inter-enterprise business processes that have become indispensable business tools. Of more immediate concern to a given operating unit is that additional procurement initiatives will surface as a result of the experienced gained from an initial project. It is likely that the growth will be explosive due to the rapid developments in trading communities and other procurement resources on the Web. Will the system being built today be flexible and extensible enough to meet tomorrow's procurement needs?

There is, fortunately, another way to build enterprise-class vendor management systems: buy and assemble components. Returning to the Meta report, "To counteract the disadvantages of monolithic EC packages and developing custom applications, organizations pursuing EPI [electronic process integration] solutions will begin constructing EC applications from best-of-breed components. Organizations will arrange, rearrange, and reuse these components as changing supply chain requirements dictate.

By leveraging common components in both DTNs [dynamic trading networks] and solutions in all three EC markets (sell-side, buy-side, and supply/value-chain management), enterprises can reduce costs and complexity for building, managing, and participating in electronic trading relationships, obviating the need to buy specific packages for every EC-facilitated process. These common components can be purchased and modified for specific buy-side, sell-side, and supply/value-chain management architectures as required by business process imperatives, while requiring minimal incremental skills from the IT department. The use of components as an underlying infrastructure enables the creation of a common EC development platform. This permits reduced time and capital investment when creating future commerce applications and solutions or evolving existing solutions to support changing trading partner and business process needs as well as shifting competitive realities."

The second key strategy issue is the degree of process integration with internal enterprise management systems and those of suppliers and other third party participants in procurement systems. Process integration is usually very tight among multiple divisions of a single enterprise. Companies and their long-term trading partners are tightly coupled while their relationship to trading communities is loosely coupled. Information can be exchanged between trading partners as data only (file transfers or through EDI messages), or through real-time transaction processing through direct interaction with application interfaces (APIs). Real-time interactions are most often the basis of integrating a

VMS with internal enterprise management systems, while EDI is the traditional form of integration via message-passing among suppliers and trading partners.

According to the Aberdeen Group, the benefits of real-time interaction across the external buyer-supplier boundaries are threefold, "1. real-time order processing compresses invoice and PO matching processes and supports real-time order tracking, thereby reducing customer service costs and improving customer service quality; 2. a single rules base can be maintained governing issues of product configuration, pricing management, and purchasing management; and 3. advanced planning engines can be more easily invoked and directly applied to improve MRP, ERP and DRP processes."[19]

Real-time interoperation requires overcoming several hurdles presented by proprietary application interfaces (APIs). Open system standards are essential and a number of e-Commerce standards for interoperation are emerging and continue to evolve. The Object Management Group and CommerceNet are pursuing standards for open e-Commerce, and industry consortia are establishing common information definitions and schemas. Companies that want to gain the benefits of real-time interoperation must embrace and evolve with these standards.

Putting It All Together

An enterprise-class vendor management system harnesses the Internet to automate the business processes of requisitioning, purchasing and receiving. A VMS can give customers access to end-to-end value-chains, and provide a company with extraordinary cost savings not possible before the advent of e-Commerce. A sustainable approach to implementing a VMS leverages legacy enterprise systems and extends them to suppliers and internal users' desktops across an enterprise. Howard Anderson, Founder of The Yankee Group and Battery Ventures confirms, "Every company has built order entry systems, customer support systems, and sales automation systems. What the smartest are doing is turning that embedded cost into "customer-facing" systems. By putting a user-friendly front end on top of a tried and true internal solution a company can build a strategic advantage. A company has achieved double leverage."[20] Anderson's prescription applies equally well to "supplier-facing" systems. Of course the tasks at hand are more than just putting a pretty face on top of existing enterprise management systems. An agile vendor management system must provide direct support for the inter-enterprise processes of next generation procurement as shown in Figure 5 - 7.

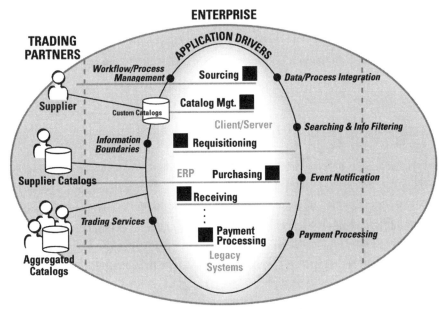

Figure 5 - 7. Putting It All Together

Companies that integrate their value-chains and master Internet procurement to reduce total costs of operations will become hyper-efficient businesses. Competing against them will be increasingly difficult. A company should start by identifying its unique requirements and issues – independent of the packages available on the market – then select low hanging fruit for initial implementation projects. Central to this approach is the reuse of a common core of e-Commerce application components to incrementally develop new applications and grow their capabilities as new integration and procurement opportunities are discovered. By adopting a component-based development approach for agile software development, companies can implement breakthrough vendor management systems today and take advantage of opportunities that will appear tomorrow.

References

[1] http://corp.ariba.com/ORM_vision/ormhome2.htm. Direct materials = 22%, Wages, Salaries and Benefits = 20%, Taxes = 11%, Depreciation = 6%, and Net Income = 6%.

[2] http://capsresearch.org/ see also, Harold E. Fearon, Ph.D., C.P.M. and William A. Bales, Ph.D., C.P.M. "Purchasing of Nontraditional Goods and Services," Center for Advanced Purchasing Studies, 1995–Focus Study, (Executive Summary), http://capsresearch.org/research/focuses/ntrad.htm

[3] http://www.summitonline.com/tech-trends/papers/killen1.html, p. 8.

[4] http://www.summitonline.com/tech-trends/papers/killen1.html p. 5.

[5] _____, Ibid.

[6] Michael Putnam et al. "Business Services on the Net," Forrester Research, January, 1999.

[7] http://www.summitonline.com/tech-trends/papers/killen1.html p. 3.

[8] Aberdeen Group, "Internet Procurement: Separating the Wheat from the Chaff," *Market Viewpoint,* Vol. 11/no. 6, March 16, 1998.

[9] http://www.summitonline.com/tech-trends/papers/killen1.html p. 10.

[10] Tom Rhineelander, Blane Erwin, and Michael Putnam, "Fourth Channel Purchasing," The Forrester Report, September 1997, p8.

[11] G. Winfield Treese and Lawrence C. Stewart. Designing Systems for Internet Commerce. Addison-Wesley. 1998. P. 54

[12] http://www.summitonline.com/tech-trends/papers/killen1.html p. 14.

[13] Tom Rhineelander, Blane Erwin, and Michael Putnam, "Fourth Channel Purchasing," The Forrester Report, September 1997, p4.

[14] Tom Rhineelander, Blane Erwin, and Michael Putnam, "Fourth Channel Purchasing," The Forrester Report, September 1997, p11.

[15] Deborah Asbrand, "Paper, pens, and floppy disks push Bellcore to develop intranet product," Infoworld, September 29, 1997, (Vol. 19, Issue 39). http://www.infoworld.com/cgi-bin/displayStat.pl?pageone/news/features/iw100.profile-3.htm

[16] Carol Sliwa, "Purchasing via Web to Save Big Bucks," Computerworld, 07/20/98. http://www.computerworld.com/home/print.nsf/all/9807205ABA

[17] Leigh Buchanan, "Procurative Powers," CIO WebBusiness, Webmaster Magazine, May, 1997. http://www.cio.com/archive/webbusiness/050197_procurement.html

[18] Meta Group, "EC Architecture Approaches," *Advanced Information Management Strategies,* February 17, 1999.

[19] Aberdeen Group, "Internet Procurement: Separating the Wheat from the Chaff," *Market Viewpoint,* Vol. 11/no. 6, March 16, 1998.

[20] http://www.battery.com/yankee.html

Notes

Chapter 6 - E-Commerce Applications: Extended Supply Chain Management

Notes

Extending the Supply Chain: the Next Frontier

Analyst Deborah Asbrand observed that "Manufacturers and distributors used to point with pride to their fully stocked, football-field-size warehouses. But no more: High inventory levels are considered evidence of an inefficient supply chain."[1]

Procurement of production goods and services (raw materials and resale items) has been the subject of automation for some time. Supply chain management (SCM) systems were implemented in the 1960s by retailers (Wal-Mart is the recognized pioneer in using SCM as a competitive weapon) and have grown to be the norm in manufacturing and distribution industries. As shown in Figure 6 - 1, SCM spans the full supply chain, from procuring raw materials to delivering finished goods to the ultimate consumers.

Supply Chain Management aims to optimize planning and execution processes to respond to market demand for goods and services. Processes that are optimized include:

- supply planning
- demand planning
- production planning, and
- inbound/outbound logistics.

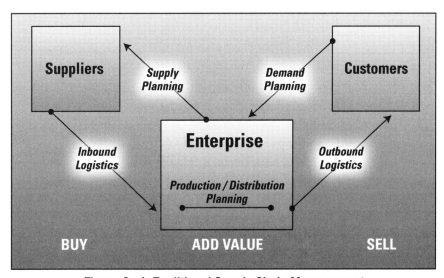

Figure 6 - 1. Traditional Supply Chain Management

The major objectives of supply chain management are getting the right product to the right place, at the right time with the right price. The goals include:

- Reduced cycle time
- Increased customer satisfaction
- Reduced inventory and associated costs
- Reduced product obsolescence
- Reduced operating expense
- Reduced working capital, and
- Increased return on assets (ROA).

Supply chain goals can be optimized by increasing communication and sharing information across the entire supply chain, from customers and their customers (demand planning) to suppliers and their suppliers (supply planning). Demand and supply planning drive production and distribution planning, which, in turn are determined by inbound and outbound logistics. By sharing information and taking a complete business ecosystem view, all parties can optimize performance and profits.

Grappling with logistics creates a compelling reason for sharing information and operational assets. According to Tim Harmon, international program director in the META Group's Application Delivery Strategies service, supply chains have become a hot issue recently because most forward-thinking companies have completed the automation of their internal operational systems and are now looking outward to their extended systems as areas of potential savings. And these savings are not small. Logistics costs in the United States alone are estimated at $760 billion to $790 billion a year. Worldwide, the annual cost of moving goods is estimated at $2 trillion to $3 trillion. Even a one-percent improvement reaps huge savings.[2]

In today's typical SCM environment, suppliers are close trading partners and are tightly integrated via costly and proprietary private Extranets as shown in Figure 6 - 2. They rely on expensive, tightly coupled electronic data interchange (EDI) systems that are point-to-point, trading partner-to-trading partner. Core applications include Materials Requirements Planning (MRP), production and logistic optimization, and raw material, work-in-progress and finished goods inventory management. SCM systems, having evolved since the 1960s, are reasonably mature. Traditional supply chain automation is, however, expensive and complex, thereby excluding small and medium sized enterprises. Many who do automate do so through coercion. Coercion? Yes, if a big fish in a supply chain, let's say Sears, tells its suppliers that they must use EDI, they either do EDI or don't do business with Sears. However, the coercive supply chain model, as the Gartner Group terms it, is about to be history. Analyst Mathew Schwartz explains, "Supply chains used to be exclusive affairs, the playthings of corporate giants who arm-twisted a few of their bigger supply-chain partners into following along."[3]

Although successful implementations certainly have optimized supply chains in many industries, the economics of the Internet have impacted traditional supply chain management systems and have opened up new possibilities for small to medium size enterprises. The Internet provides an e-Commerce platform that allows an enterprise to extend supply chain automation to its suppliers' suppliers and its customers' customers, forming dynamic trading networks: end-to-end *supply grids* containing real-time business process facilities and shared data warehouses of information for decision support. Let's look closer and develop a working definition of extended value/supply chain management.

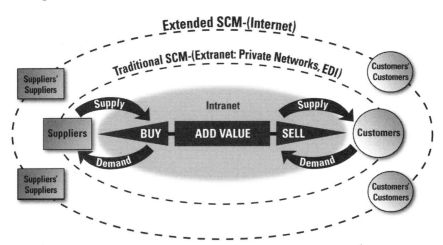

Figure 6 - 2. The Impact of the Internet on Supply Chain Management

Extended Supply Chain Management applications expand the scope of traditional SCM systems by coordinating multiple suppliers, internal/external SCM systems, and Small to Medium Enterprises (SMEs) to create collaboration and meet global market demand as illustrated in Figure 6 - 3. An *extended* supply chain management system differs with traditional SCM systems in the extent to which a company can integrate with its suppliers, trading partners and customers. As shown in Figure 6 - 3, most companies have some sort of supply chain system, albeit internal. An internal supply chain management system typically includes bill-of-material (BOM), engineering change order (ECO), and manufacturing requirements planning (MRP) applications, and may have links to one or more key suppliers that are so tightly integrated (e.g. EDI connections) that they may be considered as internal SCMs. Often these applications are a part of an ERP system.

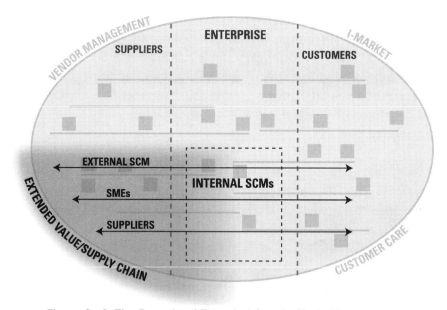

Figure 6 - 3. The Domain of Extended Supply Chain Management

According to AMR Research,[4] however, enterprise resource planning (ERP) systems deliver only 20% of the solution needed for extended supply chain management. As the name implies, *enterprise* resource planning systems span the enterprise. That pinpoints the exact problem: most of the information and business processes needed for end-to-end supply chain management reside *outside the enterprise.* Because of their inward focus, ERP systems lack advanced planning, scheduling and collaborating facilities needed across the entire supply chain. They lack the inter-enterprise processes and information sharing that is needed among all channel partners in order to gain total system efficiency for mutual advantage. Using an e-Commerce platform, on the other hand, provides loose and dynamic linkages with multiple suppliers, multiple internal supply chains in multi-line and multi-divisional corporations, and the many small-to-medium enterprise (SME) suppliers that make up to 75% of manufacturing sites.

By sharing information all the way from the point-of-sale to the inventory levels of suppliers' suppliers, all participants in an extended supply chain system can gain competitive advantage. In "The Seven Principles of Supply Chain Management," Anderson, Britt and Farve write, "Rejecting the traditional view of a company and its component parts as distinct functional entities, savvy managers realize that the real measure of success is how well activities coordinate across the supply chain to create value for customers, while increasing the profitability of every link in the chain. In the process, some even redefine the competitive game."[5] In explaining the successes and failures of SCM initiatives of over 100 manufacturers, distributors and retailers, they conclude of the successes that, "They are typically broad efforts, combining both strategic and tactical change. They also reflect a holistic approach, viewing the supply chain from end to end and orchestrating efforts so that the whole improvement achieved – in revenue, costs, and asset utilization – is greater than the sum of its parts."

"Unsuccessful efforts likewise have a consistent profile. They tend to be functionally defined and narrowly focused, and they lack sustaining infrastructure. Uncoordinated change activity erupts in every department and function and puts the company in grave danger of 'dying the death of a thousand initiatives.' The source of failure is seldom management's difficulty identifying what needs fixing. The issue is determining how to develop and execute a supply chain transformation plan that can move multiple, complex operating entities (both internal and external) in the same direction."

With Internet technologies such as Java ("write once, run anywhere") and XML (the Web's new universal file system), SCM systems of
larger players can be extended to the browsers of SME's, opening up
new sources of supply, providing new channel-wide information sharing opportunities, and superceding the coercive supply chain model.
The Internet affords breakthrough cost savings and enables new business opportunities for both big and small suppliers. And, because of the
incremental model of e-Commerce application development, an enterprise can evolve more and more functionality with growing sources of
supply – extended supply chain management is a process of sustained
evolution, not revolution.

The Business Case for Extended Supply Chain Management

"As trade in every U.S. supply chain moves in some measure to the Internet by 2003, Forrester believes that on-line sales will balloon from $43
billion to $1.3 trillion. This change will force businesses to retool their
relationships, roles, and channels."[6]
– Forrester Research.

What differentiates one company from another in the same market?
Several years ago, quality was the key. Then quality and low cost
together became the winning combination. But now, quality and cost
are givens. Responsiveness is now the key to differentiate among competitors. The enterprise that responds to customer needs fastest is the
winner. And responsiveness equals cycle time. In today's marketplace,
production of goods and services requires making products to customer demand, not to a forecast. This new model demands radical
cycle time improvements. The focus shifts to important details of pull
control methods plus specific methods for designing mixed-model production cells for maximum effectiveness. Answers lie in Kanban pull-
type systems, where material is restocked based on usage, not planned
consumption.

For years, front-office executives dismissed planning and distribution as hand-dirtying processes that were of minimal importance.
"Logistics never got senior management's attention," says Greg Girard,
senior analyst in supply-chain management for Advanced Manufactur-

ing Research in Boston.[7] "Distribution was something done at the warehouse and the loading dock." Not so today with tighter margins and faster cycle-time demands. Supply and demand planning and end-to-end logistics have become so important that logistics managers have assumed greater status in the organization, often reporting directly to CEOs and COOs.

While mid-tier businesses with $250 million to $2 billion in sales account for 75% of manufacturing sites, they purchase fewer than one-third of the products sold in the $4.8 billion ERP market, according to the Gartner Group. Although the market for supply-chain management software is much smaller, IS organizations will install $510 million worth of supply-chain management software in 1999, up from $300 million in 1996, the Gartner Group estimates.[8]

Within SME manufacturers, the opportunities to affect the bottom line are tremendous. Distribution costs typically eat up 8% of a company's sales. Software that manages inventory and forecasts capacity can trim 10% to 12% of distribution costs, estimates Rich Sherman, senior vice president for strategic research at Toronto-based Numetrix. For a $100 million business, that can amount to major savings reflected in the company's balance sheet. "Companies can save multi millions of dollars on capital appropriations by making better capacity decisions," Sherman says.[9]

Extended supply chain applications are not tools just for manufacturers. Companies in most industries can benefit from value/supply chain management: transportation, pharmaceuticals, chemicals, entertainment, and medical services, to name a few. They are relevant to any company's value-chain, as shown in the industry examples of Figure 6 - 4. GE Capital's Vendor Financial Services (VFS) has extended its unique financial service processes to its customers and partners via the Internet.

Customers of the VFS' Office Technology Financial Services (OTFS) group can create lease quotes on-line, submit credit applications, and track their leased equipment portfolios. OTFS, which offers leasing and financing programs to manufacturers, dealers and other vendors of office technology equipment, leverages the profile management and event notification capabilities of software components to quickly develop and deploy additional e-Commerce applications. The application components provide the functionality OTFS needed to extend key internal business processes to the Internet. As a result, OTFS customers are able to access personalized data on demand, including custom rate cards and pending credit applications, helping them to reduce the cost and time associated with leasing contract procurement.

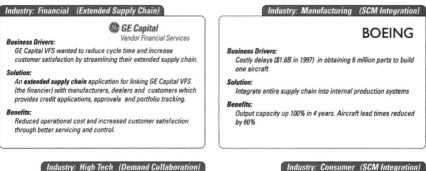

Figure 6 - 4. Industry Examples

The Boeing Company's legendary production problems finally came to a head in 1997. In the face of unprecedented demand for its airplanes, the company's supply chain ground to a halt almost instantly. Analysts Tom Stein and Jeff Sweat explain, "Boeing relies on hundreds of internal and external suppliers for the 5 million to 6 million components needed to build a large twin-aisle airplane. The goal is to put the right parts in the right airplane in the right sequence. But many of the parts often arrived late, throwing the whole process out of whack and idling half-built airplanes on the assembly line. As a result, in 1997 Boeing was forced to shut down two of its major assembly lines for a month and took a $1.6 billion charge against earnings."[10] That was then. Now, though extended supply chain initiatives, customers will no longer have to wait 3 years from the time they order a plane to the time it is finally delivered. Boeing aims to deliver them in eight to 12 months. And, the company expects to build 620 airplanes in 1999, up from 228 in 1992.

A well-oiled supply chain is a matter of life and death to Thomson Consumer Electronics Inc.[11] Jim Meyer, the company's chief operating officer, sums it up, "Our careers hang in the balance," he says. "If we are not successful here, it will be the end for Thomson." The company, which makes TVs, VCRs, and other consumer electronic products under such brand names as RCA, GE, and Proscan, knows firsthand what can befall a company that doesn't master the art of supply-chain management. A little over a year ago, Thomson's number one problem was product availability. A Kmart shopper hoping to buy an RCA product often could not because the item was likely to be out of stock. Retailers were also dissatisfied with Thomson's on-time shipping performance and its ability – or lack thereof – to fill orders exactly as requested. So in September 1997, Thomson launched its Chain Reaction program and invested in SCM, EDI and Internet technologies in an all out transformation effort. Thomson is collaborating with 55 of its top retail partners. The customers log on to a secure extranet site and feed their own forecast information and point-of-sale data directly into the system. From there, the information is automatically routed into Thomson's data warehouse, then into the supply chain planning software.

Thomson is also entering a new collaborative era with its 400-odd component suppliers. In the old world, Thomson's relationship with suppliers was based strictly on how inexpensively they could provide parts, and not necessarily on how quickly or how efficiently those parts would arrive. "Now we are talking to them about manufacturing flexibility," says Terry Reuland, manager of supply-chain integration. "We're still focused on price, but we are also focused on reducing lead times." As a result of these efforts, Thomson has reduced out-of-stock conditions to 1% and increased its forecasting accuracy above 95%.

America's fourth largest general merchandise retailer is Dayton Hudson, with Target and Marshall Fields among its chains. Some retailers pride themselves on having great forecasting software, or a great data warehouse, or a great logistics system. Dayton Hudson wants to be the best in all three areas – and more. The company claims that its electronic supply chain is one of the most complete in the business.

Its Global Merchandising System (GMS), five years in the making, is a homegrown supply chain system that integrates more than 60 applications, including forecasting, commitment management, logistics, replenishment, ordering, response analysis, and trend analysis – bearing witness that SCM is not a single application but a platform for integrating many applications that span the supply chain from point-of-sale to a dynamic supply network. They have achieved record inventory turns while increasing sales.

Analyst June Langoff writes, "Members of the supply chain form a new kind of team – the virtual supply chain. Competition shifts from individual companies to the entire chain." It is not Home Depot versus Lowes, it is Home Depot's supply chain competing against Lowes' supply chain. According to Rita Heise, program director at the Home and Building Control division of Honeywell, "The focus of competition in the marketplace is changing from companies competing against each others' products and services to companies competing against each others' supply chains as well."[12] But fine-tuned, world class supply chains do not just happen. Electronic collaboration is the key. Establishing real-time communication links among trusted trading partners is the foundation for collaborative supply chain management.

Extended Supply Chain Application Framework

Having defined what extended supply chain management systems are and why they are so important to the bottom line of a business, we can gain a deeper understanding by examining some of the key business processes that a SCM system must support (Inter-supply Chain, SME, and Supplier Collaboration and Customer Interaction) and the application drivers needed to implement these processes in software (Information Boundaries, Searching and Information Filtering, Workflow/Process Management, Trading Services, Event Notification, and Data/Process Integration).

The inter-enterprise processes are illustrated in Figure 6 - 5 along with their relationship to an enterprise's suppliers and trading partners.

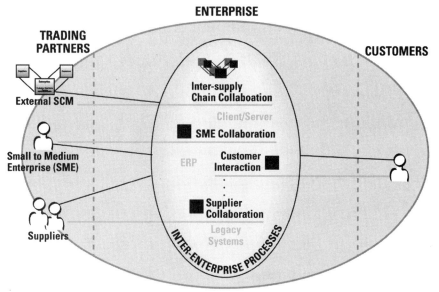

Figure 6 - 5. Vendor Management Application Framework

The key word is *collaboration* – increased collaboration with traditional suppliers, new SME suppliers, multiple supply chains and customers – all participants can gain breakthrough advantage. General Electric uses the Internet to purchase goods and services from more than 1,400 suppliers. GE's lighting division has eliminated paper requisitions and forms, blueprint retrieval and requests for low-value parts.

The request-for-quote (RFQ) process has been reduced from seven days to one and has greatly expanded the volume of RFQs going to prospective suppliers. The results of GE's collaborative supply chain management include a 15% reduction in purchasing costs from increased competition among vendors as well as volume discounts from aggregating corporate-wide purchases and lowering purchasing headcount.[13]

Key Business Processes for
Extended Supply Chain Management Systems

Figure 6 - 6 drills down to show the major elements of the key business processes that an Extended Supply Chain Management system must support.

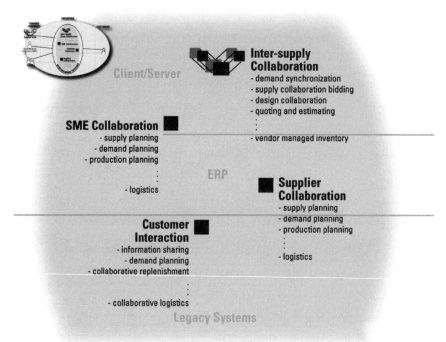

Figure 6 - 6. Extended Supply Chain Management Business Processes

Inter-supply Chain Collaboration. Through mergers and acquisitions Dayton Hudson and other multi-divisional companies typically operate multiple supply chain management systems to handle multiple plants and distribution channels. Ralph Szygenda, CIO of General Motors describes the situation, "A manufacturer, for example, can configure multiple supply chains to deal with the many supplier, distribution and customer service channels needed to reach a variety of customers around the globe. Value-chains are being made into multiple-path, multiple-node value webs."[14] Such corporations, however, rarely integrate their own internal supply chains. An extended SCM system can allow traditional, tightly linked systems to share information across channels and provide new opportunities for optimization across multiple supple chains. Some examples include demand synchronization, logistics, collaborative bidding, design collaboration, quoting and estimating and vendor managed inventory.

SME Collaboration. Small-to-medium enterprises, including 75% of manufacturing concerns, represent a whole new world of potential suppliers that can be tapped as a result of the Internet smashing the barriers of cost and complexity of traditional EDI-based systems. Supply, demand and production planning and logistics can be optimized by extending automation opportunities to SME suppliers. Even the smallest SME will likely have access to a fax machine and a Web browser. Because these simple touch points can be reached by the Web, SCM business processes can be extended to virtually any SME, anywhere. Recognizing the lack of computing resources of many SMEs, hub players in supply chains can forge new relationships by using browser/server technologies to host applications for SMEs. Fruit of the Loom hosts its SME distributors at its Activewear commerce site, creating a supply hub in its industry. Cisco Systems, makers of routers, switches and other network equipment provides another exemplar. Key Cisco suppliers use Cisco's ERP system to run their production lines, acting as adjuncts to Cisco manufacturing sites. More than 45% of Cisco's volume is directly fulfilled from third party production lines to customers.[15] Cisco allows market demand signals to flow directly through its supply chain to contract manufacturers without distortion or delay. Cisco has doubled inventory turns through this dynamic replenishment business model.[16] Direct fulfillment is especially important for globalized manufacturing and reaching international markets.

Supplier Collaboration. In the future, supply chains will function as a real-time business ecosystem. In the meantime the richness and low cost of the Internet makes it possible to add new collaboration links with existing suppliers – and their suppliers – for forecasting, logistics, replenishment, bidding and ordering. A given supplier may participate in multiple supply chains, and integrating information from them can give the supplier a consolidated information base for planning and operations. Collaborations can be ongoing or ad hoc in response to market events and conditions. While traditional SCM systems provide only 20% of the functionality needed for collaborative supply chains, the other 80% can be provided through *extended* SCM applications.

Customer Interaction. Today's leading businesses are rushing to provide their customers with e-Commerce resources. As customer-facing applications come online they must be integrated with the extended supply chain management systems. Ultimately, as such applications go live, the results can be customer-centered supply chain management. Customer information and behavior captured at the point-of-sale is the lifeblood of customer data warehouses and decision support systems. Extended SCM applications integrate customer-facing e-Commerce systems directly to the supply chain. Through a customer self-service business model, fewer customer service personnel are needed as customers gain automated access to the overall supply chain. They can independently browse and price products, configure and order them, lookup shipment schedules and track delivery. The result is increased customer satisfaction.

In addition to supporting these four key business processes, an extended supply chain management system must be integrated with ERP and other legacy systems. Throughout the procurement life cycle, the extended SCM system must interoperate with accounting applications and leverage the functionality of existing enterprise management systems where possible. Existing SCM systems can be leveraged and extended outward to provide much of the functionality needed in new collaborative supply chains. Because existing systems are already integrated with Inventory Control, Accounts Payable and the General Ledger many benefits accrue and new development is reduced. For example, if a company's existing SCM systems support ordering workflows, this functionality can be integrated to avoid redundancy of business rules and processes. Every business has its own unique processes, policies, and business rules that can be extended across external supply chains.

Key Application Drivers for
Extended Supply Chain Management Systems

A core set of application drivers is needed to implement extended supply chain business processes in software. These include Information Boundaries, Searching and Information Filtering, Workflow/Process Management, Trading Services, Event Notification, and Data/Process Integration facilities as shown in Figure 6 - 7.

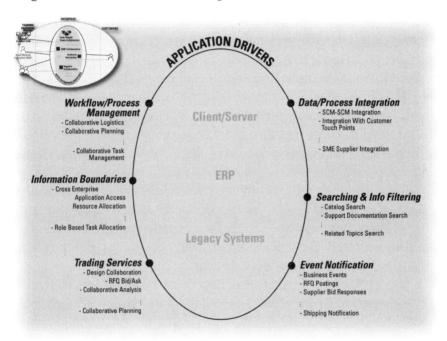

Figure 6 - 7. Key Application Drivers for an Extended Supply Chain
Management System

Information Boundaries. Profile management application facilities are needed to manage information boundaries among all participants in extended supply chain management systems – security is essential to inter-enterprise integration. User authentication, authorization and access controls are maintained by profile management software and facilities. Dynamic profiling capabilities are needed to enable cross-enterprise application access and resource allocation. Role-based task allocation is essential to accommodate organizational change and the multiple roles employees play.

Workflow/Process Management. Workflow facilities underpin collaborative supply chain management: planning, logistics and task management. Existing workflow systems of participants in the chain may be triggered by events as they occur, and new inter-enterprise workflows are needed to coordinate and route tasks to appropriate participants: transportation, storage, packaging, materials handling, order processing, forecasting and production.

Data/Process Integration. Data and process integration is required to link together multiple SCM systems, SME suppliers and customer touch points. Internally, existing ERP and legacy accounting systems must be integrated with outward-facing SCM applications. Key legacy systems include Materials Requirements Planning (MRP); production and logistic scheduling; and raw material, work-in-progress and finished goods inventory management. Data and process integration is an ongoing activity. Over time suppliers may come and go, making it essential that data and process integration facilities are easy to understand, use and administer.

Event Notification. Event notification facilities are essential for providing suppliers and customers with notifications of exceptions, changes and other situations requiring their attention. These include business events, RFQ postings, supplier bid notification, shipping notification and other business-defined events.

Trading Services. Trading services provide essential application facilities needed for collaboration: collaborative design, RFQ bid/ask, collaborative analysis and collaborative planning. With trading services facilities a company can create and maintain online collaboration (or negotiation) boards where buyers, sellers and brokers can share information and conduct business. A negotiation board can have multiple branches which can be nested to any level, as shown in Figure 6 - 8. A resource is a unit of collaboration or negotiation, such as an RFQ. Trade maker resources can be assigned directly to boards or to specific branches. Boards and branches can have multiple trade maker resources. While public boards and branches are accessible to all users, private boards and branches are accessible only to those users who have been explicitly assigned to them. A user can be assigned to many boards and many branches.

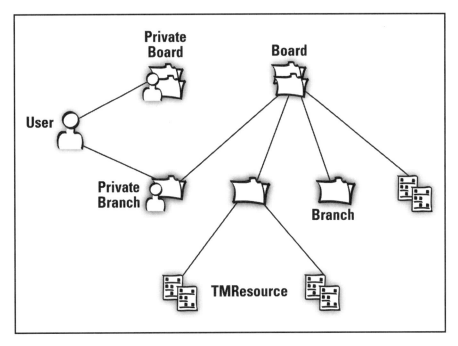

Figure 6 - 8. Trading Services Facilities

Searching and Information Filtering. Searching and information filtering facilities are needed by all users of an extended SCM system. Catalog and document search are most common. For example, Cisco saves $39 million annually through electronic document delivery and online access that enables their customers and suppliers to search for documents themselves.[17] In addition, collaborative information filtering can be extremely useful in demand analysis, helping to identify trends in buying behavior among customers in a commerce community.

These six application drivers are key not only to an extended SCM system but also can be reused for all e-Commerce applications. By establishing a common core of these e-Commerce application drivers, a company's unique business processes, rules and policies can be distributed to every desktop in the enterprise, and extended outward to suppliers, trading partners and customers.

Extended Supply Chain Management Systems Strategies

With the goal of optimizing entire supply chains, success in extended supply chain management requires "systems thinking," a business discipline derived from general systems theory. Most workers involved in supply chain management, however, are not trained to think of optimizing the whole system, just the parts of the system (silos) encompassed by their responsibilities and activities. Optimizing individual silos, however, does not optimize the overall system – these are lessons we learned from a decade of business process engineering, only now these lessons must cross company boundaries. GM's Szygenda notes, "Many people aren't trained to think from a systems viewpoint – that is, a closed-loop control and feedback mechanism. This way of thinking is essential to understand the interactions between activities and business processes within and external to a company. Change management and learning – not technology – are still the issues in transforming businesses to satisfy increasingly demanding customers and to attain ever-increasing business performance levels."[18] Learning "systems thinking," is the preparatory step that must precede any program of supply chain management transformation.

Information Week's Bruce Caldwell's report provides a concrete example of implementing systems thinking. "Take Owens Corning: Staggering with debt from fending off a takeover attempt in 1986, and hammered repeatedly over the past several years with asbestos litigation claims, the $5 billion building materials company has undergone several transformations. It snapped up 20 companies around the world and built a completely new IT infrastructure, creating a fully electronic, paperless work environment. Last year, the company took advantage of its new business and IT assets by combining its IT, customer-service, logistics, materials-management, and supply-chain planning groups into one organization called the System Thinking Information Group. "We are the linkage point with all our customers and suppliers,"[19] says Mike Radcliff, head of the new group.

Extended supply chain planning can be sophisticated and costly to implement, and definitely requires commitment. As we have discovered, an extended SCM system has many dimensions and specific applications. Point solutions do not get the job done. Instead, an extended SCM platform is needed to provide the foundation for growing a portfolio of solutions. For such an approach to work, the SCM platform must support incremental growth, allowing the enterprise to manage risks and take advantage of SCM opportunities as they arise.

Anderson, Britt and Farve describe a sustainable process, "Excellent supply chain management, in fact, transcends company boundaries to involve every link of the supply chain (from the supplier's supplier to the customer's customer) in developing forecasts collaboratively and then maintaining the required capacity across the operations. Channel-wide sales and operations planning can detect early warning signals of demand lurking in customer promotions, ordering patterns, and restocking algorithms and takes into account vendor and carrier capabilities, capacity, and constraints. Such demand-based planning takes time to get right. The first step is typically a pilot of a leading-edge program, such as vendor-managed inventory or jointly managed forecasting and replenishment, conducted in conjunction with a few high-volume, sophisticated partners in the supply chain. As the partners refine their collaborative forecasting, planned orders become firm orders. The customer no longer sends a purchase order, and the manufacturer commits inventory from its available-to-promise stock. After this pilot formalizes a planning process, infrastructure, and measures, the program expands to include other channel partners, until enough are participating to facilitate quantum improvement in utilization of manufacturing and logistics assets and cost performance."[20]

A company should start along its path to extended supply chain management by evaluating problems in its current operations: poor inventory turns, lost sales due to out-of-stock conditions, too many assets tied up in safety stock, or a competitor offering made-to-order services. Such analysis must be conducted from the perspective of the customer. Anderson, Britt and Farve explain, "By determining what customers want and how to coordinate efforts across the supply chain to meet those requirements faster, cheaper, and better, companies enhance both customer satisfaction and their own financial performance. But the balance is not easy to strike or to sustain. Each company – whether a supplier, manufacturer, distributor or retailer – must find the way to combine all seven principles [of SCM] into a supply chain strategy that best fits its particular situation. No two companies will reach the same conclusion."[21] They continue and address the barrier of companies not wanting to share information, "Excellent supply chain management requires a more enlightened mindset – recognizing, as a more progressive manufacturer did: 'Our supplier's costs are in effect our costs. If we force our supplier to provide 90 days of consigned material when 30 days are sufficient, the cost of that inventory will find its way back into the supplier's price to us since it increases his cost structure.'" The holistic view of the entire supply chain is accompanied by a holistic bottom line for the *entire* channel. Trading partners can go so far as price indexing rather than negotiated fixed prices in order to equally share gains or losses due to price fluctuations.

Once the initial investment decision has been taken, a company should implement a flexible, extended SCM platform rather than a point solution. The extended SCM infrastructure should be built from reusable components so that, as the portfolio of applications grows, components can be reused and extended rather than starting from scratch for each extended SCM initiative. By constructing solutions from best-of-breed e-Commerce application components, an enterprise can arrange, rearrange, and reuse the components as changing supply chain requirements dictate.

By leveraging common components an enterprise can reduce costs and complexity for building, managing, and participating in electronic trading relationships, obviating the need to buy specific packages for every SCM-facilitated process. These common components can be purchased and modified for specific supply chain management architectures as required by business process imperatives, while requiring minimal incremental skills from the IT department. This permits reduced time and capital investment when creating future extended SCM solutions or evolving existing solutions to support changing supplier needs as well as shifting customer demands.

Another key strategy issue is the degree of process integration with internal enterprise management systems and those of suppliers and other third party participants in extended SCM systems. Process integration is usually very tight among multiple divisions of a single enterprise. Companies and their long-term trading partners are tightly coupled, while their relationship to SMEs and external supply chains is loosely coupled. Information can be exchanged between trading partners as data only or through real-time transaction processing via direct interaction with application interfaces (APIs). Real-time interactions are most often the basis of integrating an extended SCM system with internal enterprise management systems, while EDI is the traditional form of integration via message-passing among suppliers and trading partners. Java, XML and other Internet and e-Commerce technology standards have made it possible to push the integration envelope to SME suppliers and customers that otherwise could not justify the investment and resources to implement traditional SCM systems. These advanced technologies open a whole new world of possibilities for optimizing logistics and supply chain management – in short, a new realm of possibilities for gaining competitive advantage.

Putting It All Together

Extended SCM applications harness the Internet to automate the business processes of collaborative supply chain management. They can provide a company with extraordinary planning and logistic advantages not possible before the advent of e-Commerce. A sustainable approach to implementing extended SCM systems leverages legacy enterprise systems (including traditional SCM systems) and extends them to suppliers and customers across an entire value/supply chain. Managing an extended supply chain that reaches across internal operations and networks of suppliers and customers is a balancing act requiring agility. An agile, extended SCM system must provide direct support for the inter-enterprise processes of next generation supply chains as shown in Figure 6 - 9.

A company should start by identifying its unique requirements and issues – independent of the packages available on the market – then select low hanging fruit for initial implementation projects. Central to this approach is the reuse of a common core of e-Commerce application components to incrementally develop new applications and grow their capabilities as new SCM opportunities are discovered. By adopting a component-based development approach for agile software development, companies can implement breakthrough SCM systems today and take advantage of SCM improvement opportunities that will appear tomorrow. From the loading dock to the warehouse and shop floor, what was once considered a back office drudge can become a major contributor to the bottom line. Internal and external logistic functions will blur and, with a robust supply chain infrastructure, "spot" markets will appear as companies respond to actual demand data rather than soft forecasts. This ability to sense and respond is the key to satisfying the never satisfied customer in a real-time economy.

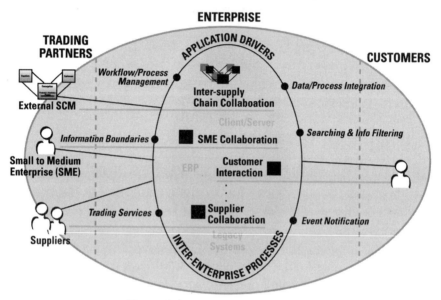

Figure 6 - 9. Putting It All Together

Companies that master their supply chains and transform them into dynamic supply grids will dominate industries. Companies that do not will be severely diminished. "They will lose out," declares Harvey Seegers, CEO of GE Information Services. "They won't be able to effectively compete in a growing global marketplace, and they will lose the ability to attract new customers, quickly reach trading partners, and penetrate new market segments."[22] Companies that do not aggressively pursue extended supply chain initiatives will be deserted by customers seeking faster delivery of customized goods and services.

References

1   Deborah Asbrand, "Squeeze out excess costs with supply-chain solutions," *Datamation,* March, 1997. http://www.datamation.com/PlugIn/issues/1997/march/03mfg.html

2   June Langhoff, "Chain of Command: Forging New Partnerships, Building Bigger Profit Margins," Oracle Magazine, *Profit,* November, 1997. http://www.oramag.com/profit/97-Nov/chain.html

3   Mathew Schwartz, "Extending the Supply Chain," *Software Magazine*, November, 1998.   http:www.softwaremag.com/Nov98/sm118eb.htm

4   http://www.advmfg.com/exec/exec9812s.htm

5   David L. Anderson, Frank E. Britt, and Donavon J. Favre, "The Seven Principles of Supply Chain Management," *Logistics Online*, 1997. http://www.manufacturing.net/magazine/logistic/archives/1997/scmr/11princ.htm

6   David Truog, "The End Of Commerce Servers," *The Forrester Report.* March 1999.

7   Deborah Asbrand, "Squeeze out excess costs with supply-chain solutions," *Datamation,* March, 1997. http://www.datamation.com/PlugIn/issues/1997/march/03mfg.html

8   _____, Ibid.

9   _____, Ibid.

10   Tom Stein and Jeff Sweat, "Killer Supply Chains," *Information Week*, November 9, 1998. http://www.informationweek.com/708/08iukil.htm

11   _____, Ibid.

12   June Langhoff, "Chain of Command: Forging New Partnerships, Building Bigger Profit Margins," Oracle Magazine, *Profit,* November, 1997. http://www.oramag.com/profit/97-Nov/chain.html

13   "The Smart Supply Chain," A White Paper, http://cisco-supply.se-com.com/

14   Ralph Szygenda, "Information's Competitive Edge," Information Week, February 8, 1999. http://www.informationweek.com/720/gmcorp.htm

15   _____, Ibid.

16   "E-commerce poster child grows up," *Datamation,* August 1998. http://www.datamation.com/PlugIn/workbench/ecom/stories/08ecom.html

17   "The Smart Supply Chain," A White Paper, http://cisco-supply.se-com.com/

18   Ralph Szygenda, "Information's Competitive Edge," Information Week, February 8, 1999. http://www.informationweek.com/720/gmcorp.htm

19   Bruce Caldwell, "Time And Money Pay Off," *Information Week*, February 8, 1999.

http://www.informationweek.com/720/payoff.htm

[20] David L. Anderson, Frank E. Britt, and Donavon J. Favre, "The Seven Principles of Supply Chain Management," *Logistics Online*, 1997.

[21] _____, Ibid.

[22] "Manufacturing Systems Orders From Chaos," *Information Week*, June 23, 1997.

Chapter 7 - Component-Based Development for E-Commerce

Notes

E-Commerce Applications Development

Developing e-Commerce applications is no trivial endeavor. Just as with all enterprise computing efforts, the task requires solid planning, systems architecture and project management. This chapter provides an overview of the development process from the requirements analysis stage to implementation.

The entire process is discussed against the backdrop of a fictitious company, OA.SYS Technologies, that requires the inter-enterprise integration of business processes. This approach is the way forward to sustainable development for the multitude of e-Commerce initiatives corporations must embrace as they build bridges to the emerging digital economy. Although a comprehensive treatment of this subject would require a book, this chapter walks the developer through the major steps of a full enterprise-scale development cycle while providing snippets of analysis, design and implementation artifacts along the way.

OA.SYS' Business Challenges

OA.SYS Technologies is a $900 million maker of computer systems for the business market. OA.SYS has one focused vision: To build custom computer systems tailored to individual business needs. OA.SYS has gained recognition as the provider of choice for business customers and government agencies and has established itself as a brand name recognized by purchasing agents across North America.

Headquartered in Flat Rock, Texas with 2,800 employees, OA.SYS' computers are manufactured to individual order specifications at facilities in Tampa, Florida; Wilton, Connecticut; and Phoenix, Arizona. The components that go into OA.SYS systems are provided by a network of suppliers located in Stamford, Connecticut; Austin, Texas; Limerick, Ireland; Penang, Malaysia; and Xiamen, China.

To accommodate its rapid growth, OA.SYS invested heavily in an enterprise resource planning (ERP) system to supplement and integrate the many legacy systems it had developed in-house during its start up years. Its inventory control system was developed on a mainframe and serves as the heart of the order entry and procurement systems. This

workhorse has been revamped to a client/server architecture to streamline the operations of remote departments and facilities.

OA.SYS' has been so successful on Wall Street that it has caught the
attention of competitors, a number of whom are in hot pursuit in the
business and government market sectors. Facing shrinking margins and
increasing competition, executive management has conducted a series
of intensive strategic planning sessions. Not wanting to rest on its past
laurels, the focus of these sessions was corporate renewal, and the planning team included managers from customer and supplier
organizations in addition to OA.SYS' CIO and executive management.

A careful analysis of OA.SYS' strengths, weaknesses, opportunities
and threats produced a number of business initiatives. Common to all
of the initiatives was the radical redesign of key, outward-facing business processes that could be enabled by the Internet. Of the 16 Internet-
enabled initiatives the team identified, two were prioritized for implementation. Procurement and establishing a Virtual I-Market thus
became OA.SYS' first forays into e-Commerce with the goals of cutting
costs and increasing revenues through a new market channel.

Using her combined business and technology expertise, OA.SYS'
CIO, Jini Martin, had to translate these business goals into requirements
and constraints. A foremost requirement was quick time-to-market – a
month earlier, a competitor with significant financial backing had
announced intentions of entering the market with Internet-based offerings. Moreover, Jini knew that the company's unique business
philosophy, policy, and processes were embedded in its legacy systems.
She recognized the wisdom of leveraging, not obliterating, these corporate assets, as they embodied OA.SYS' competitive advantage.

Jini worked through the requirements and constraints with John
Dorfman, the Systems Architect who would begin the process of designing the information and technology architectures for OA.SYS' current
and future e-Commerce initiatives. Because they were moving the company into uncharted territory, their initial risk assessment caused them
to select procurement as the first application to be developed. The
rationale was that any mistakes made along the way toward their first
e-Commerce application would be tolerated among suppliers, but abso-

lutely not tolerated by customers. Moreover, Jini and John realized that they were not just developing a single application. Instead, they knew that they must develop an overall application architecture able to sustain multiple e-Commerce development projects and integrate with OA.SYS' existing systems as well as those of their suppliers and customers.

OA.SYS' E-Commerce Strategy Formulation

Once the strategic e-Commerce initiatives were established for OA.SYS Technologies, the procurement system was confirmed as the top development priority. The goal of the system was to streamline the trading processes between the company and its suppliers. OA.SYS was to host the procurement application and integrate it with some of the critical systems at suppliers' sites. Even though several points of integration between OA.SYS and its suppliers could have been tackled, the initial goal was to integrate the suppliers' inventory systems to provide up-to-the-minute data for the procurement system catalogs, and integrate the order entry processes to automatically handle purchase orders.

After a thorough analysis of the overall systems requirements, John and his team uncovered several issues they must address:

- Should they buy a pre-packaged procurement application or build the application from scratch?
- How could they leverage OA.SYS' existing IT infrastructure of legacy applications and ERP systems?
- How could they integrate their suppliers' disparate systems, technologies, and applications?
- How could they build a framework that would both support the development of the procurement application and accommodate future e-Commerce applications?
- How could they accommodate changing business rules and models within the new e-Commerce applications in order to maintain OA.SYS' unique competitive advantage?

To address the first issue, the architecture team decided to examine the "build versus buy" dilemma, and then create a deployment strategy that was in line with OA.SYS' strategic business initiatives.

The Buy Approach

John and his team evaluated several pre-packaged procurement solutions for the Internet. Most of the solutions were fairly complete in terms of the functionality required for a procurement application, but did not address the other issues the team had identified. Some of the problems they found with the pre-packaged solutions included:

- They did not integrate with OA.SYS' legacy or ERP systems that contained OA.SYS' unique business processes. Some packages offered data integration, but not process integration. Some pre-packaged solutions required eliminating or duplicating legacy systems while others were tightly integrated with a specific ERP solution (not the one that was deployed at OA.SYS).
- While pre-packaged solutions modeled industry standard practices and processes, the business rules were hard coded into the systems. As a result, they would be very difficult to change in order to accommodate the unique business processes that embodied OA.SYS' competitive advantage.
- Customization of pre-packaged applications would be tedious and expensive. Although pre-packaged solutions were *perceived* by management to be quick and easy to deploy, John's experience in customizing them rapidly dispelled such notions.
- After the initial customization, every update to the pre-packaged solutions or changes in business processes or rules would require rewriting the "wrapper programs" used to link to legacy systems. This would be a maintenance nightmare.
- The software modules of the pre-packaged procurement systems could not be reused in OA.SYS' other e-Commerce initiatives. Each of these e-Commerce packages would exhibit the same slew of problems and would not integrate with packages from other vendors, including the procurement application.
- Every instance of integration with a supplier's systems would be a customization effort that would have to be funded by OA.SYS.

The Build Approach

After considering all of the issues brought about by pre-packaged applications, John's team decided to analyze the "build from scratch" approach. After considerable review, the team found that despite the flexibility that in-house development could deliver, several issues would have to be addressed:

- Building a solution completely in-house would be very time consuming and expensive.
- Even though they were technically competent and talented, John's team lacked experience with Internet development and was new to e-Commerce application environments. Compounding their Web expertise lag was the tidal wave of new technologies and buzzwords: EJB, XML, DNA, XQL, Servlets, JTS, DOM, RDF, OTM, IIOP, et al.
- In order to reuse common functionality across the other e-Commerce applications, John's team would have to spend considerable time building an infrastructure of reusable functional components. Designing and building such an infrastructure would have to be accomplished before even starting the first application. Without this preparation, however, major development time (and cost) as well as integration and maintenance costs would be associated with every application.
- Due to the complexity of the Internet as a computing platform, OA.SYS' application developers would end up focusing more on technology issues and less on business issues.

After assessing the trade-offs of both these development models, John's team searched for a way they could combine the benefits of both the approaches while avoiding the pitfalls of each. If they could buy a framework of application components that gave them the core business functionality they needed and yet was open enough for the team to custom code their unique business processes, most of the critical issues would be addressed, and they could simply "assemble" feature-rich and yet flexible e-Commerce solutions.

The Component Assembly Approach

During their search for a sustainable e-Commerce development strategy, John's team evaluated an emerging approach to applications development: *component-based development*. Component-based development is an architectural approach where each layer in the architecture offers *services* to higher layers while hiding the details of how those services are implemented. Although software components have been embraced since the beginnings of computing, traditionally they have been used to provide low-level technology services such as system calls and window APIs. Application components, oh the other hand, offer services that address business semantics such as user profiling and workflow routing. In order to build e-Commerce applications using component-based development, John's team realized that the architecture would have to:

- Consist of reusable software modules rich in business functionality. The software modules would have to be loosely coupled and based on open standards so that they could integrate with each other without being dependent on each other.
- Provide uncomplicated integration with legacy and ERP systems of both OA.SYS and its suppliers.
- Provide ease-of-use and flexible support for custom application logic, user interface design, configuration and post-deployment maintenance.
- Be scalable to support more users and transactions as the business grows. Scalability must be achieved via distributed computing platforms currently under evaluation by OA.SYS, including Microsoft's DCOM with its Microsoft Transaction Server (MTS) for component coordination, and CORBA Object Transaction Monitors (OTM) including IBM's Component Broker, BEA Systems' M3, IONA's OrbixOTM, and others supporting Enterprise JavaBeans (server-side components).
- Be extensible to permit additional functionality over time. As development software for the Enterprise JavaBeans specification becomes available, the architecture would have to support drag-and-drop rapid application development (RAD) to give OA.SYS and its partners the agility they would require to support business changes.

A closer look across the many e-Commerce applications that were to be developed revealed distinct patterns of functionality. If these distinct patterns were implemented and available as software components, John's team could *assemble* their new applications quickly and inexpensively by reusing these modules. Using their Java™ Integrated Development Environment (IDE) they could assemble the components into applications with "glue code" that would incorporate OA.SYS' unique business processes.

Chapter 2 discussed the framework of the core business functionality common to most e-Commerce applications and essential to inter-enterprise process integration. Some common e-Commerce application functions include profile management, collaboration and mediation, application security, workflow and process management, event notification, data and object management, and transaction processing. When implemented in software as components, these functions appear to application developers as a set of *services*. These services are part of a layered software architecture. Within each component, services are implemented by a collection of business objects. A service is simply a request protocol for a logical unit of work – for example, update employee's address, move the task to next person in queue, send the purchase order to the supplier via EDI and so on. Services can be invoked without the requester needing to know the implementation details of the software that delivers them. The process is very much like driving a car without needing to know how the engine works. It is extremely important, however, that component services are provided through a standard, published interface to ensure inter-operability, ease of use and loose coupling. To summarize, an application component is a collection of code that provides one or more services based upon a clearly-defined, standard interface as illustrated in Figure 7 - 1.

Business rules and unique business processes are embedded in the e-Commerce applications' glue code that plugs in the services provided by the components as required. The services provided by the components are very business-centric and hide the technical details of the objects they encapsulate. Application developers, therefore, can focus more on the business rather than technology issues.

Based on their domain, e-Commerce application components can be classified into three main categories: cross-application components, application-specific components and industry-specific components. *Cross-application* components provide a set of services that can be used across several different applications. They have a higher granularity when compared to other technology components such as a JDBC driver, but a lower level of granularity when compared to a specific application. *Application-specific* components, on the other hand, provide a higher level of granularity and may use cross-application components configured to provide application-specific functionality. An *industry-specific* component is unique to a given industry. To illustrate, a cross-application workflow component allows any kind of workflow to be modeled. An application-specific procurement component uses the cross-application workflow component to model a typical requisition workflow. An example of an industry-specific component is a "stock price analyzer" for the financial services industry. Any one or a combination of these e-Commerce application components mentioned above could be used to assemble customized applications as shown in Figure 7 - 2. The figure also shows where application components fit within a modern distributed computing infrastructure.

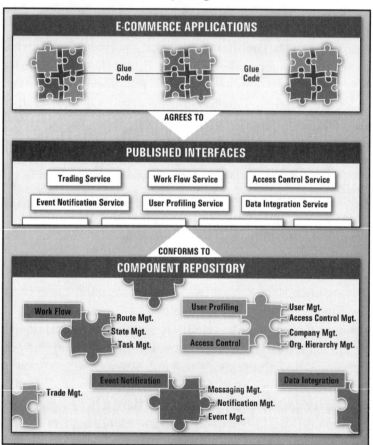

Figure 7 - 1. Component-Based Application Architecture

Having evaluated all three approaches to e-Commerce application development, John's team summarized their findings in Table 7 - 1 and presented them to management. Overwhelmingly, the component assembly approach stood out as the right choice for OA.SYS.

Table 7 - 1. Comparison of Development Approaches

Develop from Scratch (Build)	Develop using Pre-Packaged Apps (Buy)	Develop using e-Commerce Components (Component Assembly)
Requires detailed low-level implementation Technology issues seem more daunting than business issues Development focus on system design vs. application design	Hard-wired application logic doesn't suit specific business needs Customization through complex "wrapper" code lacks adaptability to change Closed environment lacks inter-operability	Focus on business logic reduces development time Feature-rich well abstracted components result in better application design Standard interfaces and open APIs ensure inter-operability and extensibility
⊗	⊗	✓

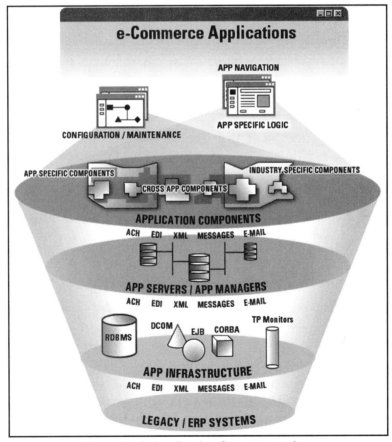

Figure 7 - 2. Application Components in a
Modern Distributed Computing Infrastructure

Component-Based Development –
Putting It All Together

Once John's team determined that components were the right way to build e-Commerce applications, they moved on to the work at hand – to execute the development and deployment strategy, beginning with the procurement application. John assigned his business analysts to start gathering requirements from the intended users of the system within OA.SYS and the suppliers. The focus of the requirements gathering team was on the inter-enterprise business processes. The team used their existing business process engineering tools, but the actors they modeled were external as well as internal. In other words, their domain modeling was aimed at Inter-enterprise Process Engineering (IPE). Their goal was to identify and eliminate duplicate processes and ineffective hand-offs across enterprise boundaries. These new inter-enterprise processes would then be jointly designed and owned.

Simultaneously, John asked his technical lead to start evaluating the components that they would need to buy that would give them the core functionality to assemble their e-Commerce applications. One of the critical features required of these application components was the ability to provide their services to not only OA.SYS, but also to their multiple trading partners. After a thorough analysis, OA.SYS acquired its initial set of application components and incorporated them into its software development repository.

Figure 7 - 3 shows the application development life cycle they adopted to create an overall architectural framework while building the procurement application. For some time, OA.SYS had been using object-oriented analysis and design methods to develop their enterprise systems. The technology team was well versed in the Unified Modeling Language (UML) and had adopted *use cases* as their requirements gathering and analysis technique. They were evaluating Fusion, the Unified Process and others for adoption as their overall systems development method, and were pleased that these methods had support for component modeling. In addition, they were delighted to learn that the shift to component-based development methods could accelerate the software development life cycle as prefabricated components shifted the focus from implementation to integration.

During all phases of development, the repository of modeling arti-facts and pre-tested components was available for reuse. The transition to component-based development did, however, affect their develop-ment culture and training was needed to refocus on architecture rather than building code. The architecture provided an infrastructure for coordination, and standards that defined what components could be plugged into it. Training extended the team's expertise from building software to component assembly

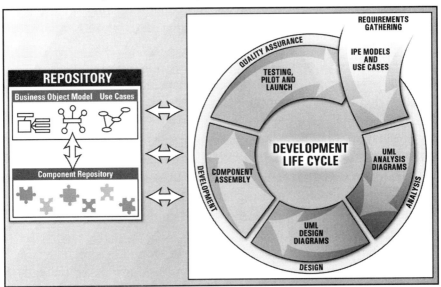

Figure 7 - 3. Component-Based Application Development Life Cycle

Requirements Gathering

During the requirements gathering phase, John's business analysts met several intended users of the proposed system, both throughout OA.SYS and within the trading partner network. They had to identify the roles that each of these entities would play, the inter-enterprise access privi-leges they needed, and how they would like to see their systems interface. One of the essential tasks assigned to the analysts was to engi-neer and streamline processes across OA.SYS and its vendors so that they could eradicate duplicate processes, eliminate inefficient hand-offs, and create new real-time interconnections.

The requirements team needed to identify points of integration between OA.SYS' new e-Commerce procurement system, their existing ERP/MRP and legacy systems, and their suppliers' ERP/MRP and legacy systems. The work involved identifying new workflows within the organization and across trading partners. Although there were several applications that needed to be integrated, the business analysts decided to use an iterative approach. The first iteration would integrate only two supplier applications: the inventory systems (for getting up-to-date catalog and pricing information) and the order entry systems (for sending orders electronically to the suppliers' order entry systems). This level of integration proved to be a challenge because the suppliers used different technologies in their inventory and order entry systems. Some larger suppliers utilized electronic data interchange (EDI) to send catalog information and receive purchase orders. Others published paper catalogs and received purchase orders via fax. To accommodate such disparate systems and business data formats, the integration simply had to be part of an overall, consistent framework.

The team used their existing business process engineering tools for gathering requirements and mapping the new inter-enterprise business processes. In addition, they developed the context level use case diagram for the system shown in Figure 7 - 4.

OA.SYS requisitioners were to be able to browse or search for the items they wished to procure, and create requisitions. Based on workflow rules, OA.SYS' requisitions would be routed to the appropriate managers for approval. The managers would receive notifications for approval based upon their preference: fax or email. Once approved, requisitions were to be routed to the Purchasing Manager to be dispatched as a Purchase Order using the supplier's preferred method of delivery (EDI, e-mail, or fax). Preferences throughout the system for both OA.SYS and suppliers were to be maintained by a profiling component. In the case of EDI, data was to flow into suppliers' order management application electronically, thus streamlining the whole procurement process from catalog maintenance to purchase order processing. Where possible, OA.SYS and its suppliers were to share their new inter-enterprise business processes in real-time.

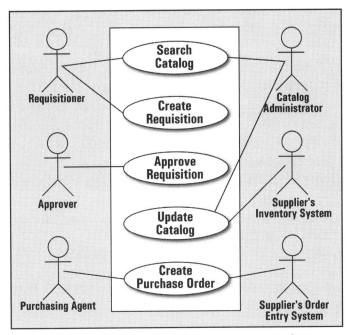

Figure 7 - 4. Context Model of the Procurement System

The team's requirements gathering work was maintained in a repository that permitted reuse of their requirement artifacts as the project moved forward into the analysis phase. The use cases in the repository would bind further steps in the development life cycle and were essential to quality assurance and systems testing.

Analysis

Once the business analysts gathered the requirements, they released the functional requirements to the technical team to begin the analysis phase. During the analysis phase, the technical team elaborated upon the context level use cases to prepare a detailed specification of the requirements of the system and to develop a logical application architecture. They also developed the initial analysis object models. The analysis artifacts they produced included a high level architecture, detailed use case diagrams, test cases, class relationship and object interaction diagrams, and sequence diagrams. Architectural decisions were critical because the many artifacts created at this stage would be held in a repository for later inspection and reuse.

Figure 7 - 5 shows a detailed use case diagram of the OA.SYS procurement system. It models the system's intended functions, its surroundings and the relationships among the actors involved in the system. Actors are not part of the system, but are either users who interact with the system or are external systems or resources that have to integrate with the system.

Each module, illustrated in the diagram above, represents a major piece of functionality that delivers value to the participants. For example, the Approve Request module provides the following functionality:

- Authenticate and authorize the user
- Display the list of requests awaiting disposition
- Allow the user to approve the request, depending upon privileges
- Route the request to the next participant in the work flow
- Notify the appropriate participant(s)

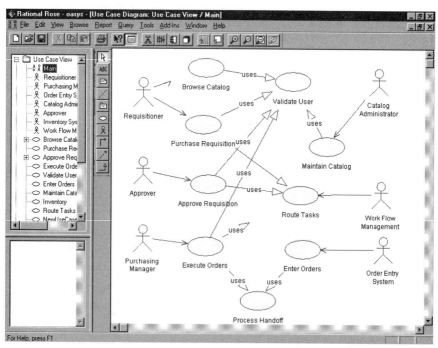

Figure 7 - 5. Use Case Diagram of the Procurement System

Design

Once the use cases and other analysis artifacts were finalized, the design team moved on to refine the logical design and transitioned from the problem space to the solution space. This entailed designing the flow of operations within each functional module of the system from the detailed requirements gathered during the analysis phase and mapping analysis models to the target platform. They packaged their deployment models so that they could be implemented in a distributed computing environment (e.g. CORBA or DCOM). Reusable components accelerated the design phase dramatically.

Figure 7 - 6 shows a sample design artifact, a sequence diagram of the Approve Requisition module discussed earlier.

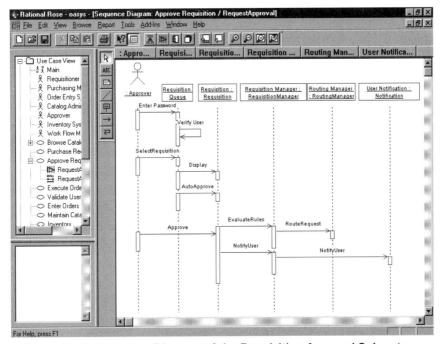

Figure 7 - 6. Sequence Diagram of the Requisition Approval Subsystem

Laying out the sequence diagram, depicting the sequential flow of events and allowed the design team to identify the interaction between objects of various functional modules in a time sequence. This activity allowed the design team to identify auxiliary objects and the messages exchanged between these objects (e.g., Approve is a message sent by the Approver object to the Requisition object). Then they structured the methods within the objects to support the desired functionality (e.g., an Approver object should have a public method called canApprove( ) and the Requisition object should have a public method called approve( )). With preexisting components available, the design team inspected the components for services that could be reused to accelerate the process.

The next step within the design phase consisted of two parts:

- The Business Object Design
- The User Interface Design

The business object design step consisted of the initial layout of the objects and their organization within a categorized hierarchy of similar packages. In this phase, the objects were modeled to encapsulate the data and provide methods (APIs or messages) for objects to communicate with each other. At this stage, the cardinality relationships were defined between the objects (e.g., one Approver object can approve many Requisition objects).

Figure 7 - 7 shows a sample object model for the Requisition Approval functionality within the procurement application.

The User Interface design addressed the effect of user task requirements on the application flow, as well as the screen design from the user's view. In this phase, the project manager worked with the graphics team and the usability group to build prototypes of the application, keeping the user-experience in mind. Some of the key design issues were the look-and-feel of the application, the ease of finding information and acting on it, the ease of initiating and tracking transactions, and user profile related functionality. In addition to authentication and access management, the user profiles needed to support *digital signatures* for nonrepudiation. Dynamic profiling was needed because purchasing agents are time constrained and want the system to bring to bear all the resources for the task at hand in a convenient manner that allows them to do their work efficiently. Often a task cannot be completed in one work session, and the user will want work in progress to continue where it left off on successive sessions.

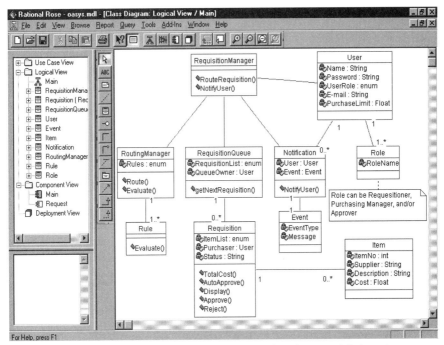

Figure 7 - 7. Class Diagram of the Requisition Approval Subsystem

Once the object model and design were finalized, the design team searched the component repository to see which of the existing objects could be reused. They found that most of the objects they required for building the procurement system either existed as part of the component framework, or could be derived from the ones that did exist. For example, an Approver object could easily be modeled with a User object from the profiling component. The basic attributes like Username, Password, and Role were available directly, whereas those attributes that were application specific (e.g. purchasing limit) could be easily associated through the Extended Attribute object provided by the component. Similarly, objects required for defining and managing workflows, user notifications and data integration of the legacy and ERP systems were available out of the box with these components.

Table 7 - 2 shows a sample mapping from application-specific objects to objects available in the application components.

Table 7 - 2. OA.SYS Application Object to Component Mappings

OA.SYS OBJECT	RELATIONSHIP	BUSINESS OBJECT	PROVIDED BY
▤ Requisitioner User	Instance of	▤ User	✹ Profiling component
Attributes:			
▩ Name	Basic Attribute of	▤ User	✹ Profiling component
▩ Password	Basic Attribute of	▤ User	✹ Profiling component
▩ Role	Instance of	▤ Role	✹ Profiling component
▩ Approval limit	Instance of	▤ ExtendedAttribute	✹ Profiling component
etc.			
▤ Requisition Created Event	Instance of	▤ ECEvent	✹ Notification component
Attributes:			
▩ Message	Instance of	▤ Message	✹ Notification component
▩ Subscribers	Instance of	▤ User	✹ Profiling component
etc.			
▤ Requisitioning Workflow	Instance of	▤ Process	✹ Workflow component
Attributes:			
▩ Req. Creation Activity	Instance of	▤ Activity	✹ Workflow component
▩ Departmental Budget	Instance of	▤ ExtendedAttribute	✹ Profiling component
▩ Within Dept. Budget	Instance of	▤ BusinessRule	✹ Workflow component
etc.			
▤ CatalogTransferAgent	Instance of	▤ DataTransferSession	✹ Data integration component
▤ CatalogItem	Instance of	▤ ApplicationObject	✹ Data integration component
▤ POEDI850	Instance of	▤ ApplicationObject	✹ Data integration component
▤ Requisition Viewer	Is a	▤ HTTPServlet	Java servlet development kit
Attributes:			
▩ Session	Basic Attribute of	▤ HTTPServlet	Java servlet development kit
▩ Current User	Custom Code	N/A	Java
▩ UI Properties	Custom Code	N/A	Java
etc.			
▩ = Attribute		▤ = Object	✹ = Component

The next step of the design phase was the configuration of the components to model the objects according to the design documents. The technical lead used the component's administrative tools to configure these objects. He defined the workflows, events, user profiles and resource access privileges, and data integration templates that would be used in the new procurement application. Figure 7 - 8 shows a sample component administration tool that was used for configuring the user profile objects while Figure 7 - 9 shows the configuration of the workflow component.

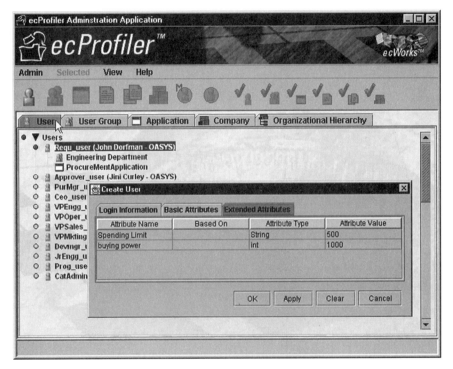

Figure 7 - 8. Configuring Objects in the Profiling Component

Once the objects were defined and the templates laid out, the system design document was updated with screen shots from the prototype, the functional description of the modules, the specifications for the implementation, and the scenarios for the regression tests. These specifications were then distributed to the entire development team and tracked using a project management tool.

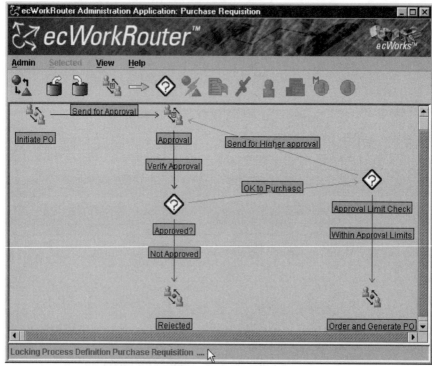

Figure 7 - 9. Configuration of the Workflow Component

Development

The developers used their existing Integrated Development Environment (IDE) to assemble the application. Figure 7 - 10 illustrates a sample IDE used for component assembly.

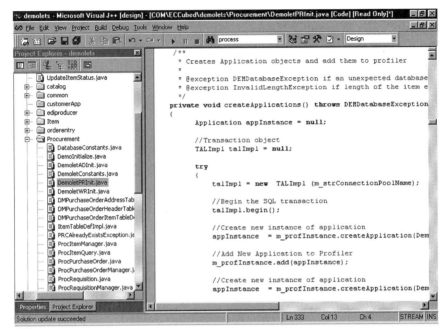

Figure 7 - 10. A Sample IDE for "Assembling" the Application

During the development phase, each developer was responsible for the unit and integration testing aspects of the glue code they built to assemble the application components. Once the coding effort was completed, the application came to life. Figure 7 - 11 is a snapshot of one of the screens in the procurement application.

Testing

Although the quality assurance (QA) team had been involved from the inception of the project, they returned to the use cases from the requirements gathering phase and went into overdrive. Their intention was to break the application at every step. They worked against a formal test plan and the functional requirements documents to ensure that the functionality in the application met the requirements specifications. In addition, the QA team tested transactions that were "not expected" by the system to see how the application would respond. All bugs and system change requests were tracked using an integrated project and configuration management system. Once the integration testing was complete, OA.SYS was ready to begin running pilot programs with some of their most strategic suppliers.

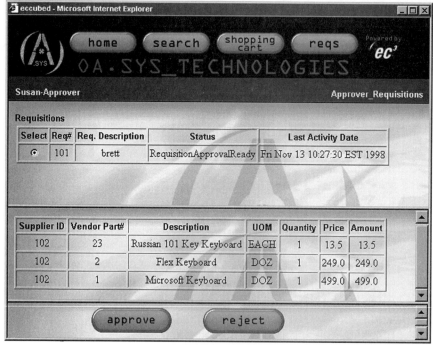

Figure 7 - 11. A Snapshot From the Procurement Application

Pilot

One of OA.SYS' close trading partners, Keyboards International, was eager to participate in the initial pilot of the new system. The technical leads shipped out the integration templates for the inventory system so that they could pull the catalogs directly out of Keyboards International's inventory system in real-time. The purchase orders were handled electronically using the traditional EDI mechanism. All that Keyboards International's MIS team was required to do was to map their existing data schema elements to those specified in the template that OA.SYS shipped to them, and have the catalog administrator initiate the transfer of item data, with contracted prices, to OA.SYS. All the items were available immediately for the requisitioners at OA.SYS'.

OA.SYS requisitioners were able to browse or search for the items they wished to procure and create requisitions. Based on workflow rules, OA.SYS' requisitions were routed to the appropriate managers for approval. The managers received notifications for approvals based upon their preference: fax or email. Once approved, requisitions were routed to the Purchasing Manager to be dispatched as a Purchase Order via EDI to Keyboards International. Once an EDI document was received by Keyboards International, the data flowed electronically into their order management application, thus streamlining the whole procurement process from catalog maintenance to purchase order processing. The two companies shared their new inter-enterprise business processes in real-time.

The Launch of the Procurement Application

After a successful pilot, OA.SYS extended the new procurement application to all its suppliers. OA.SYS' new infrastructure allowed them to roll out follow-on e-Commerce applications in record time. The component-based architecture could scale as new suppliers were added as well as integrate the disparate technologies deployed throughout OA.SYS' supplier network. In addition, the new e-Commerce framework set the stage to expand their e-Commerce applications portfolio.

After their meeting with senior management to brief them on the new procurement system, Jini and John were confident and looked forward to taking on the I-Market initiative. Although they knew that the I-Market project would not be a trivial undertaking, they now had a solid architecture on which to build (as set forth in the architectural requirements in the section, *The Component Assembly Approach*).

Conclusion

The history of business computing is demarcated by major shifts in the use of the computer for competitive advantage. Early mainframe systems brought productivity to the back office while personal computers brought productivity to the front office. With the advent of the Internet, business computing moves to the front lobby giving customers, suppliers and trading partners direct access to a company's business processes and systems. Each new era of business computing brought not only a new realm of possibility for competitive advantage, but also increased complexity and a corresponding paradigm shift in the software development processes needed to accommodate the complexity.

To tame the complexity of large-scale distributed applications and develop agile inter-enterprise systems, it is necessary to undertake the shift from a conventional development methodology to a component-based development paradigm. As we explored in this brief treatment of the subject, component-based development is not a replacement for existing development methods, it is a next step in the evolution of modern software development methods and techniques such as those found in the UML. With these needs clearly recognized, researchers, standards bodies such as the Object Management Group, and software development corporations are currently formalizing the methods and tools of component-based development. Companies wanting to remain competitive in the digital economy should act now to incorporate e-Commerce components and component-based development as strategic business weapons.

Chapter 8 - E-Commerce Business and Technology Strategies

Notes

The Importance of Architecture

The Brooklyn Bridge took thirteen years to build. An architecture was used to guide the work breakdown whereby separate components were constructed in various locations and assembled into the growing superstructure called a bridge. The architecture – the overarching design – provided the cohesion and coherence of the components so that their assembly would result in a complete, whole bridge.

Like the Brooklyn Bridge, an overarching design is needed to guide the construction and assembly of e-Commerce initiatives into the growing superstructure called a *digital enterprise*. Unlike the Brooklyn Bridge, where traffic could not commence until the entire structure was constructed, the digital enterprise need not be fully built before a company can implement its digital business initiatives. Business goals, objectives and constraints will determine which initiatives and how much infrastructure will be implemented at each step along the way. Developing a solid business and technology architecture is hard work but results provide the cohesion and coherence needed so that as a company's e-Commerce initiatives grow, they fit in and interact with the growing superstructure of the fully digital enterprise.

Corporations and their value-chains are large, dynamic and complex systems. Further, they must evolve within even larger systems including the industries in which they participate and the overall economy. *Large, complex* and *rapidly changing* are three facts of life for the corporation and its business ecosystem. Given these fundamental characteristics, how does a company manage its business and its technology?

Business and technology leaders have grappled with the complexity of enterprise-class information systems for some years. They have learned that an architectural approach is essential to conceiving, designing, building and maintaining these large and complex business systems. The design goal of an enterprise architecture, containing robust and interchangeable business and technology elements, is to provide a coherent framework for managing complexity and change.

An *enterprise architecture* provides the blueprints, the structural abstractions, and style that rationalize, arrange and connect business and technology components to achieve a corporation's purpose – now and in the future. All businesses have an architecture, albeit implicit. The components usually include past, present, and next generations of business policies and processes as well as past, present, and next generations of technologies. For example, adding new electronic sales channels with their unique policies and processes requires that a company continue supporting present sales channels while incorporating the new processes and systems of the new channels.

Without explicit enterprise architecture, chaos will reign. Business and technology changes are certain, and thus an enterprise architecture must provide a framework for change. The changes that result from designing new business models or from adopting new technologies should not hinder the other. Thus change itself is one of the strategic goals of enterprise architecture and enterprise architectures must be living documents.

While a complete discussion of best-practice enterprise architecture is beyond the scope of this book, the suggested readings will be useful to those readers who are new to architecture-centric business and technology processes and methods. The focus here moves beyond enterprise architecture to *inter-enterprise architecture*. The primary principles of enterprise architecture are extended to form an overarching structure for the business and technology components needed at the boundaries between and among enterprises: customers, suppliers and trading partners.

In addition to the elements of enterprise-scale architecture, inter-enterprise architecture adds new dimensions, challenges, and complexity. At the boundaries, technologies and business models are not only disparate, they are beyond the control of any one participant. Thus rules of engagement must accommodate collaborative integration that maintains the integrity of the participants' business policies and processes. These rules of engagement, because they are in the nether land between participants, must be explicit, unambiguous and universally agreed to – in short, they must be based on standards.

Standards are essential to inter-enterprise architecture and those standards must include both *technology standards* (e.g. XML, EJB, COM+, and CORBA) and *business standards* (e.g. OFX for payments, OBI for open MRO procurement, ICE for information content exchange, and SWAP for Simple Workflow Access Protocol). Third wave companies have learned that e-Commerce has so many facets that reach into the core of the business that its architecture should mirror that of not only the enterprise, but of the business ecosystem in which it lives. Thus, standards-based inter-enterprise architecture is the linchpin of third wave e-Commerce.

The problem with standards, of course, is that there are so many de facto and de jour standards from which to choose. The best strategy is to pay close attention to standards most relevant to a company's industry and to adopt *open* standards, where possible, or to migrate to open standards when they become available. Open standards provide the greatest opportunity to achieve the critical goals of *portability* and *interoperability*. Standards are integral components in a sound inter-enterprise architecture. The well designed architecture should be able to accommodate change in its standards-related components.

The task of transitioning to a digital enterprise is, of course, not a single event. It will not happen overnight or be implemented as a "project" to be handled by the IS staff. Companies are not changing their information systems, they are changing the very way they conduct business, the way they operate. E-Commerce is first and foremost the extension of *business*, not technology. The nature, size and sheer complexity of building the ultimate digital enterprise demands that companies develop an overall inter-enterprise architecture, and implement the architecture's components in a step-wise fashion. Because of the absolute need for quality in each component in these mission-critical systems, business and software engineering disciplines are essential. Architecture and these engineering disciplines are the keys to building the ubiquitous business.

Inter-enterprise Architecture

Jim Champy, known for helping to launch the business process reengineering (BPR) revolution, describes a new age of business engineering, "Re-engineering has been mostly about breakthroughs in getting the right stuff out the door. But there are huge productivity gains left in processes that link companies to their suppliers and customers. It goes well beyond the outsourcing of a single function, and it will be driven by the need to deliver a higher level of customer service than a single company can. To make all this work, a company's technology architecture now will have to encompass what's external as well as internal to its operation."[1]

People, process and technology are the ingredients of business architecture. As shown in Figure 8 - 1, inter-enterprise architecture addresses "process" from three key perspectives: *existing business processes* (and the systems that implement them), *value-chain processes*, and *customer-facing processes*. For companies that have changed from product-centric to customer-centric, *customer-facing processes serve as the capstone, binding together all other elements of the architecture.* By focusing first and foremost on customer-facing processes, context is provided for the other components of the architecture, including technology and people.

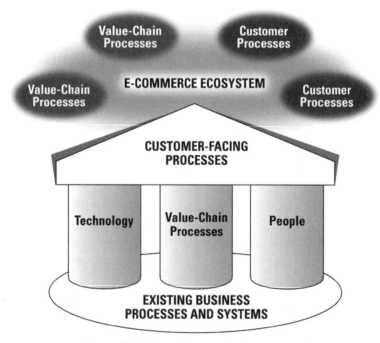

Figure 8 - 1. Inter-Enterprise Architecture

At the center of the architecture, emphasis is given to value-chain processes which are the essence of business-to-business e-Commerce. Having determined the requirements, goals and constraints of customer-facing processes, architecting value-chain processes is a matter of reconciling and optimizing the value delivered by a company's trading partners and its existing business processes. Value-chain processes will likely be subject to new forms of electronic mediation and aggregation different to those in the physical, paper-based world. An early effort aimed at these notions is Hewlett-Packard's e-Services. Industry analyst Patricia Seybold explains, "We're about to embark on a new era in which most companies will begin to focus on a few very strategic business processes. Innovative companies will package up their strategic processes as services that can be provided and/or launched via the Internet. Soon, many business-to-business activities will be handled by a series of e-services locating one another, negotiating with one another, and handling each other's requests."[2] Service-oriented, interenterprise architectures are essential to value-chain innovation. The foundation for a company to participate in new value-chain structures and processes is a company's existing business processes and systems. They must be adapted to participate in the new service-based systems.

Together, these three process architectures identify how the people and technology pillars need to be realigned to support successful e-Commerce transitions and programs. Corporations will have to adopt new technologies and transition staff to new roles and new skills. An overall inter-enterprise architecture allows change to be carefully managed by explicitly identifying those facets (architectural elements) that need to be monitored and controlled as a company transitions to and manages e-Commerce as a new platform for business.

The Inter-enterprise Process Engineering Process

E-Commerce is not an end state. It is a new business platform that will grow and evolve. The secret to sustainable e-Commerce success is to think and plan in terms of overall architecture, but act in incremental steps. To manage risk, a company's very first e-Commerce initiative might well be a simple "paper replacement" project to demonstrate the proof-of-concept in a well controlled, internal environment. Processes are untouched, just the user interface is modified. Then the scope of the project can be expanded to include easily managed process changes. With experience gained, the program can move on to engineering processes that cross corporate boundaries.

Figure 8 - 2 shows the major steps in transitioning to e-Commerce as a way of business. Companies cannot go it alone. Before inter-enterprise teams can be effective they need to build *shared vision*. This can be accomplished through educating all participants about e-Commerce and its many business dimensions. With an initial working knowledge in hand, *inter-enterprise assessments* are needed to identify the capabilities and readiness of participants in new e-Commerce ecosystems, which in turn will lead to an initial inter-enterprise architecture describing the levels of e-Commerce integration: simple hand-offs, process alignment, or joint execution of business processes. A combination of these process arrangements may need to be supported in a given ecosystem. Assessment provides the foundation for developing the *initial inter-enterprise architecture* and development plans. Such plans must be validated before opening e-Commerce systems to the world. It is, therefore, essential that a *proof-of-concept pilot* be carried out in order to manage risk. Because e-Commerce introduces change in virtually all facets of business operations and technology development, a proof-of-concept project provides a controlled environment. A proof-of-concept project must incorporate the dimensions relevant to any other e-Commerce project, but its scope, duration and pace of development allow for climbing the learning curve.

After successful completion of one or more proof-of-concept pilots, the development of e-Commerce initiatives should proceed in a sustainable manner. By implementing a *program management* organization, the architecture can be refined and infrastructure resources added as projects come on stream. As shown in Figure 8 - 2, parallel initiatives can be undertaken, sharing a common architecture and management organization. Each project or initiative should adopt an incremental delivery approach. Deliverables should be time-boxed to six months or less. By providing deliverables frequently, changes in business priorities and direction can be accommodated. Frequent deliveries build credibility with customers and enhance developer morale. The multi-year monolithic development cycles of the past cannot be tolerated in the world of e-Commerce.

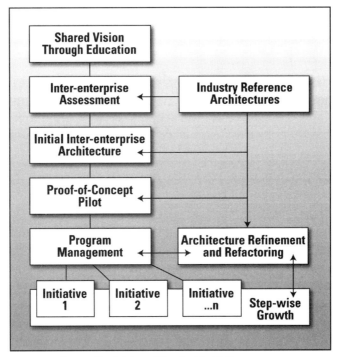

Figure 8 - 2. Transitioning to E-Commerce

Key Processes of E-Commerce Program Management

Both program and project management are needed to oversee the development and growth of e-Commerce initiatives. Program management involves three critical processes: building shared vision, conducting gap analysis and building inter-enterprise work teams.

1. Build Inter-enterprise Shared Vision through Education. A picture of the future is required if a company is to know where it is going and what it is trying to build. Corporations cannot possibly arrive at their destinations if they do not have a clear vision of where that is. Few concepts are more mysterious than corporate vision: shared visions are not pearls of wisdom handed down from an enlightened CEO. Instead, shared vision bubbles up from individual vision – from customers, suppliers and individual employees. Shared vision brings about common directions, focus, and the motivation for personal, team and organizational learning. With genuine shared vision, not imposed corporate vision statements, all workers across the organizations of inter-enterprise endeavors are able to keep their eyes on the prize.

2. Conduct Inter-enterprise Architectural Assessments and Gap Analysis. Peter Senge is Director of the Systems Thinking and Organizational Learning Program at MIT's Sloan School of Management. Senge calls *systems thinking* the "5th discipline" and the cornerstone of the *learning organization.* To be successful, e-Commerce teams must be masters of *general systems thinking.*

Systems thinking provides a new perspective to business process analysis and redesign. For example, can you imagine holding up your hand a foot before your face and blocking your view of the earth, the entire earth? Astronauts have been able to do that. The world looks drastically different from their perspective. They see the whole earth. Unfortunately, we only see bits and pieces of our company and industry in our earthly day-to-day work. Today's businesses need an astronaut's perspective of whole, end-to-end, value-chain processes. Systems thinking is a formal discipline of management science that deals with whole systems and with the interconnections and interactions of the individual parts. Systems thinking is also a learning method. Business team members can make assumptions about improved business processes and test those assumptions with the systems model. Feedback closes the loop and causes learning.

If it ain't broke, break it. One of the key principles of systems thinking and architecture is to envision what could be in a perfect world. Then, the real world is assessed against the desired state. The resulting gap analysis is used to plan the resources and tasks needed to reach the desired state in the desired timeframe. Innovative business processes are not extensions of existing processes; they are discovered by new ways of thinking, unencumbered by entrenched mental models and ways of conducting work.

Applying the first principles of systems thinking, e-Commerce teams can analyze the entire business ecosystem and discover opportunities for breakthrough value propositions made possible by the e-Commerce business platform. The analysis will focus on the new business capabilities afforded by the Net:

- What is it that we can now do that we couldn't do before the

availability of the Net?
- Who is our current and future e-Commerce customer?
- What can and should we outsource to our customers?
- How can we add compelling value to our present and future customers?
- How would we design a value-chain if were just starting a business, a digital business?
- Should we cannibalize our own business?
- How should we reintermediate our present and future value-chain? What roles should we play: standalone web site, aggregator, open I-Market, supply-chain portal?
- How deeply do we integrate business processes in our new value-chains: data hand-offs, process hand-offs, or shared real-time processes?
- What e-Commerce competitive threats do we face?
- What is the readiness of our trading partners to participate in e-Commerce?
- How does e-Commerce change our pricing policies?
- How can we create or play a leading role in communities-of-interest?
- What customer touch points do we need to reach now and in the future?
- Should we create niche portals that may even host our competitors?
- What organizational and ownership forms should we create?
- What are the people and technology requirements of the new architecture?

These questions guide the assessment of inter-enterprise architecture from two perspectives. First, a green field or "could be" architecture is envisioned and documented. Then current architectural elements can be documented, providing a description of the "as is" architecture. Gap analysis then ensues, revealing the people, processes and technology needed to implement elements of the new architecture. The result of assessment and gap analysis forms the basis for developing an initial strategic (strategy) plan for e-Commerce.

3. Build Inter-enterprise Organizations and Work Teams. Peter Senge asserts it is possible to create *learning organizations*. In addition to the cornerstone, systems thinking, he describes four other core disciplines required to build such an organization. The core disciplines include *personal mastery, working with mental models, building shared vision, and team learning.* These disciplines are not necessarily in the policy manuals of personnel departments of today's corporations nor in the realm of our individual thinking. They are, however, central to the success of e-Commerce in the new business ecosystem.

With the focus on general systems thinking and an architecture-centric approach to systems development, the tasks, knowledge and skills inherent in e-Commerce environments can be packaged into new roles and organizations for handling the work responsibilities. A few of the new roles are highlighted below, although a much longer list can be associated with architecture-based development of e-Commerce systems: reuse managers, quality assurance managers, configuration management specialists, business object modelers, object-oriented programmers and Internet technology specialists. If a company already has adopted object-oriented development approaches, many of the needed roles are probably already in place. After exploring some of the new roles we can then look at how e-Commerce affects organizational design.

E-Commerce Program Managers have line authority over enterprise-wide e-Commerce initiatives and projects. They are tasked with e-Commerce integration and managing an overall business and technology architecture and infrastructure. They are senior-level line managers who are effective at bridging the divides between business and technology units within an organization and across the extended enterprise.

Enterprise Architects define, align and refine the overall inter-enterprise architecture. They carry out many of the tasks of program management and provide guidance so individual projects can make optimum use of infrastructure resources for e-Commerce. They do the balancing act between business requirements and technological capabilities. On individual projects, enterprise architects help identify the requirements, goals and constraints of the project. They allocate responsibilities for each of the architectural elements and coordinate the modeling and design activities for the overall enterprise architecture. They are the chief architects of e-Commerce and coordinate the work information, infrastructure and application architects.

All architects and modelers should be completely versed in *design patterns* common to the many facets of business and technology. The design pattern movement has affected all aspects of analysis, design, and implementation of component-based systems. Design patterns are the reusable material of architecture and represent a watershed in the way complex, distributed information systems are conceived and developed. Much of the activity in software design patterns reflects the work of Christopher Alexander who developed the first principles of the discipline in relation to building architecture.[3]

Business and Information Architects are steeped in business domain knowledge including business processes and logical information structures. They coordinate the work of business and technology analysts and modelers who develop abstract representations or business object models of the subjects, rules, roles, events, tasks, activities and policies of the business domain. Business object models describe a logical domain irrespective of applications. Such application-neutral models enable the reuse of business engineering analysis and design patterns and artifacts.

Infrastructure Architects identify the technical services required of the technology infrastructure to empower and support the logical business and information architecture. They evaluate existing infrastructure services, select those appropriate to a given project and acquire (via build or buy) new components needed in the infrastructure. They oversee the work of technical specialists in modeling the services architecture of the technical infrastructure. They maintain the technical components of the development repository.

Application Architects coordinate the business process modeling activities across multiple projects and business domains. They coordinate the work of domain modelers and maintain the repository of business and component models. They evaluate existing business component services, select those appropriate to a given project and acquire (via build or buy) new components needed in the evolving business model. They maintain the business application components of the development repository. Most importantly, they guide solution developers in blending the business object model with the infrastructure services needed to implement the models in an e-Commerce platform.

Solution Developers are application developers. They develop the use cases for the specific application at hand, compose solutions through extensive use of business object models and use case repositories. They assemble application components to implement e-Commerce applications. Unlike conventional programmers or programmer/analysts, they do not build or program components. Instead they assemble or glue together business solutions from prefabricated components. They use highly integrated development environments (IDEs) such as IBM's VisualAge, Symantec's Visual Café, Sybase's PowerJ and Inprise's Jbuilder. Emerging Computer Assisted Software Engineering (CASE) tools and related methods will likely appear that tighten the link between business modeling and software development. Tools for understanding and managing business processes, such as Intellicorp's LiveModel™, will likely evolve to the e-Commerce development space. Today, LiveModel™ allows solutions developers to build logical business models that can automate the configuration and management of the SAP/R3 ERP system.

Solution developers likely come from the ranks of experienced object-oriented developers since the component paradigm is the next step beyond objects, not a replacement. Their knowledge and experience can be levered and built upon for component-based development.

Component Developers build components. They are masters of component technology and know the intricacies of composition, delegation, and object-oriented systems analysis and design. They are proficient in component development languages (such as Java and C++), modeling standards (such as UML and XMI), and distributed computing platforms (such as CORBA, DCOM, and EJB). They understand and think in terms of architectural design patterns.

As high quality business components and application frameworks become commercially available, component developers working directly in business enterprises will be fewer and fewer as they will likely work for software development companies. In the meantime they will close the gap between business requirements and available components. Component developers must be highly qualified software engineers since quality components do not just happen. They are carefully constructed using quality software engineering disciplines.

Component developers, therefore, must be highly trained specialists and masters of software quality processes such as CMM and ISO as well as masters of component-based development methods.

Human Factors engineers are needed to design the next generation of user interfaces. While the graphical user interface (GUI) is recognized as the enabler of wide-spread personal computing, *task-centered user interfaces* provide assistance to end-users and can be a boon to productivity in the world of e-Commerce. E-commerce transactions can involve a multitude of complex steps and processes. Well designed user interfaces can help navigate and guide the user through these tasks, keeping track of progress, and picking up where users leave off when transactions span multiple sessions of work.

Human factors engineering has never been of such importance to applications development. In the race to engineer customer processes that delight, the differentiating factor among e-Commerce systems is *helpfulness*, not just the prettiness of the GUI. Researchers in the field of Human Computer Interaction (HCI) are very active in researching and developing task-centered user interfaces. Whether through hiring experts or engaging them as consultants, winning e-Commerce development teams will have a human factors specialist at the planning table and at the development workbench. All participants in any e-Commerce development effort should read Donald Norman's *Design of Everyday Things*[4] before even thinking about designing customer-facing processes.

The new business models of e-Commerce require new organizations. In today's interconnected economy, companies discover that they cannot innovate alone. James Moore[5] explains that organizational form follows function. "The old multidivisional firm (the M-form) is giving way to the ecosystem form (E-form) where networks of complimentary functions are established to deliver end-to-end business processes to existing and potential markets." It is the degree of integration made possible by the Internet that allows this new business form. In the future, connections in the E-form will occur dynamically, on the fly. The value-grid will replace the value-chain in business-to-business ecosystems.

Transitioning a company to the E-form is certainly no short term proposition. Building and maintaining trading partner relationships is a lot of work requiring a lot of time, energy and insight. Even for the short term, where initial e-Commerce initiatives are launched to go after low-hanging fruit or in response to competitive pressure, new organizations are needed. As a new channel of business, the embarking on an e-Commerce path can be likened to starting a new business, whether from scratch or through merger or acquisition. As with any business endeavor, e-Commerce initiatives require human, financial and technology resources. In addition, it is reasonable to assume that the employees and organizations conducting today's business are fully occupied, if not overworked as a result of downsizing. Furthermore, e-Commerce initiatives introduce radical change in the ways work is done to a workforce already entrenched in the current ways of working and thinking. Changing the mental models of an established workforce is often costly and painful. As a result, it is not uncommon for corporations to spin off separate e-Commerce companies to gain agility and the benefits of green-field development – to wit, barnesandnoble.com, Inc., owned equally by "bricks-and-mortar" retailer Barnes & Noble and German media giant Bertelsmann. In both the short term and long, organizational design is a critical issue of e-Commerce strategy.

Key Processes of E-Commerce Project Management

With an overall function of program management established, multiple e-Commerce projects may be undertaken simultaneously, in parallel. Four key processes are involved in project management: engineer customer processes; engineer value-chain processes; engineer internal business processes; and incrementally develop e-Commerce applications.

1. Engineer Customer Processes. The task of engineering customer processes is paramount, and can only be done with the full and direct participation of customers themselves. After all, in business engineering terms, the customer is the process *owner*. Through a process of outside-in design, customer processes become the requirements specifications for value-chain process engineering. Customer processes are expressed in terms of the services they require. Each customer will want to customize those services and subsets of them to optimize their information and buying activities.

In business-to-consumer applications, customers will increasingly seek total solutions to their buying needs. For example, buying a car involves financial, legal and insurance services. Customer processes must have access to all the information and all the services needed to form a total solution. In business-to-business applications the customer's internal business processes must interact with those on the e-Commerce boundary. For example, a typical purchasing application will require internal requisitioning workflows, approvals and processes as well as those related to the external e-Commerce transaction.

2. Engineer Value-chain Processes. Process integration between and among actors in the value-chain is the essence of inter-enterprise process engineering and business-to-business e-Commerce. As shown in Figure 8 - 3, e-Commerce process integration can be measured at three levels: data hand-offs, process hand-offs and shared real-time processes.

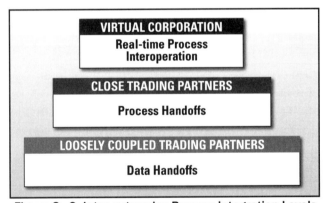

Figure 8 - 3. Inter-enterprise Process Integration Levels

Without process integration, simple data hand-offs occur between participants in e-Commerce transactions. At this level of integration, e-Commerce is simply a media replacement for paper. At the next level, e-Commerce transactions trigger the processes in the systems of other participants. For example, an order processing system of a retailer may trigger inventory status processes within a supplier's system – the processes in the e-Commerce transaction are aligned via process hand-offs.

At the highest level of inter-enterprise process integration, processes in the e-Commerce space are jointly owned and interoperate in real-time. The user of such systems cannot tell which sub processes are running on whose internal systems – the user is interacting with and consuming ubiquitous e-Services. Full process integration gives each player in a value-chain full access to information and services, both up and downstream in the value-chain. For example customer information is available throughout the value-chain, not just to the "seller." Such information sharing can allow each participant in the value-chain to optimize its performance. These fundamentals are essential in value-chain to value-chain competition.

As open markets continue to emerge, a combination of these three process arrangements need to be supported simultaneously in a given ecosystem. Players in a value-chain will have differing technological capabilities and readiness for process sharing. For example, a 'mom-and-pop' specialty manufacturer of components may not have a computer but can participate in an e-Commerce value-chain by fax, just like in the traditional world of commerce. Others in the same value-chain may participate only by email, while yet other participants are connected in real-time, 7x24. New Web standards for data and document sharing, such as the eXtensible Markup Language (XML), will ease the interoperation challenges and bring the benefits of traditional EDI systems to all businesses, big or small.

In addition to the internal business processes that are the object of traditional business engineering of a company, inter-enterprise processes add new dimensions of functionality and new players that must be addressed. Some of the key new processes that come into play beyond the boundary of a given company are shown in Figure 8 - 4.

One of the challenges of inter-enterprise process engineering is the mapping of the processes to trading partners whose processes are integrated at various levels, from data hand-offs to fully integrated processes. Inter-enterprise process engineering adds new dimensions to traditional business engineering because we are modeling business ecosystems, not just a single company.

3. Engineer Internal Business Processes. Internal business processes must be adapted in order to participate in e-Commerce. With a component-based development approach "wrappers" are developed for legacy information systems that implement internal business processes. In addition, new e-Commerce processes for which there are no legacy implementations will require data to be integrated from legacy systems directly into the e-Commerce applications.

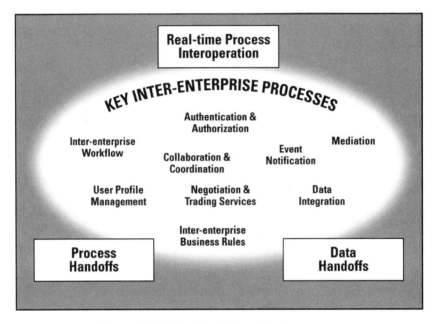

Figure 8 - 4. Key Inter-Enterprise Processes

4. Pilot, Deploy and Iterate. Building ultimate, all encompassing e-Commerce systems does not happen in one big step or one big project. These systems are too large and complex and, when doing business at Internet-time, time is short. The goal is to deliver fast and often. Using a minimalist approach, incremental delivery is the key to sustainable development. The minimal functional business requirements should be developed, piloted to manage risk, and deployed as "Release 1." Business requirements determine the functionality to be delivered in Releases 2 to …n. Release 1 embodies the key business process innovation, Releases 2 to … n represent continuous process improvement. In the battle for competitive advantage in the digital economy, e-Commerce development never ends. Each iteration of development must raise the bar for competitors.

Technology Issues and Strategies

Issue 1: E-Commerce Integration and Program Management

Leading companies recognize e-Commerce as a complete business platform than can span business-to-consumer activities all the way back through business-to-business collaboration: product conceptualization, engineering manufacturing and distribution across an inter-enterprise value-chain. They likely have multiple e-Commerce initiatives underway on both the buy and sell-sides of the business. These companies now have their eye on a prize much larger than the sum of all the individual initiatives: customer self-selling and self-service. Putting the customer in complete control of the value-chain is the ultimate outcome of the customer-driven business.

Companies that are taking the path toward becoming a fully digital, customer-driven business realize that no e-Commerce application is an island. Rather than creating islands of e-Commerce, they design enterprise and inter-enterprise architectures whose centerpiece is e-Commerce integration. The process of integration begins with identifying the patterns of business logic and data common to e-Commerce applications. Those patterns are translated into specifications for core e-Commerce application components and often include user access and role-based profiles, event management and notification, data and business object integration, trading services, business policies and rules, process management and workflow. Establishing and managing these "e-Commerce engines "as a shared business asset is the singular defining step toward e-Commerce integration and the brave new world of e-Services. These assets may be jointly designed, managed and shared across the enterprise and across trading partners, suppliers and customers.

Having an infrastructure in place that fosters e-Commerce integration does not guarantee success. Those assets must be well managed through *a program management organization* that is empowered to coordinate people, projects and business resources. While governance of each e-Commerce initiative remains with business units, the shared commerce infrastructure should grow in synchronization with the evolution of the overall business architecture. Successful program and project management are the keys to an orderly transition to becoming a digital business. Well managed corporations are experienced with program management and will extend their management processes to the needs of inter-enterprise program management, coordinating multiple projects in multiple organizations. The program management organization should be chartered as a business unit to ensure that e-Commerce is totally business-driven, now and throughout the greater transition to becoming a virtual corporation.

Issue 2: Security is Prerequisite

The Internet allows a company to open its business to the world. The potential benefits of giving customers, suppliers and trading partners direct access to the business are compelling – increased revenues and decreased costs. The Internet proposition has, however, one very serious implication – security concerns are often cited as *the* greatest barrier to electronic commerce. A business does not want the outside world to have unrestricted or unauthorized access to company information and business processes. Likewise for customers.

Security is concerned primarily with managing risk. The degree of security needed will depend on the importance of what is being secured, how much money is available to implement and maintain the system and the number of weaker links. It is more expensive to add security after the fact than to design security into the system from the beginning.

Security must be built-in at both the technical and business process levels. At the technical level, data vulnerabilities while in transit are usually dealt with though a combination of encryption schema and transmission protocols such as Secure Sockets Layer (SSL). The Secure Sockets Layer security approach adds a layer that negotiates a secure transmission connection on top of the existing network transport protocol and beneath the application layer. Secure Hypertext Transfer Protocol (HTTP-S) adds a set of security headers used to negotiate what type of scheme (such as bulk encryption) and which specific algorithm (such as RSA public key encryption) to apply to information transfers. In addition, corporate *firewalls,* consisting of hardware and software combinations, control and limit access to a private e-Commerce network from the public Internet. Firewalls function as Internet Protocol

(IP) packet filters, application relays, monitors and logging devices. They provide proxy masquerading of information and concentration of security administration. IP packet filters enforce rule sets as to what types of packets can enter or leave through the gateway.

At the business process level, what is needed is authentication so that no one else can pretend that he or she is an authorized user, and access control so that a particular user can gain access to only those portions of the business for which he or she is authorized. On the state-less and session-less World Wide Web, the user needs to know he is communicating with the right server, called server authentication, and the server needs to know it is communicating with the right user, client authentication. Prior to the advent of e-Commerce, methods of identifying an individual's position, role or authority were accomplished via phone calls, meetings, correspondence and contracts. In retail industries, driver's licenses, photo IDs, PIN numbers, passports and birth certificates are used to vouch for identity. These means of identification now have their counterparts in the digital world.

Authentication procedures must provide convenience as well as security. For example, in a business-to-business context, authentication should provide a single, universal user logon to multiple applications running on multiple servers while controlling access to resources on the system: files, directories and server universal resource locators (URLs). In fact, a single sign-on is a requirement in many business-to-business e-Commerce environments. Authentication procedures typically involve something known, something possessed or something a user is. High-level security applications often demand a combination of factors such as something possessed, like a smart card with a private key, in conjunction with something known, such as a PIN number. Parties to an e-Commerce transaction must feel comfortable in their belief that they are in fact doing business with whom they believe they are. Doubt as to the identity of other parties must be done away with by a security system that authenticates by verifying information that the user provides against what the system already knows about the user.

E-Commerce access management requires an authentication and profiling capability that enables the access control processes to be managed electronically, and extended globally to suppliers, trading partners and customers. Authorization involves the control of access to a particular information space once the user has been authenticated and, accordingly, identified to the server's satisfaction. Authorization is intended to limit the actions or operations based on their security clearances that various authenticated users are able to perform in an internetworked space. Corporations already have internal business and technical controls over the use of information systems by their employees, but business-to-business e-Commerce requires extending this controlled access to outside companies, outside employees, and outside computer systems. Information boundaries must be designed to control access and manage sessions as well as assign rights and privileges to trusted partners and new customers or suppliers. Information boundary management (i.e., who is allowed to view what and when) addresses the security, directory services, and access control aspects of content and application functionality necessary to support inter-enterprise business processes, collaboration and application-to-application integration.

Access control mechanisms are based on access rights, or permissions, that define the conditions under which the user can access network resources. Access controls delineate the user's privileges or permissions such as 1) creating and destroying information, 2) reading, writing and executing files and programs, 3) adding, deleting and modifying content, and 4) exporting and importing abilities. The site administrator controls the permissions using an access control list that itemizes the privileges of authenticated users on a resource-by-resource basis. Integrity is concerned with protecting data from unauthorized modification both while in transit over the network and while stored on the system servers or in accessible databases. Changes that the integrity services component of access management must protect against include data additions, deletions and reordering as well as modifications. Security management services support the integrity of e-Commerce.

Secure it, or forget it! Security is a non-functional yet absolute requirement of all e-Commerce applications. As with all business controls, the cost of the controls must be in line with the assets they protect. The security, control and auditability of e-Commerce applications require the same primary principles that are needed in the physical world of management control. The primary principles of business con-

trols cover the nine major risk exposures of any corporation whether it
is using pencil-and-paper or digital media in its operations. A corporation's auditing team, therefore, is a vital part of the e-Commerce team.

Issue 3: Nonrepudiation: Signing the Contract

In the physical world, business contracts are not legally executed and
binding until they are signed. The same must hold true for e-Commerce
if nonrepudiation is to be achieved in cyberspace – the document must
be signed. What is needed is a digital infrastructure for handling
signatures.

The public key infrastructure (PKI) is a comprehensive set of functionalities for encryption and digital services that consists of several
components, including a directory, certification authority (CA) and
certification revocation lists. PKI's most popular feature is its two sets of
keys – a public key and a private key. PKI simultaneously addresses the
four issues:

- authentication (a user is who he says he is),
- authorization (the user is authorized to be where he is on the
  network),
- nonrepudiation (the user is the one who really sent the message)
  and
- privacy (no one has read or tampered with a user's message).

Secure Sockets Layer (SSL) protocols, now supported by all popular
browsers, are capable of presenting client public key certificates to any
Web server configured to require client authentication. To create a client certificate, the user goes to the Web site of a *certificate authority* and
fills-out a form with personal identification information needed to create a public key pair. The public half of the key pair is then submitted
along with the personal identification data to the certificate-issuing Web
server which then uses its certificate authority root key to digitally sign
the user's public key. The signed certificate is then returned to the
browser for storage together with the corresponding private key.

A certification authority is the trusted third-party who issues certificates for public keys. Individuals can also generate their own private
and public keys and send the latter to the CA for validation. Public keys
may be kept in white pages-like directories. Typically, two key-pairs are

generated – one pair for encryption and one for digitally signing documents. The term "asymmetric keys" means the use of separate public and private keys. Suppose "Alice" wants to send "Bob" a digitally signed and encrypted document. "Alice" will sign it using her private key and use "Bob's" encryption key to encrypt the message. "Alice" will go to the directory to obtain "Bob's" public key. When "Bob" receives the message, he will use "Alice's" public signing key to see if "Alice" is indeed the originator of the document and that the content has not been tampered with in transit. "Bob" will use his own private key to decrypt the message.

In addition, certificate revocation lists are repositories of invalid certificates and key histories that are for decrypting old information. Cross certification means two separate certificate authorities recognize each others certificates. Nonrepudiation involves digital signatures and time stamping, so senders cannot deny they sent a message in question. Client software is used for certificate validation, storage of the private key and applications that use secure PKI. Directories are essential to implementing PKI and function as a repository for cryptographic information. Support for the Lightweight Directory Access Protocol (LDAP) is important. E-Commerce applications must reside on a solid PKI infrastructure. Nonrepudiation is as essential in cyberspace as it is in the traditional world of commerce.

Issue 4: Trust and Privacy in Cyberspace

In both business-to-consumer and business-to-business e-Commerce, trust and privacy are critical issues that must be dealt with electronically. Trust is a measure of confidence, and TRUSTe, an independent, non-profit privacy organization has taken the initiative. TRUSTe focuses on a company's unaudited, voluntary commitment to meeting certain standards for electronic commerce related to privacy. TRUSTe has developed a third-party oversight "seal" program that alleviates users' concerns about online privacy, while meeting the specific business needs of each of their licensed Web sites. A TRUSTe *trustmark* is awarded to sites that adhere to established privacy principles and agree to comply with ongoing TRUSTe oversight and resolution procedures, including audits by CPA firms. All Web sites that display the trustmark must disclose their personal information collection and privacy practices – what personal information is being gathered, how the information will be used, who the information will be shared with, choices available to the browser regarding how collected information is used, safeguards in place to protect information from loss, misuse, or alteration, and how a user can update or correct inaccuracies in information.

"Privacy principles embody fair information practices approved by the U.S. Department of Commerce, Federal Trade Commission, and prominent industry-represented organizations and associations. The principles include 1) adoption and implementation of a privacy policy that takes into account consumer anxiety over sharing personal information online, 2) notice and disclosure of information collection and use practices, 3) choice and consent giving users the opportunity to exercise control over their information, and 4) data security, quality and access measures to help protect the security and accuracy of personally identifiable information. To become a TRUSTe licensee, a candidate creates a privacy statement with the help of a TRUSTe online wizard, reads and signs a TRUSTe license agreement, and pays annual fees."[6]

Privacy is a major concern of Internet users and can be divided into concerns about what personal information can be shared with whom, and whether messages can be exchanged without anyone else seeing them. The World Wide Web Consortium's Platform for Personal Privacy Project (P3P) is developing specific recommendations for practices that will let users define, control and share personal information with Web sites. The P3P incorporates a number of industry proposals, including the Open Profiling Standard (OPS). Using software that adheres to the P3P recommendations, users will be able to create a personal profile, all or parts of which can be made accessible to a Web site as the user directs.

In an open network such as the Internet, message privacy usually requires encryption and decryption. The most common approach is through a public key infrastructure (PKI). Providing a trusted and private presence on the Web is essential to any e-Commerce initiative.

Issue 5: Agility and Software Components

Because they span multiple unique enterprises and disparate hardware platforms, e-Commerce applications require the *services* of a robust distributed object computing infrastructure – they require a Web object model. The key requirement of the underlying object platform is that it separates technology and business concerns and that it be service-based. The components of the architecture supply high level business and technology services that can be used without having to know how those complex services are implemented or delivered. This layered architecture is essential to the separation of concerns needed for agile software development.

Software components throughout the architecture may be changed without affecting the others, and e-Commerce applications can be assembled, disassembled, and reassembled without leaving the semantics of the business to dip into the technology plumbing. It is critical that abstractions used to model e-Commerce application components stay above the distributed object computing infrastructure (DCOM or CORBA). These logical models should be platform independent and conform to Meta Object Facilities such as the XML Metadata Interchange (XMI) format specification so that they may be incorporated into disparate modeling methods and tools. Although UML is the standard for component modeling, differing analysis and design methods and tools are used by corporations. XMI makes it possible for separate enterprises to share UML models and is essential to inter-enterprise development of e-Commerce applications. The whole idea of component-based development is that an application solution to a business problem is an assembly and configuration of defined services. By staying above the technology platform, component models can be distributed and incorporated to gain maximum benefit from technology now and in the future, both at the business modeling and systems deployment phases.

In *A Framework for Business-IT Alignment Using Components,* Paul Allen describes the range of activities involved in component-based development. "Traditional software engineering techniques are geared to individual applications. CBD goes far beyond traditional software development in its range of activities:"[7]

Table 8 - 1. Component-Based Design Activities

Architect: Achieve an overall software structure for components adaptable to business needs.	Extend: Specialize component interfaces; a form of black-box reuse.
Assemble/Develop: Plug together components, with the minimum of newly developed code, to produce a business solution as rapidly as possible.	Wrap: Build component interfaces based on legacy systems; a form of black-box reuse.
Acquire: Purchase application components.	Upgrade: Replace or evolve existing software to component status.
Subscribe: Use published services from an external component provider.	Engineer: Build new components.
Modify: Specialize component models; a form of white-box reuse used with frameworks.	Integrate: Ensure the various types of components work consistently and coherently together.

Component-based development strategies are the key not only to software agility, but they also help eliminate the disconnect between business engineering and software engineering. Traditionally, models of innovative business processes are developed by business people and thrown "over the wall" to software developers to transform them into software. One group thinks with business mental models, the other with computer mental models – disconnects are sure to arise. But what if there were another way? What if the business engineering process was carried out with business components as the modeling medium? After all, business application components are the implementation of the business processes and entities being modeled. Assuming that existing sets of business processes have been implemented as business components and registered in a *repository,* the existing component model represents the "as is" analysis model of business engineering. The "should be" model results from customizing and reconfiguring the components, and conducting gap analysis to discover requirements for additional components. This *compositional approach to business engineering* can unlock

- rapid business engineering, and
- rapid application development.

When the business world operates in Internet-time, the ability to sense and respond to new threats and opportunities is paramount. Rapid business engineering and rapid application development must be fused into a single activity in order to meet the new competitive realities. In short, the Business Object Model and the System Object Model can and must be aligned, integrated and synchronized.

The notion of aligning business and technology is not new, but tangible progress toward this noble goal has been slow in coming. Object-oriented technologies and methods have made significant contributions to business modeling and business engineering. Methods such as Enterprise Engineering's Object-Oriented Business Engineering (OOBE™) and Jim Odell's Object-Oriented Information Engineering (OOIE) are powerful approaches to aligning technology with business. For example, Odell's notion of multiple dynamic classification is essential to open markets where actors must play multiple and changing roles in an e-Commerce ecosystem. Object-oriented technologies and development methods, however, are new and sometimes complex. As we explored in Chapter 2, O-O technologies and methods require new ways of thinking and present steep learning curves – on to components. Component frameworks are the next step in the progression of object-oriented theory and practice and can overcome the drawbacks and obstacles of O-O to deliver on the promise of O-O. Component frameworks can make the business and technology alignment notion real. An agile business powered by agile software can be built with component frameworks – this is the component breakthrough for competitive advantage.

The methods and tools of compositional business and software engineering are just emerging. The move beyond the object to the component paradigm has been underway for only a few years. Most methods associated with software engineering are top-down and decompositional, and they are still fully viable approaches. This long entrenched way of thinking will take time to be extended by mature compositional methods and tools. Fortunately, the key players in the software development industry are committed to the component model and early methods and tools have already appeared (e.g. CSC's Lynx method, Riverton Software's HOW, ICON Computing's Catalysis, and Sterling Software's COOL). An essential corporate software strategy for e-Commerce is to adopt component-based architectures, development methods and tools, and evolve with them – today's methods and tools are quite powerful and will only get better.

Software architectures are generally tiered and divided into two broad categories: *information architectures* that deal with the business domain and *technical architectures* that deal with the computing infrastructure services needed by the application domain. While information architecture partitions the business logic across components and arranges the collaborations needed to meet functional requirements, technical architecture includes domain-independent design decisions such as middleware, database management, fail over, event management and persistence. Technical architecture should be developed early as it provides the technical services upon which applications will be built and reinforces the separation of concerns so critical to rapid component-based development.

Issue 6: Server-side Component Models, Platforms and Frameworks

Software component architectures are *service-based*: end-user services, business process services and data services. Application components rely on distributed computing infra-structure services, freeing solution developers from the complexity and intricacies of the underlying technologies. Component builders are technologists who use component-based software engineering disciplines to *produce* components of extreme quality. Solution developers *consume* these prefabricated components during business process modeling and rapid application assembly.

Component architectures divide software into construction and consumption: once built in compliance with standards, newly constructed software components can register the services they provide, while other components can subscribe to and consume these services. Components do not act alone, they plug into *component frameworks* that connect participating components and enforce rules of component interaction. Component frameworks mediate and regulate component interaction. Component frameworks are arranged in a tiered architecture. Figure 8 - 5 illustrates components and how they plug into an interoperability framework that in turn calls on the services and facilities of a distributed computing platform.

Three leading component models are Microsoft's' COM+, Sun Microsystems' Enterprise JavaBeans (EJB) and the Object Management Group's CORBA Component Model (CCM), an extension of EJB. They are *server component models,* as opposed to client-side components such as JavaBeans or ActiveX. The chief difference among these models is that the Microsoft model is restricted to Microsoft runtime systems and communication protocols. For example, although COM and DCOM have been ported to Solaris and other Unix platforms, COM containers are not available on these platforms. EJB, on the other hand, adheres to the write once, run anywhere (WORA) philosophy that made Java the overnight success for programming the Internet.

EJB and the CORBA middleware standard go hand-in-hand. EJB provides software *portability* (allowing EJB components to run on any operating system) and CORBA provides software *interoperability* with platform services written in languages other than Java, such as C++ and Smalltalk. Rather than reinvent the wheel, EJB's application programming interfaces (APIs) provide access to underlying enterprise-class, standards-based infrastructure services. For example, the Java Transaction API defines a distributed transaction management service based on CORBA's Object Transaction Service (OTS) standard. In turn, the Java IDL creates a remote interface to CORBA communication and includes a lightweight object request broker (ORB) that supports CORBA's Internet Inter-ORB Protocol (IIOP).

Business and e-Commerce application components will not be delivered to corporations as a big pile of parts and pieces. Instead the components will be pre-assembled into industry specific application *frameworks* as illustrated by the Financial, Manufacturing, and e-Commerce components shown in Figure 8 - 5.

The e-Commerce components provide essential inter-enterprise functionality for e-Commerce (e.g. negotiation, mediation, inter-enterprise user access management, inter-enterprise workflow management and event notification). These frameworks represent applications that are almost, say 60% to 80%, complete. The task of solutions developers is to customize and extend the frameworks to incorporate the unique business rules and processes of a company. Thus, solution developers concentrate on the unique character and knowledge of the company that provides its competitive advantage. They are insulated from the technology plumbing.

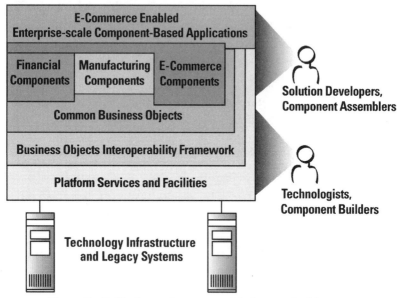

Figure 8 - 5. Business Component Software Architecture

IBM's SanFrancisco™ is a leading example of a component-based application framework that includes most of the code needed for developing server-side, mission-critical business applications. SanFrancisco's component architecture is layered and services-based, using an architecture similar to that portrayed in Figure 8 - 5. It includes four layers. The *Foundation* layer utilizes the distributed object services of the EJB component platform that, in turn, are based on definitions of the Object Management Group (OMG) (e.g. object transaction services, collections, object communication and persistence). The Foundation layer provides the base classes and utilities needed to support the distributed, mission-critical applications for which SanFrancisco was designed. Built on the Foundation layer is the *Common Business Object* layer that provides cross-application business objects common to most commercial domains (e.g. Company, Address, Business Partner, Bank

Accounts, Unit of Measure and Credit Check). The *Core Business Process* frameworks layer provides the prefabricated components for applications in a specific business domain (e.g. General Ledger, Accounts Receivable, Accounts Payable, Warehouse Management and Order Management). The final *Application* layer is built by solution developers who map business requirements to the core business processes, configure their properties to reflect unique business needs, and extend the prebuilt functionality to add specific requirements, the user interface, business rules, competitive differentiators and complimentary application functionality.

SanFrancisco makes extensive use of design patterns derived from classical architecture. Design patterns are techniques used to solve recurring design problems. As we mentioned, Christopher Alexander defined the concept of patterns in architecture, "Each design pattern describes a problem which occurs over and over again in our environment, and then describes the core of the solution to that problem, in such a way that you can use this solution a million times over, without ever doing it the same way twice."[8] In the worlds of objects and software components, design patterns form the cornerstone of software reuse and provide consistency throughout the SanFrancisco frameworks.

The breakthrough of server-side component architecture is the clear separation of business and technology concerns that simplifies the process of building enterprise-class e-Commerce applications. Solution developers can concentrate on business models and logic while the component framework manages the complex middleware services for the applications. For an architectural approach to software development to be practical, enterprise-class e-Commerce systems and their component frameworks must have certain characteristics. These nonfunctional characteristics include the requirements and constraints shown in Table 8 - 2.

In a DARPA research report, Thompson, Linden and Filman[9] list the architectural properties required of the non-functional, technology-level environment.

Table 8 - 2. Requirements and Constraints

loosely coupled	self-organizing
self-describing	event-driven
asynchronous	reliable
secure	survivable
intuitive	collaborative
embody business controls	auditable

As shown in Table 8 - 3, their list is dominated by property names suffixed with "ility," and thus the list is referred to as the *ilities* of architecture. "Software is designed primarily to meet functional specifications – that is, to achieve particular input and output behavior. However, a well-designed system achieves an appropriate balance of other [non-functional] properties: those that encompass its ability to exist in its environment and evolve as that environment changes. Following evolving practice, we call these *ilities*. Ilities are architectural properties that often can cut across different levels or components of a system's architecture to be properties of the whole. Unlike simple functionality, ilities can include trade offs – for example, enhanced interoperability may have been produced at the cost of lesser security. Although ilities are sometimes invisible properties of the system as a whole, they represent real (though perhaps unspoken or even unrealized) customer requirements. The enterprise architect or system architect is responsible for ensuring such ilities, and a most appropriate task for an architectural framework is to support them." In total, these ilities create the ab*ility* to evolve and meet new demands of the business.

Third wave companies embrace component-based architecture and their ultimate strategy is to implement an architected approach to rapid application development. Components accelerate the entire application development life cycle and, when used directly in business process modeling, they eliminate the disconnect between business and technology. This approach is the essence of business and software agility. Although component-based development is an emerging approach, sufficient methods and tools are available to begin using the approach now, and gain even greater benefits as the approach grows to full maturity.

Table 8 - 3. Some "ilities"

interoperability	composability
scalability	evolvability
extensibility	tailorability
security	reliability
adaptability	survivability
affordability	maintainability
understandability	performance
quality of service	nomadicity

Issue 7: The XML Factor: Industry Vocabularies

Open markets require the interoperation of e-Commerce applications and consistent protocols and formats for information interchange. The complexity of building such virtual commerce places mandates a common vocabulary based on standards if there is to be any hope of interoperability at the commerce level. The ultimate purpose of e-Commerce interoperability standards is to develop consistent business semantics that can be used by all participants – a common language of digital commerce. These semantics provide commonality to the names of and relationships between processes, workflows, and data across value and supply chains.

The World Wide Web Consortium (W3C) adopted a new standard for defining and naming data on a Web page in 1998. It is likely that the eXtensible Markup Language (XML) will revolutionize the Web because it allows structured data – with standard names and consistent semantics – to be moved around the Web in a simple, straightforward way, as easily as HTML does today. XML is a native Web approach that enables extensible data-exchange formats, and gives industries the flexibility to create their own data tags to develop a shared Internet file system.

XML is being touted as the next big thing on the Internet since the introduction of Sun Microsystems' Java. XML, however, is not a replacement for Java – XML and Java go hand-in-hand. In fact, Sun engineer, Jon Bosak, who chaired the W3C XML Coordination Group, is generally regarded as the father of XML. In Bosak's words, "XML and Java technologies are the yin and yang of vendor-neutral programming. Put them together and you have a complete, platform-independent, Web-based computing environment."[10] Java provides a way for software programs to be shuttled around the Internet, XML does the same thing for data, offering a universal data interchange format. With Java and XML working together (XMLbeans[11]), the result is much like the science fiction films where all the information (data, process and control) needed to perform an activity moves seamlessly from computer to computer throughout cyberspace. Java turns the Internet into a single, ubiquitous computer, XML turns the Internet into a single, ubiquitous filing cabinet for information.

The contents of an XML document, however, need not be only data. In fact the term "smart data" may be more appropriate. Anne Thomas of the Patricia Seybold Group explains, "Combining Java and XML technologies produces portable 'smart' data. XML supplies a universally portable structured data format, and Java technology supplies universally portable code. Since code written in the Java programming language can be embedded into a document written in the XML language, we can create a data structure that includes its own data manipulation applications. It's a great combination."[12] Thus XML can play a role at all three levels of process integration as illustrated in Figure 8 - 3: simple data hand-offs, process hand-offs and real-time interoperation.

XML is a document-centered technology ideally suited for message passing between trading partners in an e-Commerce ecosystem. Document messaging is a way for e-Commerce applications to interoperate in a loosely-coupled, request-for-service, communication process. The document type definition (DTD) alone can identify a given document type in a business-to-business transaction. This is similar to the various document types defined for the EDI community. For example, an ANSI X12 EDI 850 is a Purchase Order transaction set. By sending such a document to an EDI enabled system, the receiving organization knows what processing services to perform on the data. Such data hand-offs trigger business processes in the receiving organization based simply on knowing the document type contained in the message sent to it.

On the other hand, process tags (<Process>) tags can be included in an XML document to indicate the business process or system process to be launched or invoked by the receiving organization as a result of the process hand-off. The Document Object Model (DOM) is a platform- and language-neutral interface that allows programs and scripts to dynamically access and update the content, structure and style of documents. DOM allows XML content (including all markup and any Document Type Definitions) to be accessed and manipulated as a collection of objects. The document can be further processed and the results of that processing can be incorporated back into the presented page. Java code thus embedded in an XML document enables real-time process integration. Regardless of the techniques used to add "behavior" to XML documents, the result is a *document services architecture* that allows trading partners to combine and request services needed to process business documents marked up in XML.

XML also is being embraced by the Enterprise Application Integration (EAI) community whose central goal is to achieve interoperability between legacy and Enterprise Resource Planning (ERP) systems. ERP integration has been a long-standing problem that has become a burning issue with the advent of e-Commerce. Using the same principles described above, ERP vendors (SAP, Baan, Peoplesoft and Oracle) and the non-profit Open Applications Group (OAG) are turning to XML to solve some of the chronic interoperability problems between and among ERP systems. Today companies have a choice of digging in and dealing with the proprietary application program interfaces (APIs) such as SAP's BAPI, or they can turn to third party companies like Crossworlds, Active Software or Visual Edge to provide adapters for higher-level interfaces to the leading ERP systems. The ERP vendors are developing means to take lower-level function calls to their systems and translate them into standardized XML documents. Thus, XML can be used to greatly simplify and lower the costs of legacy and ERP interoperation just as it can simplify and lower the cost of EDI.

XML is, however, not a silver bullet, and in some ways it is little more than the reintroduction of the "unit record concept" that was introduced with the punched card in the 1950s, where chunks of data (fields) were tagged with names that gave us attribute/value pairs bound together as a standalone document (a record). After all, XML is simply text (ASCII) data, and it must have links to a powerful, underlying object infrastructure (based on a Web Object Model) to handle the adaptive business processes and workflows that e-Commerce requires. The truly difficult part of this process is gaining global agreement on the semantics – an effort that has eluded information systems designers since the introduction of centralized corporate databases in the 1960s. Ask any experienced data administrator and they will tell you that they cannot even get departments within the same company to agree on data names, much less their meaning.

Rik Drummond, CommerceNet's XML/EDI project leader, put it this way in his research note, *Is XML Dead in the Water?*, "Just like the Clinton 1992 presidential race 'It's the economy dummy! – In XML, 'It's the semantics dummy!' Since XML is a Meta language [a language used to define other languages], it is easy to define the structure of the document to describe how things relate to each other. It also allows one to establish data element names, that is, names such as <price>, <DiscountPrice> or <size>. The syntax is not the problem, because the XML parsers can read the syntax. The semantics are the issue. This is especially true with semantic interoperability. For example, how do we agree with what <size> means? Is it length, width, depth, or some combination of all three? Is it in feet, yards or meters? These are semantic issues."[13] Because XML can be used to describe sub-structures, <size> can be further broken down into <dimension> and <value> yielding a meaningful information structure rather than a simple data tag. Facilties such as the XML schema definition language are essential to forming complete information structures and enabling knowledge representation.

Thus, XML is simply an enabler, not a guarantor, of the consistent business semantics required for e-Commerce. XML can be used within a single company with little debate over vocabulary and semantics. Two trading partners could do the same, although this process could require mapping the DTDs of each company if each had its own definitions.

Add more trading partners and the mapping problem grows exponentially. What is really needed for open e-Commerce are standard XML industry vocabularies for DTDs and schema. Then companies that adhere to the standards can all talk to each other digitally in the same tongue, no mapping required.

Some industries will do better than others at establishing semantic consensus. For example, groups such as the XML/EDI Group and Data Interchange Standards Association (DISA) may have early success because they are dealing with an established body of inter-enterprise business semantics. The task is one of mapping EDI document definitions to XML, and, DISA, which maintains the ANSI ASC X.12 EDI standards, has already undertaken XML initiatives.

A number of XML industry vocabularies are being developed by individual companies, vertical industry consortia and software industry groups. Some of these are listed here and a brief description of each appears in Appendix A:

- Open Financial Exchange (OFX/OFE) for consumer finance
- Information Content Exchange (ICE) for content syndication and exchange
- Open Trading Protocol (OTP)
- Open Buying on the Internet (OBI) for MRO procurement
- DISA XML/EDI
- Open E-Book (OEB) for electronic book publishing
- Financial Products Markup Language (FpML) for financial derivatives
- FinXML™ for trading and risk management for capital markets.
- FIX/FIXML for securities transactions in the equities market.
- Signed Document Markup Language (SDML) for digital signatures
- Electronic-Commerce Modeling Language (ECML) for electronic wallets
- XMLNews for the news industry
- RosettaNet for the PC industry supply chain
- cXML for e-Commerce transactions
- XML Metadata Interchange (XMI) for interoperating UML and Data Warehousing models and artifacts
- Channel Definition Format (CDF), a Microsoft push standard
- Bank Internet Payment System (BIPS)
- OpenMLS – Real Estate DTD Design

- Legal XML Working Group
- Customer Support Consortium
- Electronic Component Manufacturer Data Sheet Library Specification (ECMData)
- XML-HR for recruiting and placement
- SWAP – Simple Workflow Access Protocol
- XML for the Automotive Industry – SAE J2008
- HL7 for healthcare
- ACORD for insurance

The list of standards and industry vocabulary initiatives will surely grow, probably until it comes close to the number of global standards related to commerce in the physical world. The sheer number of new and evolving industry vocabularies causes obvious problems. What happens when connections are needed between them in a given e-Commerce ecosystem? What is needed is a common repository of XML schema that can be shared by participants globally over the Net. The ideal goal would be to establish an XML portal for industry vocabularies. The portal should serve as a repository and a registry of vocabularies. Within the registries, XML tags must be managed using the Namespaces standard for XML so that names do not overlap and collide in documents containing multiple vocabularies.

While registries must be organized into a meaningful taxonomy, such taxonomies must be more than a way to classify information. They must encode and represent knowledge to get at the meaning of the information. While XML *data* and Java *processing* bring the *information* needed for e-Commerce, *ontologies* bring *knowledge representation* to the e-Commerce table. Open markets require smart software acting on behalf of all participants.

Knowledge representation is a discipline within the artificial intelligence community and can be captured in the form of *ontologies*. What is an ontology? In its general meaning, ontology is the branch of metaphysics that deals with what kinds of things exist in the universe – the classification and essence of things. Tom Gruber of Stanford University provides the short answer in context of artificial intelligence, "An ontology is an explicit specification of a conceptualization." He explains, "A body of formally represented knowledge is based on conceptualization: the objects, concepts, and other entities that are assumed to exist in some area of interest and the relationships that hold among them." An ontology defines the basic terms and relations comprising the vocabulary of a topic area, as well as the rules for combining terms and relations to define extensions to the vocabulary. All domain models embody an ontology – albeit mostly implicitly. An artificial intelligence approach to defining business objects emphasizes the use of explicit ontologies as implementation-neutral representations of knowledge that can then be mechanically translated into different target modeling tools.

Ontology.org, sponsored by Computer Science Corporation (CSC), was founded by Howard Smith and Kevin Poulter in 1998. Ontology.org is working with CommerceNet to develop ontologies for e-Commerce and XML vocabularies. Smith and Poulter elaborate on the goals of Ontology.org, "Although taxonomy contributes to the semantics of a term in a vocabulary, ontologies include richer relationships between terms. It is these rich relationships that enable the expression of domain-specific knowledge, without the need to include domain-specific terms."[14] The adoption of a shared ontology allows e-Commerce software (especially software agents) to simultaneously "interoperate without misunderstanding, and retain a high degree of autonomy, flexibility and agility." Without ontologies, the tasks of integrating, or in any way unifying the rapidly growing list of XML vocabularies will be as monumental as building the Tower of Babel.

A neutral, non-profit organization makes the most sense for governance of XML repositories and registries. CommerceNet, the non-profit electronic commerce consortium, has announced that it is developing an e-Commerce Registry service. Another organization, OASIS, the Organization for the Advancement of Structured Information Standards, is a non-profit, international consortium dedicated to accelerating the adoption of product-independent formats based on public standards, including SGML, XML and HTML. XML.ORG is an industry Web portal operated by OASIS. The most important function of XML.ORG is to serve as a trusted, secure, persistent repository and registry for DTDs, namespaces, schemas, and other specifications that must be globally accessible in order to make possible the use of XML for data exchange within particular industries.

Owning and governing XML repository portals means power and influence with software developers, so commercial companies including Microsoft have made moves into this space. Using the ".org" top-level domain name, Microsoft rushed in to fill the registry gap by establishing BizTalk.org. The web site is "free," and Microsoft will be happy to store companies' private XML schema in secure areas on the site as well as public vocabularies.

In summary, XML by itself is little more than a markup language. When XML is used as a meta language to define industry vocabularies so that trading partners can interoperate, then it will be those very vocabularies that thrust XML center stage as the language of e-Commerce. Reaching this goal will not be as easy as it may sound and many requirements must be met. The XML/EDI Group amply describes these requirements. "What does it take for a document/format to meet the challenges of delivering on the concept of enabling the "Electronic Enterprise" of the future? One can foresee that the requirements would include:

1. Message objects containing all the information (rules and data) necessary to process them without reference to the originator for clarification. [self-describing and introspective business objects]
2. A self-validating and authenticating message.
3. Displayed as requested by the author or reader, including local styles, and also tailoring itself automatically to the particular device or media available.
4. Dynamic links from various sources/servers and object components from around the world.
5. A web presence with common tagged elements.
6. A legacy interface with the new system without having to redesign expensive business processes.
7. Extended EDI messages with multimedia-based objects and content.
8. Searchable via today's and enhanced object-based engines of the future.
9. Encapsulated internal routing and security elements.
10. An easily assimilated protocol via today's software.
11. Manipulated and viewed with your Web browser, word processor or spreadsheet program.

12. Dynamically updateable industry codes cross-linked to reflect the local language.
13. Compatible with internal workflow subsystems and external business-to-business pipelines.
14. Automated on-line E-business.
15. Intranet access to local databases without the use of complex middleware."[15]

As industry vocabularies mature, XML will bring the benefits of traditional EDI to the masses, ease the legacy and ERP interoperability problems, and level the playing field for small and medium-sized enterprises (SMEs). Although adapting to the new XML-enabled world of e-Commerce will require a lot of transition planning and work (no technology introduction is trivial), XML is in every company's e-Commerce future.

Issue 8: Open Markets: Standards-based Rules of Engagement

The telephone was the first universal, fully interactive information highway. Standards made it possible for any phone company's proprietary system to interoperate with any other phone company's proprietary systems. As a result, today anyone can phone anyone anywhere at anytime. Without global standards, however, the telephone would not be universal and would not have its impact on society and the economy.

In the third wave, e-Commerce transforms closed, isolated markets to dynamic open markets. Standards are prerequisite to such dynamic markets and market interoperation. We have discussed the Tower of Babel problem of the growing XML industry vocabularies. Creating standards, *open standards,* between and among these semantic towers of e-Commerce Babel is essential to digital commerce. Open e-Commerce standards (tying together the XML Towers of Babel) to watch for include CommerceNet's eCo system architecture and the Object Management Group's Electronic Commerce Reference Architecture Model.

A January 1999 report from CommerceNet documents the status of the eCo system framework and the problem it aims to solve. "Using XML and Objects to construct an Electronic Commerce Framework – CommerceNet announced its eCo Framework workgroup in August 1998. Its purpose is to select and integrate various existing technologies into a framework for all commerce. Many efforts, proprietary, industrial and international in nature, are working to establish electronic commerce standards. Efforts such as OFX (Open Financial Exchange), ICE (Information Content Exchange), or OTP (Open Trading Protocol), while well done, focus on only part of the whole Electronic Commerce process and do not offer a total solution. The eCo Framework Workgroup hopes to solve this problem through the use of new and existing object-oriented technologies, XML, Object-Oriented XML, Agents, EDI and other existing semantic and syntactical technologies. This is a formable undertaking – to accomplish this goal, expertise from many related standards groups is required for constructing the final framework. The work group has two efforts underway. One effort is to establish the architecture of services and how they interact and fit together. The other effort is to research existing technologies and recommend those that should be used to construct the framework."[16]

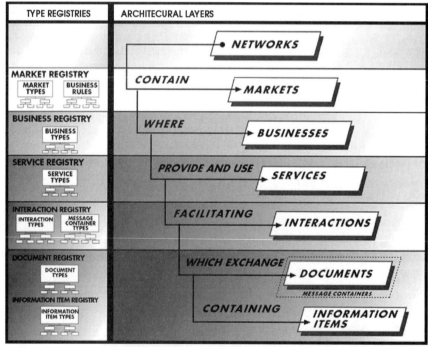

Figure 8 - 6. CommerceNet's eCo Architecture for Open E-Commerce

"Marketware is the generic name for a class of eCo applications and services that would bring together buyers and sellers. The services are based on a common platform that would be customized by plugging in different application modules. Depending on the modules used, a variety of value-added market services could be implemented. CommerceNet's eCo framework is centered on advanced semantic models and technique derived from the world of artificial intelligence such as ontologies developed by the European Enterprise Project."

"The primary focus of CommerceNet's eCo framework project is to demonstrate the value of the integration of three common component-based electronic commerce services. These services are semantic integration of multiple database types with multiple data constructs and data libraries; trusted open registries; and agent-mediated buying. It is our belief that these three core services will serve as the foundation for next generation, component-based commerce applications and services. These core services will provide interoperability between many commerce services and serve as a foundation to operate Web-based trading communities." The eCo Architecture is presented in Figure 8 - 6.

To help put the eCo Framework in perspective, Figure 8 - 7 shows an instance of the eCo framework at work.

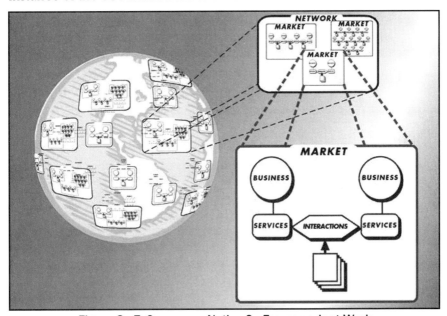

Figure 8 - 7. CommerceNet's eCo Framework at Work

"Using the eCo Architecture specification, the figure illustrates the following e-Commerce scenario, two companies are represented as eCo Businesses (implementations of the eCo Business Layer). These Businesses exist together in an eCo Market that provides a venue for the type of e-Commerce that they are conducting. The eCo Market is indexed within a Network of Markets so that it can be located on the Internet. Each of these Businesses offers a set of e-commerce 'Services' to each other. Each Service represents an interface to a business process. Example Services might be 'Become a VAR', 'Order some product', or 'Review a catalogue of products.' At the highest level, Businesses interact by using the Services of each other."

"A Service is composed of a set of document exchanges. We call these exchanges 'Interactions'. An Interaction occurs when a request (consisting of one or more Documents) is sent from one Business to another and a response (again consisting of one or more documents) is received."[17]

Distributed object computing sets the foundation for both enterprise computing and the inter-enterprise computing that is essential to open e-Commerce. In fact, it is the distributed component paradigm that has made it possible for e-Commerce to aspire to open digital markets.

Like business objects in general, the interoperation of open market processes must rise above technology interoperation ("above the ORB") to a level of abstraction where business information models can interoperate using the vocabulary of e-Commerce. In other words, common business semantics must be available to all participants in an open digital market.

Yet common business semantics are not enough. Interoperation at the e-Commerce semantic level is the focus of CommerceNet. Interoperation at the information systems level is the focus of the Object Management Group's Common Object Request Broker Architecture (CORBA) specification. In addition to CORBA middleware, and rising above the "orb," the OMG's Electronic Commerce Domain Taskforce (ECDTF) combines e-Commerce interoperation with distributed, heterogeneous systems interoperation. The greater business world will benefit if these two organizations closely collaborate with each other, W3C and DISA.

The OMG EC Domain Task Force group is developing standards for *open* markets: Negotiation, PKI, Payments, and Brokerage specifications, with more to come within the framework of OMG's overall reference architecture. The Electronic Commerce Reference Model sets the stage for open market standards backed by a robust distributed computing infrastructure. No organization has contributed more to creating open, standard "middleware that's everywhere" – an OMG slogan.[18] We can understand the OMG's Electronic Commerce Reference Model and the goals of the ECDTF by reading from its draft mission statement:

"The Electronic Commerce Domain Task Force (ECDTF) exists to define and promote the specification of OMG distributed object technologies for the development and use of Electronic Commerce applications by: (1) developing an object-oriented framework for open commerce that promotes the interoperation and reuse of applications and services, and (2) supporting an ongoing process for achieving broad consensus on issues of interoperability and reuse.

The ECDTF will focus on defining and influencing OMG specifications for technology areas related to EC, including:
- Security
- Certificates (e.g., Authentication)
- Asynchronous (e.g., queued) Communications
- Information Transfer Protocols
- Transactions
- Quality of Service

The ECDTF will work with other OMG elements to leverage existing activities and specifications. As new requirements are identified, the ECDTF will collaborate with other OMG elements to develop new OMG specifications. Finally, the Electronic Commerce TF will work with outside organizations (such as, CommerceNet, ANSI X12, EDIFACT, CEFACT, TINA-C) through the OMG Liaison committee to leverage and influence related activities and specifications."[19] In recognition of the requirement for knowledge representation in e-Commerce, the OMG ECDTF includes an Agent Technology Work Group that has participants with world-class experience in the commercial intelligent agent community.

The OMG's initial draft *Service Architecture for Open Electronic Markets,* the Electronic Commerce Reference Model, is shown in Figure 8 - 8. The model is of sufficient depth to address such issues as "policy management" which affects market participant behavior and enterprise system rule enforcement. The architecture reaches deeply into the interactive relationship between participants such as customer and supplier (and their respective agents). Negotiation may equally occur over agreement on policy in order to establish a common, temporary domain. This concept of "dynamic policy domains," built using sophisticated policy management tools, opens up new markets in third-party policies, used for the duration of a transaction and then discarded.

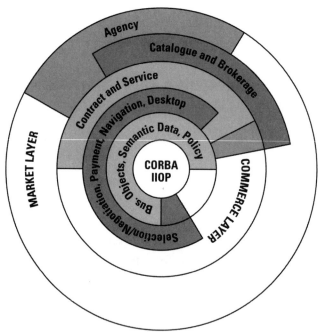

Figure 8 - 8. OMG's Electronic Commerce Reference Model Architecture

The e-Commerce related standards being evolved by OMG and CommerceNet, as well as the Workflow Management Coalition (WfMC), DISA (EDI) and the World Wide Web Consortium (W3C) are works-in-progress. Corporations wanting to excel in emerging, open markets should participate directly in the work of these organizations. Participation will help a company keep abreast of developments and offers the opportunity to help shape the standards that will serve as the rules of engagement.

The Critical Success Factors

In this chapter and throughout this book, we have explored the challenges and strategies of the third wave of e-Commerce. From working with the pioneers of e-Commerce on large-scale initiatives such as GE's TPN Register, we have seen some common patterns and gained valuable insight through observing traits common to those who have developed sustainable and flexible initiatives. We can now recap and summarize the critical business and technology factors of success.

Inter-enterprise Architecture

We have stressed the need for an inter-enterprise architecture to provide an underlying structure that is consistent, easily understood and comprehensive (it includes both business and technology elements). In his column, "Peopleware, Re: Architecture" Larry Constantine writes, "Architecture, whether in the organization of the internal functionality or in the structure of the user interface, is often among the first victims felled by today's time-boxed software projects, short release cycles, and rapid applications development. There seems to be no time to think through the consequences of architectural decisions. Often there is barely time to think. Full stop."[20] The facts, however, remain. The development of a strong architectural vision and the adoption of incremental development cycles are keys to sustainable e-Commerce success. In turn, success in e-Commerce architecture will be determined largely by five key business imperatives: *adopting the customer paradigm, optimizing the value-chain, achieving time-to-market, governance,* and *measuring progress and effectiveness.*

Customer Paradigm

In the "old days" producers would determine what consumers could have. They would take their products and push them on their customers. Now, the shoe is on the other foot, subordinating production to the demands of the customer.

With the new production-consumption equation, customers must be provided complete self-service access to a company's business processes and those of the company's value-chain. The customer-centric company of the 21st century changes the customer relationship by engineering customer-facing processes from the outside-in, creating the "open" corporation where the customer initiates and conducts his or her own business using the open (yet secure and auditable) resources of the corporation.

Value-Chain Optimization: business-to-business.com

With the customer in control, a business must realign its value-chain around the customer, from end-to-end, squeezing out inefficiencies – and customizing information, products and services. The open corporation is extended to suppliers and trading partners so that when customers touch the resources of a corporation they also touch the resources of the value-chain.

The customer drives the entire value-chain, determining what is to be produced, when and at what price. Pricing will ultimately behave as is does in the stock market, changing in real-time. As in the stock market, pricing will fluctuate with overall perceived value which, in turn, will be influenced by cyberbranding. The customer will interact with the whole ecosystem, not just the individual company, making *general systems theory* a core business competency. Companies must directly participate in building the new business ecosystem, or competitors will do it for them. Inter-enterprise architecture provides the framework for customer-driven, value-chain optimization.

Time-to-Software, Time-to-Market

In the domain of e-Commerce, time-to-market is governed by time-to-software. Component-based development is the next logical step in modular software development, a trend that has been underway since the advent of "structured" programming, then structured analysis and design, and then on to object-oriented development. By packaging software constructs and implementations into components, software can be removed from the critical path in time-to-market. Component-based development is the current best practice in software development because it combines strong architectural notions with rapid applications development.

Governance: Put the CEO In Charge of E-Commerce

The question of e-Commerce governance summons a short and simple answer. Business users of information systems are the most thorough source of business and market knowledge, and the most accountable for business success. E-Commerce is, therefore, a business unit responsibility – with IT playing a role of enablement and support.

Looking at the chain-of-command in Fortune 1000 corporations, and considering that e-Commerce will form a completely new platform for operating a business, it is logical to conclude that, ultimately, the CEO must also become the CECO, Chief Electronic Commerce Officer. As a company transitions to a fully digital business, the CEO will assume bottom-line responsibility for e-Commerce – to wit, Jeff Bezos, CEO at Amazon.com where e-Commerce *is* the business.

What's good for the CEO is good for the board of directors. In his provocative article, *"Directors' Boards are Clueless About the Internet,"* Thorton Mays, Vice President of Research and Education at Cambridge Technology Partners, reflects on Emerson, "Ralph Waldo Emerson once observed that 'we learn geology the morning after the earthquake.' The emerging digital economy, and how it's affecting boards of directors, is being studied post-Web-quake by some top business scholars. Their conclusion: The directors of most mainstream companies don't understand the implications of the Internet, aren't aware of their ignorance and are taking no steps to remedy their dangerous strategic blind spot." For one, existing boards are too grounded in vision limiting experience in their industries, the very industries they need to transform. In addition, the ability to unlearn or forget entrenched mental models is a very difficult learning proposition. Boards need to learn new things and forget many of the ways they operated in the past. To overcome this behavioral inertia, Mays contends that boards of directors need to "add new tech-savvy DNA to the board, hire a technology coach for each board member and collectively educate the entire board on the competitive implications of IT."[21]

Balanced Scorecard ROI

Measurement is a critical element in any system of management. As a new platform for conducting business, e-Commerce is a long-term business proposition – a company cannot go out and buy e-Commerce, it must make it a way of business and grow it. Measures of e-Commerce's value should include the long-term value of the business infrastructure it provides as well as the individual return-on-investment (ROI) of specific e-Commerce initiatives.

Because e-Commerce changes the way a company operates, it calls for new measures of business performance. While *financial* (ROI) measures have dominated Industrial Age corporations, the business reengineering movement of the early 1990s gave birth to Information Age measures of performance. It follows that if companies were reengineering to do new things, they needed new, consummate, measures of business-critical performance. How else could they measure their progress in translating vision and strategy into day-to-day business reality?

A modern jet airliner requires many more instruments to measure flight-critical performance than an automobile needs for its simpler operating environment. Business-critical performance in the e-Commerce environment requires measuring the right things, those things that create competitive advantage in digital age competition.

Robert S. Kaplan and David P. Norton, developers of the Balanced Scorecard method, write, "The emergence of the information era in the last decades of the twentieth century made obsolete many of the fundamental assumptions of Industrial Age competition. The balanced scorecard retains traditional financial measures. But financial measures tell the story of past events, an adequate story for industrial age companies for which investments in long-term capabilities and customer relationships were not critical for success. These financial measures are inadequate, however, for guiding and evaluating the journey that Information Age companies must make to create future value through investment in customers, suppliers, employees, processes, technology, and innovation." More than a financial measurement system, the Balanced Scorecard, is a strategic management system for achieving long-term goals. Kaplan and Norton show how to use measures in four categories – *financial performance, customer knowledge, internal business processes*, and *learning and growth* – to align individual, organizational and cross-departmental initiatives and to identify entirely new processes for meeting customer and shareholder objectives. These measures are portrayed in Figure 8 - 9.

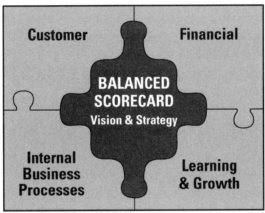

Figure 8 - 9. Kaplan and Norton's Balanced Scorecard

The Balanced Scorecard serves as a learning system for testing, gaining feedback and updating an organization's strategy. The four perspectives provide a balance between short-term and long-term performance, and include subjective as well as objective measures. When applied to e-Commerce initiatives, measures may include process cycle-time, transaction per employee ratios, cost per transaction, volume of transactions, percent of customers supported by e-Commerce, time to fulfill service requests, and inventory costs. Kaplan's recent research initiatives have extended activity-based analysis to technology and product development and interorganizational measurement systems between manufacturers and retailers that capture supplier and customer profitability.

Whether it is the Balanced Scorecard or another equally robust system of measurement, measuring "the right things," in addition to financial ROI is crucial to successful e-Commerce. The following anecdote tells the story of measuring the *right things*, "The concept is interesting and well-formed, but in order to earn better than a 'C,' the idea must be feasible," wrote a Yale University management professor in response to Fred Smith's (founder of Federal Express Corporation) paper proposing reliable overnight delivery service.[22] Is "well-formed" or "competitive breakthrough" the right thing to measure? We can wonder what grade the professor would have given Amazon.com's Jeff Bezos.

The Ultimate Success Factor

A company deliberating its future in the brave new world of e-Commerce may seek out lessons learned from past experiences with disruptive technologies. "Dear Mr. President: The canal system of this country is being threatened by a new form of transportation known as "railroads." ... As you may well know, Mr. President, "railroad" carriages are pulled at the enormous speed of 15 miles per hour by "engines" which, in addition to endangering life and limb of passengers, roar and snort their way through the countryside, setting fire to crops, scaring the livestock and frightening women and children. The Almighty certainly never intended that people should travel at such breakneck speed," wrote Martin Van Buren, Governor of New York (1828).[23] Like it or not, e-Commerce, along with its many side-effects, is *quietly* roaring and snorting its way through the business landscape, scaring investors and frightening Industrial Age thinkers and leaders. Whether by evolution or revolution, e-Commerce will create winners and losers in every industry. Who will they be? Who knows? In uncharted territories and in uncertain times, prediction is of dubious value. Through a stream of assimilation, individuals, departments, companies, industries, and markets must learn as they go. They must learn a little, do a little, learn a little, do a little. At each step in the journey, more information will become available and knowledge will grow from experience.

Rather than being overwhelmed by rapid, discontinuous change, the winners will look back and learn that it was their total commitment to the underlying factors of success that enabled them to arrive at the future first. An inter-enterprise architecture allowed them to build learning organizations that used the first principles of general systems thinking to transform their companies into customer-centric businesses. With this architectural approach, they were able to rationalize, arrange and connect business and technology components to produce the desired results. For them, e-Commerce mastery provided the bridge to the Customer Age. Over a decade ago, Arie DeGeus of Royal Dutch/Shell wrote words in the Harvard Business Review that today describe *the* critical success factor for enterprise-class e-Commerce, "The ability to learn faster than your competitors may be the only sustainable competitive advantage."[24]

References

[1] Jim Champy, "Goodbye Info Age; Hello Age of Logistics," *Computerworld*, p. 54, August 24, 1998.

[2] Patricia B. Seybold, Preparing for the E-services Revolution: Designing your next Generation E-Business, April 30, 1999, http://www.hp.com/e-services/article_sey_1.html

[3] Alexander, Christopher, *Timeless Way of Building*, Oxford Univ. Press, 1979.

[4] Donald A. Norman, *The Design of Everyday Things*, Currency/Doubleday, 1990.

[5] James F. Moore, "The New Corporate Form," in *Blueprint to the Digital Economy*, McGraw Hill, 1998.

[6] http://www.truste.org/about/

[7] Paul Allen, *A Framework for Business-IT Alignment Using Components*. Distributed Computing Magazine, December, 1998.

[8] Christopher Alexander, Sara Ishikawa, Murray Silverstein, *A Pattern Language: Towns, Buildings, Construction*, Oxford University Press, 1977.

[9] Craig Thompson, Object Services and Consulting, Inc.; Ted Linden and Bob Filman, Microelectronics and Computer Technology Corporation (MCC). *Thoughts on OMA-NG: The Next Generation Object Management Architecture*. DARPA Research. September 1997.

[10] Jon Byous, Co-Stars in Networking: XML and Java™ Technologies, http://java.sun.com/xml/co-stars.html

[11] For an informative set of articles on XMLbeans, see Mark Johnson, "XML JavaBeans," *JavaWorld*, 1999, http://www.javaworld.com/javaworld/jw-07-1999/jw-07-beans.html

[12] _____, Ibid

[13] Rik Drummond, *Is XML Dead in the Water?*, CommerceNet, Research Note #99-07, February 15, 1999.

[14] Ontology.Org, Frequently Asked Questions, http://ontology.org/main/papers/faq.html

[15] The XML/EDI Group, *The Future of Electronic Business*, http://www.geocities.com/WallStreet/Floor/5815/executive.htm

[16] Rik Drummond, Executive Consultant to CommerceNet. *Report from the Jointly-sponsored CommerceNet and Veo Systems eCo Framework Workgroup*, January, 1999.

[17] CommerceNet, eCo Architecture for electronic commerce interoperability, 1999. http://www.commerce.net/eco/spec/eCoArchitecture.htm#Section_2

[18] OMG, ECDTF, Draft Electronic Commerce Domain Task Force Mission Statement, Revised 5/18/99.

[19] OMG, ECTD, Draft Mission Statement revision, May, 1999.

[20] Larry Constantine, *"Peopleware, Re: Architecture,"* Software Development Magazine, January, 1996, p. 87.

[21] Thornton May, XMLrfc: "Directors' boards are clueless about the Internet," Computerworld, July 12, 1999.

[22] Science and Technology Quotes located at http://busboy.sped.ukans.edu/~adams/sciquot.htm

[23] _____, Ibid.

[24] DeGeus, Arie, "Planning as Learning," Harvard Business Review, p. 74 (March-April 1988).

Notes

Appendix A   XML Industry Vocabularies and Consortia

Agency Company Organization for Research and Development (ACORD)

ACORD is a not-for-profit standards-setting association for the insurance industry. It is a resource for information about object technology, EDI, XML and electronic commerce in the United States and abroad.

Ad Markup / Advertising Index DTD

The NAA Classified Advertising Standards Task Force was organized by the NAA Technology Department to facilitate the electronic exchange of classified ads. Standards developed will pave the way for aggregation of classified ads among publishers on the Internet, as well as enhance the development of classified processing systems.

Alexandria Digital Library (ADL)

The goal of the Alexandria Project is to develop a user-friendly digital library system providing a full range of services in relation to collections of maps, images, and spatially-referenced information that are dispersed geographically over a number of sites.

Bank Internet Payment System (BIPS)

The Bank Internet Payment System (BIPS) is a project of the Financial Services Technology Consortium (FSTC). The BIPS specification includes a protocol for sending payment instructions to banks safely over the Internet and a payment server architecture for processing those payment instructions.

Channel Definition Format (CDF)

Microsoft submitted this specification to the W3C in 1997. Related to push technologies, the specification permits a Web publisher to offer frequently updated collections of information, or channels, from any web server for automatic delivery to compatible receiver programs on PCs or other information appliances.

Chemical Markup Language (CML)

CML is a tool for management of molecular and technical information, especially geared to Inter- and Intra-net use. Based on Java and XML it covers a wide range of chemical disciplines.

Commerce XML (cXML)

cXML is an XML vocabulary created to facilitate the exchange of catalog content and transaction information between buyers and suppliers.

Common Business Library (CBL)

Common Business Library is being developed as a set of building blocks with common semantics and syntax to insure interoperability among XML applications.

Customer Support Consortium

Founded in 1992, the Customer Support Consortium is a group of over 70 technology companies who work together to improve customer support by developing innovative new strategies, standards and programs. A subgroup is developing a set of mappings from standards specifications to XML.

Data Interchange Standards Association (DISA) ANSI ASC X12 and XML/EDI

XML may be the means to bridge EDI into Electronic Commerce by making the existing EDI knowledge base available to e-Commerce developers. CommerceNet, the XML/EDI Group and ANSI ASC X12 have entered into a joint project to investigate how to translate ANSI ASC X12 and CEFACT data elements, segments and transactions into XML.

Digital Receipt Consortium

DRC consists of representatives from various financial institutions, accounting firms and software development companies. The consortium is developing a standard to describe the content, creation, exchange and management of digital receipts.

Electronic-Commerce Modeling Language (ECML)

ECML is currently defined as an IETF draft proposed by Microsoft, America Online, Sun, Visa, MasterCard and American Express. It provides a common interface for electronic wallets. Interestingly, the value of an electronic wallet for consumers may be less in the fact that it holds money, but rather than it holds personal information. Electronic wallets may help users give out information selectively as well as receive information that results from a transaction, such as a receipt.

Electronic Component Manufacturer Data Sheet Library Specification (ECMData)

ECMData is a standard proposed by Marshall Industries that would enable the automatic retrieval, indexing, and cataloging of electronic component manufacturers' data sheets and contents of those datasheets.

European Association of Aerospace Industries (AECMA)

AECMA Specification 1000D has been produced to establish standards for the documentation of any civil or military air vehicle or equipment. It is based on international standards such as SGML and CGM for production and use of electronic documentation. In addition, Spec 1000D defines a Common Source Data Base (CSDB) to enable production/interchange of common documentation and to provide source information for compilation of the publications.

Financial Products Markup Language (FpML)

J.P. Morgan & Co. Incorporated and PricewaterhouseCoopers LLP's FpML deals with information sharing of financial derivatives, initially handling interest rate and foreign exchange products. FpML enables Internet-based integration of a range of services, from electronic trading and confirmations to portfolio specification for risk analysis.

FinXML™

Integral (www.integral.com), a provider of browser-based trading and risk management systems, developed FinXML™ with the intention of it becoming a standard language for describing capital markets instruments and transactions

FIX/FIXML

The Financial Information eXchange (FIX) protocol is a messaging standard developed specifically for the real-time electronic exchange of securities transactions for the equities market. FIX is a public-domain specification owned and maintained by FIX Protocol, Ltd.

Information Content Exchange (ICE)

The ICE, which comprises Vignette, Sun Microsystems, CNET, Adobe, News Internet Services, and Channelware Inc., defines the roles and responsibilities of syndicators and subscribers, defines the format and method of content exchange, and provides support for management and control of syndication relationships. ICE is useful in automating content exchange and reuse, both in traditional publishing contexts and in business-to-business relationships.

Legal XML Working Group

A small group named the XML Work Group has been formed within the scope of the Utah Electronic Law Project. "The purpose of the XML Work Group is to develop one or more model Document Type Definitions (DTDs) for the filing and exchange of legal documents using the recently released XML standards.

News Industry Text Format (NITF)

This is an XML DTD designed to allow news information to be transferred with markup and be easily transformed into an electronically publishable format. This new version uses the XML syntax but otherwise meets the design aims of the original NITF.

Open Applications Group (OAG)

The Open Applications Group, Inc. is a non-profit industry consortium aimed at the interoperation of ERP systems. OAG's XML vocabularies define interoperability for Financials, Human Resources, Manufacturing, Logistics and Supply Chain.

Open Buying on the Internet (OBI)

The Open Buying on the Internet (OBI) Consortium is a non-profit organization dedicated to developing open standards for business-to-business Internet commerce. OBI is the industry standard for business-to-business commerce developed to address the low-dollar, high-volume transactions that account for approximately 80% of all purchases. OBI has not yet released a DTD for its standards implementation.

Open Financial Exchange (OFX/OFE)

Microsoft, Intuit, and CheckFree joined together to develop XML specifications for the online transfer of financial data. Open Financial Exchange (OFE) integrates Microsoft's Open Financial Connectivity, Intuit's OpenExchange, and CheckFree's electronic banking and payment protocols. Features supported include: 1) Bank statement download, 2) Credit card statement download, 3) Funds transfers including recurring transfers, 4) Consumer payments, including recurring payments, 5) Business payments, including recurring payments, 6) Brokerage and mutual fund statement download, including transaction history, current holdings and balances, 7) Bill presentment and payment.

Open Trading Protocol (OTP)

"The Internet Open Trading Protocol (OTP) provides an interoperable framework for Internet commerce. It is a payment system that encapsulates other payment systems such as SET, Mondex, CyberCash, DigiCash and GeldKarte. OTP is able to handle cases where such merchant roles as the shopping site, the payment handler, the delivery handler of goods or services, and the provider of customer support are performed by different parties or by one party.

Real Estate Markup Language (REML)

An initial design document by 4thWORLD Telecom models information relevant to real estate listings.

RosettaNet

RosettaNet is aimed at the IT supply chain: manufacturers, distributors, resellers and end-users of computer equipment and related services.

Signed Document Markup Language (SDML)

The XML-Signature WG is a joint Working Group of the IETF and W3C. The XML Digital Signature specification provides syntax used for representing signatures on Web resources and procedures for computing and verifying such signatures. Digital signatures provide data integrity, authentication, and non-repudiatability.

Simple Workflow Access Protocol (SWAP)

SWAP is a protocol designed to allow for interoperability between workflow systems and between workflow systems and other applications.

vCard

This Document Type Definition (DTD) corresponds to the vCard, electronic business card format.

XML for the Automotive Industry – SAE J2008

In response to requirements from the 1990 US Clean Air Act, The Society of Automotive Engineers (SAE) has adopted a number of standards under the 'SAE J2008' family of standards designed to provide easy access to emission-related automotive service information.

XML Metadata Interchange (XMI)

XMI, XML Metadata interchange, enables easy interchange of metadata between modeling language tools based on the UML (unified modeling language) industry standard. It combines XML with OMG's UML and MOF standards. XMI makes it practical for distributed development teams in heterogeneous environments to work together. XMI is expected to be used in additional key domains such as data warehouse metadata and business object metadata.

XML-HR

In partnership with Applied Theory Communications (ATC), the America's Job Bank (AJB) Service Center has begun the XML-HR Initiative. The purpose of the initiative is to collaborate on the creation and standardization of human resource/electronic recruiting XML definitions.

XMLNews

XMLNews is an XML and RDF-based news industry format developed by David Megginson for WavePhore for its NewsPak product.

More Information

For more information on the growing number of XML industry vocabularies, see Robin Cover's SGML/XML Web Page at http://www.oasis-open.org/cover/xml.html#applications

Notes

Appendix B   E-Commerce Information Portals on the Web

A number of comprehensive sources of information about electronic commerce are available on the Web. We have listed some of our favorites for quick reference. They are available as hotlinks at http://home1.gte.net/pfingar ... see Essential Links.

@Brint.com: Electronic Commerce & Electronic Markets
http://www.brint.com/Elecomm.htm

All eCommerce
http://www.allec.com

Carnegie Mellon University Institute for eCommerce
http://www.ecom.cmu.edu

Center for Information Strategy and Policy
http://www.cisp.org

The Center for Research in Electronic Commerce at the Graduate School of Business, the University of Texas at Austin, Texas
http://cism.bus.utexas.edu

CETUS: 15,473 Links on Objects & Components
http://www.cetus-links.org

CIO magazine's Electronic Commerce Research Center
http://www.cio.com/forums/ec

The CommerceNet Consortium
http://www.commerce.net

CommerceNet's Research Report #98-19 on the Future of E-Commerce
with Software Agents
http://home1.gte.net/pfingar/eba.htm

Competence Network Electronic Commerce (CNEC)
http://www.cnec.org

Computerworld's eCommerce Site
http://www.computerworld.com/emmerce

The Department of Defense Joint Electronic Commerce Program Office
(JECPO)
http://www.acq.osd.mil/ec

DigitalTimes™
http://www.digitaltimes.com/Commerce

e-CentreUK
http://www.eca.org.uk

Electronic Commerce Association
http://www.ecassociation.org

The Electronic Commerce Guide
http://ecommerce.internet.com

Electronic Commerce Resources
http://www.cs.nccu.edu.tw/~jong/agent/EC/ecr.html

The Emerging Digital Economy, U.S. Commerce Secretary William M.
Daley
http://www.ecommerce.gov/emerging.htm

The Enterprise Resource Planning (ERP) Supersite
http://www.erpsupersite.com

The European Commission: Electronic Commerce and the European
Union
http://www.ispo.cec.be/ecommerce

The European ESPRIT and ACTS projects related to Electronic
Commerce
http://cordis.lu/esprit/src/ecomproj.htm

The Federal Electronic Commerce Program Office
http://www.ec.fed.gov

The Fisher Center for IT and Marketplace Transformation at the Haas
School of Business, University of California
http://www.haas.berkeley.edu/~citm/research
http://www.haas.berkeley.edu/~citm/OFFER

A Framework for Global Electronic Commerce, The White House, 1997
http://www.ecommerce.gov/framewrk.htm

Glossary of EDI and Transport Terms
http://www.webcom.com/pjones/gloss.html

Harvard Information Infrastructure Project
http://ksgwww.harvard.edu/iip

Hewlett Packard's eBusiness magazine
http://www.hp.com/Ebusiness/

IBM's eBusiness Forum
http://www.ibm.com/e-business

IBM's Institute for Advanced Commerce
http://www.ibm.com/iac

IBM's SanFrancisco Site: Excellent Eight Chapter eBook on Component
Frameworks
http://www.software.ibm.com/ad/sanfrancisco/concepts/concepts.html

IDG.net
http://www.idg.net

The Information Economy: Commerce (The University of California
Berkeley)
http://www.sims.berkeley.edu/resources/infoecon/Commerce.html

InformationWeek
http://www.informationweek.com/

InfoWorld's I-Commerce News
http://www.infoworld.com/cgi-bin/displayIcommerce.pl?/icomm.htm

The International Center for Electronic Commerce
http://icec.net

The Internet Economy Indicators™
http://www.internetindicators.com

The Internet Society
http://www.isoc.org

Internet.com's E-Commerce News
http://www.internetnews.com/ec-news

JavaOne™: Electronic versions of JavaOne presentations
http://java.sun.com/javaone

Jeff Sutherland's Business Object Component Technology Web Site
http://jeffsutherland.org

The Object Management Group
http://www.omg.org

Ontology.org
http://ontology.org

Organisation for Economic Co-operation and Development (OECD)
http://www.oecd.org/dsti/sti/it/ec

The Organization for the Advancement of Structured Information
Standards (OASIS)
http://www.oasis-open.org

The Owen Graduate School of Management,
Vanderbilt University, Project 2000
http://ecommerce.vanderbilt.edu

Roger Clarke's Electronic Commerce Pages and EC Definitions
http://www.anu.edu.au/people/Roger.Clarke/EC
http://www.anu.edu.au/people/Roger.Clarke/EC/ECDefns.html

The Society for Electronic Commerce and Rights Management
(ECARM)
http://marcella.ecarm.org

The Software & Information Industry Association's
Electronic Commerce Web Resource (ECWR)
http://www.siia.net/ecwr

TechWeb's NetBusiness
http://www.techweb.com/netbiz

The Wharton School Forum on Electronic Commerce
http://ecom.wharton.upenn.edu

Whatis.com: Look up those pesky acronyms
http://www.whatis.com

Wired magazine's Encyclopedia of the New Economy
http://www.hotwired.com/special/ene

The Workflow Management Coalition (WfMC)
http://www.aiim.org/wfmc

The World Wide Web Consortium (W3C)
http://www.w3.org

XML.org: The XML Industry Portal
http://xml.org

The XML/EDI Group
http://www.xmledi.com

ZD Net's e-Business
http://www.zdnet.com/enterprise/e-business

Notes

Appendix C   Suggested Readings

The bibliography contains a comprehensive list of business and technology books on e-Commerce. In it, the reader will find books of general interest and specific titles that will prove useful to individual needs. The suggested readings, on the other hand, annotate some of the essential reading and reference materials. Some of the titles are just off press while others are much older but included because their content applies just as much today as when they were written.

Readings on E-Commerce Strategy and New Business Models

Patricia B. Seybold and Ronni T. Marshak (Contributor), *Customers.Com: How to Create a Profitable Business Strategy for the Internet and Beyond,* **Times Books (1998).**

Well-known technology consultant, Patricia Seybold is founder and CEO of the Boston-based Patricia Seybold Group, which consults with Fortune 500 companies. Her book centers on case studies of 16 large companies, ranging from American Airlines Inc. to Wells Fargo & Co. The book provides an excellent discussion of the need to transform a company from being product-centric to customer-centric.

G. Winfield Treese and Lawrence C. Stewart. *Designing Systems for Internet Commerce,* **Addison-Wesley (1998).**

This book is packed with information, including both management and technical information. It is written by two technologists at Open Market, Inc., so the dense, bulleted lists that make up the bulk of the book are not too surprising. In addition, the "putting it all together" chapter drops into Open Market's products and packaged software approach. With these distractions aside, the book provides a good balance between the business dimensions and technical building blocks of e-Commerce.

Opening Digital Markets: Battle Plans and Business Strategies for Internet Commerce. Walid Mougayar. McGraw-Hill (1997).

This book, by the founding chairman of CommerceNet Canada, offers broad theoretical foundations for global e-commerce. Strategic perspectives and strategy formulations are its essence, making it an important read for decision-makers who must guide their corporations through the new realities of global electronic commerce.

McKenna, Regis, *Real Time.* Harvard Business School Press (1997).

McKenna describes how and why we need to take advantage of real-time information in today's marketing battles. As he explains, "It's about giving customers what they want when, where, and how they want it."

Ware, James (Editor), Judith Gebauer, Amir Hartman and Malu Roldan. *Search for Digital Excellence*, McGraw-Hill (1998).

A CommerceNet flagship book, this work was compiled by the folks at the Fisher Center for Management and Information Technology at the Haas School of Business. It is full of case studies that reveal successful and unsuccessful strategies of the early pioneers. Definitely belongs on the manager's e-Commerce bookshelf.

Porter, Michael E., *Competitive Strategy: Techniques for Analyzing Industries and Competitors*, Free Press (1980), *Competitive Advantage: Creating and Sustaining Superior Performance*, Free Press (1985), and *On Competition.* Harvard Business School Press (1998).

Micheal Porter produced the seminal work on value-chain management and his thoughts and insight are contained in these three volumes. They are required reading for Fortune 1000 leaders.

Champy, James, *Reengineering Management: The Mandate for New Leadership*, HarperBusiness (1995).

In follow-up to the publication of *Reengineering the Corporation*, Champy asserts that a familiar pattern has emerged in the application of reengineering: too often reengineering stops in its tracks at the executive suite. He provides the guidelines needed by managers to lead, measure, and reward the new work created by reengineering.

Davidow, William H. and Michael S. Malone, *The Virtual Corporation: Structuring and Revitalizing the Corporation for the 21st Century,* Harper Collins (1992).

The authors provide an integrated picture of the customer-driven company of the future. The book is at the cutting-edge and describes the future global marketplace that depends on corporations producing virtual products high in added value and available to customers instantly.

Gibson, Rowan, *Rethinking the Future: Rethinking Business, Principles, Competition, Control & Complexity, Leadership, Markets and the World,* Nicholas Brealey (1997).

The thinking of 17 thought leaders under one book cover.

Kaplan, Robert S., and David P. Norton, *The Balanced Scorecard: Translating Strategy into Action,* Harvard Business School Press (1996).

The Balanced Scorecard retains financial measures, such as return-on-capital-employed and economic value added, and supplements these with new measures on value creation for customers, enhancement of internal processes, including innovation, to deliver desired value propositions to targeted customers, and the creation of capabilities in employees and systems.

Goldman, S. L., R. N. Nagel, and K. Preiss. *Agile Competitors and Virtual Organizations: Strategies for Enriching the Customer.* Van Nostrand Reinhold (1994).

The publisher of this book practices what the book preaches. They offer corporate customers with customized editions to meet their specific needs. This book explains the business impact of mass customization and what it does to the legacy of mass production where one size fits all.

Hamel, Gary, and C. K. Prahalad, *Competing for the Future: Breakthrough Strategies for Seizing Control of Your Industry and Creating the Markets of Tomorrow,* Harvard Business School Press (1994).

The authors challenge executives to stop the unrewarding process of dead-end downsizing and enter the realm of dynamic business transformation. The book reframes what it means to be strategic.

James, Geoffrey, Business *Wisdom of the Electronic Elite: 34 Winning Management Strategies from CEOs at Microsoft, Compaq, Sun, Hewlett-Packard, and Other Top Companies,* **Random House (1996).**

This book offers a composite of the best management methods of some of the most innovative leaders in industry today. The author has spent months interviewing senior high-tech executives including Bill Gates of Microsoft, Lewis Platt of Hewlett-Packard, Jim Manzi of Lotus, Ann Winblad, the high-tech venture capitalist and others to find out why their companies have been able to maintain a competitive edge and high level of profitability in today's fierce marketplace.

Kelly, Kevin, *Out of Control: The Rise of Neo-biological Civilization,* **Addison-Wesley (1994).**

Reengineered processes lead to redesigned organizations. This work makes a significant contribution to organizational design as it applies to the business enterprise of the coming century.

Martin, James. Cybercorp: *The New Business Revolution,* **Amacom Book Division (1996).**

Martin's cybercorp is a corporation that is designed for fast change; that can learn, evolve, and transform rapidly; and that can use cyberspace to its advantage. Martin believes we have entered the early stages of a total corporate revolution, which will require us to think in completely new ways. As superhighways and software become more powerful, corporate structures will need to be reinvented. Martin uses examples from real-life global organizations that are designed to succeed.

Moore, James F., *The Death of Competition: Leadership and Strategy in the Age of Business Ecosystems,* **HarperBusiness (1996).**

Moore presents a new vision of competitive systems. He dispenses with simplistic models of corporate competition to argue that the complex, interdependent nature of today's business relationships is best understood as a form of ecosystem. He examines the strategic and managerial implications of this dynamic vision.

Newell, Frederick, *The New Rules of Marketing: How to Use One-To-One Relationship Marketing to Be the Leader in Your Industry,* **Irwin (1997).**

Database and relationship marketing and customer management represent the fastest growing marketing investment in North America today, but very few businesses know how to leverage these tools in order to gain a decisive competitive advantage. Newell is an expert with database and relationship marketing who has used techniques and strategies of both to develop customer-focused marketing programs.

O'Dell, Susan M. and Joan A. Pajunen, *The Butterfly Customer: Capturing the Loyalty of Today's Elusive Consumer,* **Wiley (1997).**

The Butterfly customer's first instinct is to try something new, something better, and something different, and their last instinct is to stay loyal to any one offering. This book is about building trust and gaining loyal customers.

Peppers, Don and Martha Rogers, *Enterprise One to One: Tools for Competing in the Interactive Age,* **Currency/Doubleday (1997).**

This book is a marketing classic on how to sell more products to fewer customers through one-to-one marketing. In this brave new world, where technology is making it possible for businesses to know their customers better than ever before, there is incredible opportunity to build unbreakable customer relationships. Peppers and Rogers explain the strategies needed to achieve killer competitive advantages in customer loyalty and unit margin.

Peppers, Don and Martha Rogers, *The One to One Future: Building Relationships One Customer at a Time,* **Currency/Doubleday (1997).**

The *One to One Future* revolutionized marketing when it was first published. Then considered a radical rethinking of marketing basics, this best selling book has become today's bible for marketers.

Peters, Tom, *Liberation Management: Necessary Disorganization for the Nanosecond Nineties,* **McMillan (1992).**

In the new economy, hierarchical business structures are being consigned to the shredder and replaced with flexible, fast-responding, ad hoc groups of brainworkers. Tom Peters, author of the best selling *In search of Excellence*, demonstrates that the key to success in the business of future is total engagement, dynamism, speed and independence.

Preiss, Kenneth, Rogel N. Nagel and Steven L. Goldman, *Cooperate to Compete: Building Agile Business Relationships*, Wiley (1997).

The day of the stand-alone business is over. This book is about building strategy as an "interprise," forming closer, more interactive relationships with customers, suppliers, and even competitors.

Preiss, Kenneth, Rogel N. Nagel and Steven L. Goldman, *Agile Competitors and Virtual Organizations: Strategies for Enriching the Customer*, Wiley (1997).

What is agility and why do we need it? This book is a product of the authors' research at the Iacocca Institute at Lehigh University. This book presents a vision of agile competition, which promises to affect life in the 21st century as profoundly as mass production-based competition affected life in the 20th century. By focusing on practice rather than on theory, the book describes in detail how this new form of competition is rapidly differentiating winners from losers, not just in the U.S. but around the world.

Sakaiya, Taichi, *The Knowledge-Value Revolution, or A History of the Future*, Kodabsha International (1991).

A former official at Japan's Ministry of International Trade and Industry, Sakaiya prophesies a brave new postindustrial world in which leisure time and wisdom abound but material as well as human resources are in short supply. He envisions that the mass-produced manufactures that underpin modern consumer societies will yield to goods that somehow combine utility with the equivalent of intelligence and distinctively personal appeal.

Savage, Charles M., *Fifth Generation Management: Co-Creating Through Virtual Enterprising, Dynamic Teaming, and Knowledge Networking*, Butterworth-Heinemann (1996).

Savage assists corporations in "unlocking the future" using virtual enterprising and knowledge era/knowledge worker information. In this revised edition of Savages groundbreaking work, the author covers lessons learned over the past five years since 5th Generation Management was first published, emphasizes dynamic teaching of core capabilities, and much more.

Schwartz, Evan I., *Webonomics: Nine Essential Principles for Growing Your Business on the World Wide Web,* **Broadway Books (1997).**

Wired Magazine's Jeffrey Mann reviewed this book – "The book's real value comes from Schwartz's analysis and anecdotes of what works, what doesn't and why. This book reads like a scrawled message warning about dead ends and easy passages left by explorers just ahead of us."

Senge, Peter M., *The Fifth Discipline: The Art and Practice of the Learning Organization,* **Doubleday/Currency (1990).**

Senge's focus on "systems thinking" represents a discipline that is central to reengineering business processes. This seminal work has had a major impact on business reengineering.

Tapscott, Don, *The Digital Economy: Promise and Peril in the Age of Networked Intelligence,* **McGraw-Hill (1995).**

Tapscott takes a comprehensive look at how the new technology has fundamentally transformed the way we do business, and offers practical advice on moving into the digital age. Using examples from leading-edge organizations who are successfully riding the IT wave, he describes how the new technology has immutably altered the way products are created and marketed; how they have shifted the dynamics of competition, and, in fact, have transformed all of the rules which govern business success.

Tapscott, Don, et al, *Blueprint to the Digital Economy: Wealth Creation in the Era of E-Business,* **McGraw-Hill (1998).**

Tapscott puts on an editor's hat and, along with Alex Lowy and David Ticoll, presents a collection of 20 articles that speak to all aspects of doing business in the digital age. The articles, written by members of the alliance, cover a wide range of topics from business design at GM and the role of banking in the digital economy to creating communities in cyberspace and the role of government in the networked world. The real strength of books in this genre is not their writing and presentation, which tend to be uneven, but rather the breadth of experience and perspective they communicate.

Taylor, Jim, Watts Wacker and Howard Means, *The 500-Year Delta: What Happens After What Comes Next. HarperBusiness* (1977).

Wired magazine had this to say about this book, "Wacker and Taylor sound a wake-up call for businesses interested in speculating on tomorrow's tomorrow." The authors argue that our world is on the precipice of massive change. They believe this transformation will manifest itself as a shift from reason-based to chaos-based logic; the collapse of producer-controlled consumer markets; and a splintering of social, political, and economic organization. They outline strategies to help companies and individuals succeed in the increasingly unpredictable future they describe.

Thurow, Lester C., *The Future of Capitalism: How Today's Economic Forces Shape Tomorrow's World,* William Morrow (1996).

Recognized around the world for his views and analysis of the global economy, Thurow identifies the many factors responsible for the enormous changes occurring around the globe: the rise of man-made brain-power industries, changing demographics, the impact of a global economy, the lack of a dominant world leader, and the conversion of the communist world to capitalism. With this knowledge, and asserting that the future holds great opportunity for those equipped to weather the storm of change, Thurow helps to chart a course for survival and success in the 21st century.

Weinzimer, Philip, *Getting It Right!: Creating Customer Value for Market Leadership,* Wiley (1998).

Management guru, Thomas H. Davenport says that if it's not in this book, "you don't have to worry about it." The three "Ps" model stands for Prepare, Percieve, and Provide and sets a context for market positioning and competing for the future.

Readings on Business and Technology Architecture

Martin, James, *The Great Transition: Using the Seven Disciplines of Enterprise Engineering to Align People, Technology, and Strategy,* **AMACOM, New York (1995).**

Martin describes the essential disciplines corporations need to come to grips with: advanced information technology, business reinvention, and global competition.

Steven H. Spewak and Steven C. Hill, *Enterprise Architecture Planning: Developing a Blueprint for Data, Applications and Technology,* **John Wiley & Sons (1993).**

Enterprise Architecture Planning (EAP) is a high-level blueprint for data, applications and technology. It outlines a stable business model independent of organizational boundaries, systems and procedures.

Bass, Len, Paul Clements and Rick Kazman, *Software Architecture in Practice,* **Addison-Wesley (1998).**

Drawing on their extensive experience building and evaluating architectures, the authors cover the essential technical topics, and they emphasize the importance of the business context in which large systems are designed. Their aim is to present software architecture in a real-world setting, reflecting both the constraints and the opportunities that companies encounter. Key points of both technical and organizational discussions are illustrated by a selection of "industrial-strength" case studies. These studies, undertaken by the authors and the Software Engineering Institute, describe how successful architectures have led to the fulfillment of demanding requirements and enhanced an organization's position in its business community.

Brown, William J., Raphael C. Malveau, Hays W, III McCormick, William H. Brown, and Thomas J. Mowbray, *AntiPatterns: Refactoring Software, Architectures, and Projects in Crisis,* **John Wiley (1998).**

While patterns help you to identify and implement procedures, designs and codes that work, AntiPatterns do the exact opposite; they let you zero-in on the development detonators, architectural tripwires, and personality booby traps that can spell doom for a project. Written by a team of object-oriented systems developers, AntiPatterns identifies 40 of the most common AntiPatterns in the areas of software development, architecture, and project management. The authors then show you how to detect and defuse AntiPatterns as well as supply refactored solutions for each AntiPattern presented.

Buschmann, Frank, Regine Meunier, Hans Rohnert, Peter Sommerlad, Michael Stal, *Pattern-Oriented Software Architecture – A System of Patterns*, Wiley and Sons (1996).

Pattern-oriented software architecture is an approach to software development for large-scale applications and systems. This book represents the progression and evolution of the pattern approach into a system of patterns capable of describing and documenting large-scale applications. It is a serious book for systems architects and developers of large-scale systems. This book is the winner of the 1996 Software Development "Jolt" Productivity Award.

Cook, Melissa A., *Building Enterprise Information Architectures: Reengineering Information Systems*, Prentice Hall (1996).

Less technical and detailed than other like texts, this book sets out to put business executives and managers back in control of their information systems architecture. The work is strongly influenced by Zachman frameworks.

Gamma, E., R. Helm, R. Johnson, and J. Vlissides, *Design Patterns: Elements of Reusable Object-Oriented Software*, Addison-Wesley (1995).

Lines formed at the 1994 OOPSLA conference to buy this book. The authors show how object-oriented systems exhibit recurring patterns and structures that let developers reuse successful designs and architectures without having to rediscover solutions.

Jacobson, Ivar, Martin Griss, Patrik Jonsson, *Software Reuse: Architecture, Process, Organization for Business Success*, Addison-Wesley (1997).

The book introduces the notion of software reuse as an enabler of business success. It describes how architecture, properly designed, can facilitate the graceful evolution of applications and components. The authors provide process guidelines and advise on organizational issues related to the software life cycle.

Shaffer, Steven L. and Alan R. Simon, *Transitioning to Open Systems: Concepts, Methods, & Architecture,* **Morgan Kaufman Publishers (1996).**

Organizations of all sizes have begun the process of transforming their legacy information systems into modern environments that take advantage of "open" information technologies. Emphasizing the important combination of technology and methodology, Shaffer and Simpson help readers determine a clear, realistic view of how open information technology should be deployed throughout their organization to ensure that costly, timely efforts in this realm succeed.

Shaw, M. and D. Garlan, *Software Architecture Perspectives on an Emerging Discipline,* **Prentice Hall (1996).**

Shaw and Garland examine the useful abstractions and paradigms of system design as well as key notations and tools. They present an introduction to software architecture that illustrates the current state of the discipline and examines ways in which architectural issues can impact software design.

Alexander, Christopher, *Timeless Way of Building,* **Oxford Univ. Press (1979).**

A reader writes, "This book needs plenty of reading, as it is full of ideas and images that slowly come together to form a whole. It describes "the quality with no name" that make some buildings come "alive" and be wonderful to live in. It is this same quality that makes nature so appealing. The quality is formed from patterns – the second book in the trilogy "A Pattern Language" describes a large number of patterns for architecture in detail. Another reader writes, "It is amazing how a book that propounds revolutionary architectural theory has stirred up the computer software industry. This deeply philosophical book, which is very practical and rigorous, lays the foundation for developing "pattern languages".

Eberhardt Rechtin, *Systems Architecting: Creating and Building Complex Systems,* **Prentice Hall (1991).**

From the author, "Systems architecting is the use of architecting tools and techniques (e.g., analysis, insights, heuristics metaphors, practice, ethics and modus operandi) to systems (collections of different things which collectively produce results not producible by the components, alone." The book elaborates on the first principles of the activity of systems architecting.

Readings on Component-Based Software Development and Project Management

Brown, Alan W. (Editor).*Component-Based Software Engineering:* **Selected Papers from the Software Engineering Institute. IEEE Computer Society. 1996.**

This book is a collection of works on research efforts at Carnige Mellon University's Software Engineering Institute. The papers address the development and evolution of component-based systems.

D'Souza, Desmond F. and Alan Cameron Wills, *Objects, Components and Frameworks With UML: The Catalysis Approach,* **Addison-Wesley (1999).**

This book introduces Catalysis, a next-generation method for constructing open component systems from frameworks, based on UML and OMG standards. Even if you do not actually adopt the Catalysis process, this authoritative and clear book offers a wealth of design expertise. The method's simple core, on-demand precision, and separation of concerns support component technologies and standards based on Java, CORBA and COM+.

Jell, Thomas (Editor), *Component-Based Software Engineering,* **Cambridge University Press (1998).**

This book includes coverage of the most important and current topics covered at the first Component Users Conference. The eighteen contributors address such issues as componentware platforms, component design and architecture, distributed object computing, componentware languages, patterns and frameworks, interoperability, and debugging and testing.

Szyperski, Clemens, *Component Software: Beyond Object-Oriented Programming,* **Addison-Wesley (1998).**

This book is essential to any software engineer working with component-based development. Dion Hinchcliffe of Object news describes the book – "*Component Software* is a fascinating study of the practical aspects of making components work in software development. Touching on Java, CORBA, COM, architectures, frameworks, component assembly, domain standards and much more, the author gives the reader an impressive panorama of the state-of-the-art in component technology.....But this doesn't do justice to the expressiveness, insight, and impressive range of integration between fields of component study that Szyperski puts into this book."

Frost, Stuart and Paul R. Allen, *Component-Based Development for Enterprise Systems: Applying the Select Perspective*, Cambridge Univ. Press (1998).

As businesses become increasingly adaptive and call for software that is more flexible, enterprise software development presents challenges of sheer scale and complexity that continue to accelerate at a terrific pace. The approach in this book offers a streamlined set of modeling techniques based on Unified Modeling Language (UML). It also uses a service-based architecture that provides an overall design philosophy for reusable software.

Goldberg, Adele and Kenneth S. Rubin, *Succeeding with Objects: Decision Frameworks for Project Management*, Addison-Wesley Publishing (1995).

This is a great book for object-oriented project management based on a manageable approach of work products. Written for technical project managers and their teams, this book is filled with advice distilled from the authors' extensive experience in the creation and use of object technology. It is an invaluable guide to evaluating, selecting, and working with objects for software development projects, covering programming languages, development tools, and methods for analysis and design.

Norman, Donald A., *The Design of Everyday Things*, Currency/ Doubleday (1990).

Simply put, do not attempt to build any e-Commerce applications before you read this book! The cover says it all. Amazon.com's review explains, "Anyone who designs anything to be used by humans – from physical objects to computer programs to conceptual tools – must read this book, and it is an equally tremendous read for anyone who has to use anything created by another human. It could forever change how you experience and interact with your physical surroundings, open your eyes to the perversity of bad design and the desirability of good design, and raise your expectations about how things should be designed."

Bibliography

The number of books on the business and technology aspects of e-Commerce is large and growing. We have made every attempt to include those titles that would be of the greatest interest at the time we went to press with this book. To keep abreast of the latest titles or to obtain reviews of these books, visit The Essential Object-Oriented Library for Business Engineering – it's on the Web at (http:// home1.gte.net/pfingar) and its categories include: Directions in Business, e-Commerce, Object-Oriented and Component Development, XML, Java and more. The Library contains reviews and comments from business and software practitioners.

ABA Professional Education, *A Commercial Lawyer's Take on the Electronic Purse: An Analysis of Commercial Law Issues Associated With Stored-Value Cards.* ABA Professional Education. 1998.

Adam, Nabil R and Yelena Yesha, *Electronic Commerce: Current Research Issues and Applications,* Springer Verlag (1996).

Adam, Nabil R., *Electronic Commerce: Technical, Business and Legal Issues (With CDROM),* Prentice Hall (1998).

Ahuja, Vijay, *Secure Commerce on the Internet,* AP Professional (1996).

Aklecha, Vishwa, *Object Oriented Frameworks Using C++,* The Coriolis Group (1999).

Aklecha, Vishwajit. *Object-Oriented Frameworks Using C++ and CORBA.* Coriolis Group Books. 1999.

Aldrich, Douglas F, *Mastering the Digital Marketplace: Practical Strategies for Competitiveness in the New Economy,* John Wiley & Sons (1999).

Alexander, Christopher, Timeless Way of Building. Oxford Univ. Press (1979).

Alexander, Christopher, Sara Ishikawa, Murray Silverstein, *A Pattern Language: Towns, Buildings, Construction*, Oxford Univ Press (1977).

Alexander, Michael, *Net Security: Your Digital Doberman: Sure-Fire Strategies for Wired Businesses*, Ventana Communications Group (1996).

Allen, Paul, Stuart Frost and Edward Yourdon, *Component-Based Development for Enterprise Systems: Applying the Select Perspective*, Cambridge University Press (1998).

Allen, Cliff, Deborah, Kania and Beth, Yaeckel, *Internet World Guide to One-To-One Web Marketing*, Wiley (1998).

Ambler, Scott W., *More Process Patterns : Delivering Large-Scale Systems Using Object Technology*, Cambridge University Press (1999).

Amirfaiz, Farhad, *Official Microsoft Site Server 2.0 Enterprise Edition Toolkit*, Microsoft Press (1998).

Anderson, Thomas (Editor). *Java for Business: How Companies Are Using Java to Win Customers and Make Money Now*. Van Nostrand Reinhold. (1997).

Arnold, Ken and James Gosling, *The Java Programming Language*, Addison-Wesley (1996).

Asbury, Stephen, and Scott R. Weiner, *Developing Java Enterprise Applications*, John Wiley & Sons (1999).

Baker, Abercrombie Stewart, *The Limits of Trust: Cryptography, Governments, and Electronic Commerce*, Kluwer Law International (1998).

Baker, Mike, *Strike It Rich On eBay* (The World's Largest Online Internet Auction Site), Mike Baker Publishing (1999).

Bass, Len, Paul Clements and Rick Kazman, *Software Architecture in Practice* (SEI Series in Software Engineering), Addison-Wesley (1998).

Bekkers, J. J. M., Bert-Jaap Koops and Sjaak Nouwt (Editors), *Emerging Electronic Highways: New Challenges for Politics and Law (Law and Electronic Commerce*, Kluwer Law International (1996).

Benesko, Gary G., *Inter-Corporate Business Engineering: Streamlining the Business Cycle from End to End,* Research Triangle Consultants (1996).

Berg, Cliff, *Advanced Java Development for Enterprise Applications,* Prentice Hall (1998).

Bernstein, Jake, *Strategies for the Electronic Futures Trader,* McGraw-Hill (1999).

Berry, J. A. and Gordon Linoff, *Data Mining Techniques: For Marketing, Sales, and Customer Support,* Wiley (1997).

Betancourt, Marian, *The Best Internet Businesses You Can Start,* Adams Media Corporation (1999).

Beyer, Hugh and Karen Holtzblatt, *Contextual Design: A Customer-Centered Approach to Systems Designs,* Morgan Kaufman Publishers (1997).

Birznieks, Gunther and Selena Sol, *CGI for Commerce: A Complete Web-Based Selling Solution,* IDG Books Worldwide (1997).

Bishop, William, *Strategic Marketing for the Digital Age,* NTC Business Books (1998).

Bollier, David, *Future of Electronic Commerce,* Aspen Inst. Publications Office (1996).

Bollier, David, *Sustainable Competition in Global Telecommunications: From Principle to Practice,* Aspen, Inst. Publications Office (1998).

Bollier, David, *The Globalization of Electronic Commerce,* Aspen Inst. Publications Office (1998).

Bonnett, Kendra, *The IBM Guide to Doing Business on the Internet,* McGraw-Hill (1998).

Booch, Grady, Jim Rumbaugh, and Ivar Jacobson, *Unified Modeling Language User Guide,* Addison-Wesley (1998).

Booch, Grady, *Object Solutions: Managing the Object-Oriented Project. 2nd Ed.,* Addison-Wesley (1995).

Booch, Grady. *Object-Oriented Analysis and Design With Applications,* 2nd Ed., Addison-Wesley (1994).

Boumphrey, Frank, *Professional Stylesheets for HTML and XML,* Wrox Press Inc. (1998).

Bowman, Jim, *Novell's Certified Internet Business Strategist Study Guide,* IDG Books Worldwide (1998).

Brad, Harris, *Microsoft Site Server 3.0 Bible,* DG Books Worldwide (1998).

Brown, Alan W. (Editor), *Component-Based Software Engineering:* Selected Papers from the Software Engineering Institute, IEEE Computer Society (1996).

Brown, William J., Raphael C. Malveau, Hays W, III McCormick, William H. Brown, and Thomas J. Mowbray, *AntiPatterns: Refactoring Software, Architectures, and Projects in Crisis.* John Wiley (1998).

Bruner, Rick E., *Cybernautics and USweb Corporation,* Net Results: Web Marketing that Works, Hayden Books (1998).

Bullis, Douglas, *Preparing for Electronic Commerce in Asia,* Quorum Books (1999).

Burnham, Bill, *The Electronic Commerce Report,* McGraw-Hill (1998).

Buschmann, Frank, Regine Meunier, Hans Rohnert, Peter Sommerlad, and Michael Stal (Gang of Five), Pattern-Oriented Software Architecture-A System of Patterns, Wiley and Sons (1996).

Cairncross, Frances, *The Death of Distance: How the Communications Revolution Will Change Our Lives,* Harvard Business School Press. (1997).

Cameron, Debra, *E-commerce Security Strategies: Protecting the Enterprise,* Computer Technology Research Corporation (1998).

Cameron, Debra, *Electronic Commerce: The New Business Platform for the Internet,* Computer Technology Research Corporation (1997).

Camp, L. Jean, *Trust and Risk in Internet Commerce,* MIT Press (1999).

Cashin, Jerry, *E-Commerce Success: Building a Global Business Architecture,* Computer Technology Research Corporation (1999).

Cashin, Jerry, *Web Commerce: Developing and Implementing Effective Business Solutions,* Computer Technology Research Corporation (1998).

Cataudella, Joe, Dave Greely and Ben Sawyer, *Creating Stores on the Web: Insider's Guide to Setting Up a Profitable Cybershop (On the Web Series),* Peachtree Press (1998).

Champy, James, *Reengineering Management: The Mandate for New Leadership,* HarperBusiness (1995).

Chan, Sally, Hal Stern, Peter Keen and Craigg Balance, *Gaining Control of Electronic Commerce,* John Wiley & Sons (1998).

Chang, Dan and Dan Harkey, *Client/Server Data Access With Java and XML,* John Wiley & Sons (1998).

Charles, Ann Carol, Christopher P. Foss and Shamita R. Dewan, *Globalizing Electronic Commerce: Report on the International Forum on Electronic Commerce,* Center for Strategic & Int'l Studies (1996).

Chase Larry, *Essential Business Tactics for the Net,* John Wiley & Sons (1998).

Chesher, Chesher and Rukesh Kaura, *Electronic Business Communications* (Practitioner Series), Springer Verlag (1998).

Chissick, Michael and Alistair, Kelman, *E Commerce,* Sweet & Maxwell (1998).

Chung, David R., *Component Java: Developing Components With Java Beans and Activex (JavaMasters Series),* McGraw-Hill (2000).

Cleary, Timothy, *Business Information Technology (Frameworks),* Pitman Pub Ltd. (1998).

Clemente, Peter, *State of the Net: The New Frontier,* McGraw-Hill (1998).

Coad, Peter, Eric Lefebvre and Jeff De Luca, *Java Modeling in Color With UML: Enterprise Components and Process,* Prentice Hall (1999).

Coad, Peter, Mark Mayfield and Jon Kern, *Java Design: Building Better Apps and Applets, 2/e,* Prentice Hall (1998).

Cobb, Stephen, and Michael Cobb, *Implementing SET: A Guide to the Visa/MasterCard Secure Electronic Transaction Specification,* Computing McGraw-Hill (1997).

Cohan, Peter S., *Net Profit: How to Invest and Compete in the Real World of Internet Business,* Jossey-Bass Publishers (1999).

Columbus, Louis, *Deploying Electronic Commerce Solutions with Microsoft BackOffice,* Microsoft Press (1999).

Cook, Melissa A., Building Enterprise Information Architectures: Reengineering Information Systems, Prentice Hall (1996).

Coplien, James O. and Douglas C. Schmidt (Editors), *Pattern Languages of Program Design,* Addison Wesley (1995).

Cornell, Gary and Cay S. Horstmann. *Core Java.* Prentice Hall (1997).

Coyle, Diane, *The Weightless World: Strategies for Managing the Digital Economy,* MIT Press (1998).

Cross, Thomas B, *Digital Money - Building and Expanding an Online Business Internationally,* VHS Tape (1996).

Dahl, Andrew, Leslie, Lesnick and Lisa, Morgan, *Internet Commerce,* New Riders (1996).

Danish, Sherif and Patrick Gannon, *Building Database-Driven Web Catalogs,* McGraw-Hill (1998).

Davenport, Thomas and Laurence Prusak, *Working Knowledge: How Organizations Manage What They Know,* Harvard Business School Press (1997).

Davidow, William H. and Michael S. Malone. *The Virtual Corporation: Structuring and Revitalizing the Corporation for the 21st Century,* Harper Collins (1992).

Davis, Stan and Christopher Meyer, *Blur: The Speed of Change in the Connected Economy,* Hardcover (1998).

De Kare-Silver, Michael, *Electronic Shock: How Retailers and Manufacturers Can Shape the Coming Shopping Revolution,* AMACOM (1999).

De Kare-Silver, Michael, *Strategy in Crisis: Why Business Urgently Needs a Completely New Approach,* New York University Press (1998).

Denning, Dorothy E. and Peter J. Denning, *Internet Besieged: Countering Cyberspace Scofflaws,* Addison-Wesley Pub Co, (1997).

Department of Defense, *Introduction to Department of Defense Electronic Commerce: A Handbook for Business,* Version 2. DIANE Publishing Co. (1997).

Douglass, Bruce Powel, *Doing Hard Time: Developing Real-Time Systems with UML, Objects, Frameworks and Patterns,* Addison-Wesley (1999).

Downes, Larry, and Chunka Mui, *Unleashing the Killer App: Digital Strategies for Market Dominance,* Harvard Business School Press (1998).

Drew, Grady N., *Using Set for Secure Electronic Commerce,* Prentice Hall (1999).

Drucker, Peter Ferdinand, *Management Challenges for the 21st Century,* HarperBusiness (1999).

D'Souza, Desmond F. and Alan Cameron Wills, *Objects, Components and Frameworks With UML*: The Catalysis Approach. Addison-Wesley (1999).

Eager, Bill, *Complete Idiot's Guide to Marketing Online,* Que (1999),

Easton Jaclyn, *Strikingitrich.com (Striking It Rich.com): Profiles of 23 Incredibly Successful Websites You've Probably Never Heard Of,* McGraw-Hill (1998).

Eckel, Bruce, *Thinking in Java,* Prentice Hall Computer Books (1999).

Edwards, Jeri, *3-Tier Client/Server at Work,* Wiley (1999).

Edwards, Paul, Sarah, Edwards and Linda Rohrbough, *Making Money in Cyberspace,* J. P. Tarcher (1998).

Ellsworth, Jill H., and Matthew V. Ellsworth, *The New Internet Business Book*, John Wiley & Sons (1996).

Emmerson, Bob and David Greetham, *Computer Telephony and Wireless Technologies: Future Directions in Communications Computer,* Technology Research Corporation (1997).

Evans, David S., and Richard Schmalensee, *Paying With Plastic: The Digital Revolution in Buying and Borrowing,* MIT Press (1999).

Fayad, Mohamed, and Ralph Johnson (Editors), *Domain-Specific Application Frameworks: Frameworks Experience by Industry,* John Wiley & Sons (1999).

Fayad, Mohamed, Douglas C. Schmidt and Ralph Johnson (Editors), *Building Application Frameworks: Object-Oriented Foundations of Framework Design,* John Wiley & Sons (1999).

Fayad, Mohamed, Douglas C. Schmidt and Ralph Johnson (Editors), *Implementing Application Frameworks: Object-Oriented Frameworks at Work,* John Wiley & Sons (1999).

Figallo, Cliff, *Hosting Web Communities: Building Relationships, Increasing Customer Loyalty, and Maintaining a Competitive Edge,* Wiley (1998).

Fingar, Peter, Dennis Read and Jim Stikeleather, *Next Generation Computing: Distributed Objects for Business,* Foreword by Chris Stone, CEO of OMG, Prentice Hall (1996).

Fingar, Peter, Steven Hagy and Michael Fuller, *Climb from Chaos: Achieving CMM Level 2 Quality in E-Commerce,* Meghan-Kiffer Press (2000).

Fingar, Peter, *The Blueprint for Business Objects,* Prentice Hall (1996).

First International Workshop on Agent-Mediated Electronic Trading, *International Workshop on Agent-Mediated Electronic Trading,* 1998, Springer Verlag (1999).

Fischer, Layna, *New Tools for New Times: Electronic Commerce,* Future Strategies (1996).

Flanagan, David, and Mike Loukides, *Java in a Nutshell: A Desktop Quick Reference,* O'Reilly & Associates (1997).

Flanagan, David. *Java in a Nutshell.* O'Reilly & Associates (1997).

Flynn, Peter, *Understanding SGML and XML Tools: Practical Programs for Handling Structured Text,* Kluwer Academic (1998).

Ford, Warwick and Michael S. Baum, *Secure Electronic Commerce: Building the Infrastructure for Digital Signatures and Encryption,* Prentice Hall Press (1997).

Freeman, Eric, Susanne Hupfer and Ken Arnold, *JavaSpaces: Principles, Patterns and Practice (The Jini™ Technology Series),* Addison-Wesley (1999).

Frost, Stuart and Paul R. Allen, *Component-Based Development for Enterprise Systems*: Applying the Select Perspective. Cambridge Univ. Press (1998).

Gamma, E., R. Helm, R. Johnson, and J. Vlissides (Gang of Four), *Design Patterns: Elements of Resuable Object-Oriented Software.* Addison-Wesley (1995).

Gardner, Karen M., Alexander R. Rush, Michael Crist, Robert Konitzer, James J. Odell, Bobbin Teegarden and Robert Konitzer, *Cognitive Patterns: Problem-Solving Frameworks for Object Technology,* Cambridge University Press (1998).

Garfinkel, Simson and Gene Spafford, *Web Security & Commerce* (Nutshell Handbook), O'Reilly & Associates (1997).

Geary, David M, Graphic *Java 2, Mastering the JFC: Swing* (Sun Microsystems Press Java Series), Prentice Hall (1999).

Gerlach, Douglas, *The Complete Idiot's Guide to Online Investing,* Macmillan Publishing Company (1999).

Ghosh, Anup A., *E-Commerce Security: Weak Links, Best Defenses,* John Wiley & Sons (1998).

Gibson, Rowan. *Rethinking the Future: Rethinking Business, Principles, Competition, Control & Complexity, Leadership, Markets and the World,* Nicholas Brealey (1997).

Gielgun, Ron E, *How to Succeed in Internet Business by Employing Real-World Strategies; Business Approaches,* Actium Publishing Inc. (1998).

Goldberg, Adele and Kenneth S. Rubin, *Succeeding with Objects: Decision Frameworks for Project Management,* Addison-Wesley (1995).

Goldfarb, Charles F., Steve Pepper and Chet Ensign, *SGML Buyer's Guide: A Unique Guide to Determining Your Requirements and Choosing the Right SGML and XML Products and Services,* Prentice Hall (1998).

Goldman, S. L., R. N. Nagel, and K. Preiss. *Agile Competitors and Virtual Organizations: Strategies for Enriching the Customer,* Van Nostrand Reinhold (1994).

Goncalves, Marcus McSe, *Implementing and Supporting Web Sites Using Microsoft Site Server 3* (Prentice Hall Ptr McSe Certification Series), Prentice Hall (1999).

Gonzalez, Fernando and William Rhee, *Strategies for the On-Line Day Trader: Trading Techniques for On-Line Profits,* McGraw-Hill (1999).

Goossens, Michel and Sebastion Rahtz, *The Latex Web Companion: Integrating Tex, HTML and XML* (Tools and Techniques for Computer Typesetting Series), Addison-Wesley (1999).

Goralski, Walter, *Virtual Private Networks: Achieving Secure Internet Commerce and Enterprisewide Communications,* Computer Technology Research Corporation (1999).

Gore, Jacob, *Object Structures: Building Object-Oriented Software Components With Eiffel,* Addison-Wesley (1996).

Gosling, James , Bill Joy and Guy L. Steele, *The Java Language Specification.* Addison-Wesley (1996).

Gosling, James and Frank Yellin, *The Java Application Programming Interface.* Addison-Wesley (1996).

Govoni, Darren, Java *Application Frameworks,* Wiley (1999).

Grady, Drew, *Using Set for Secure Electronic Transactions* (With CDROM), Prentice Hall (1998).

Grand, Mark, *Patterns in Java, Volume 1,* Wiley (1998).

Grand, Mark, *Patterns in Java, Volume 2,* Wiley (1999).

Grand, Mark, *Patterns in Java, Volume 3,* Wiley (2000).

Grand, Mark. *Java Language Reference.* O'Reilly & Associates (1997).

Grant, Gail, *Understanding Set: Visa International's Official Guide to Secure Electronic Transactions,* McGraw-Hill (2000).

Gurian, Phil H., *E-Mail Business Strategies,* Grand National Press (1999).

Gutterman, Alan S., *The Professional's Guide to Doing Business on the Internet,* Harcourt Brace Professional Publishers (1999).

Hackathorn, Richard D., *Web Farming for the Data Warehouse,* Morgan Kaufman Publishers (1998).

Haddad, Jane, *Going, Going, Gone! How To Sell On eBay™ In 4 Easy Steps,* Jane Haddad (Spiral Bound) (1999).

Hagel, John and Arthur, G Armstrong, *Net Gain: Expanding Markets through Virtual Communities,* Harvard Business School Press (1997).

Haggard, Mary, *Survival Guide to Web Site Development,* Microsoft Press (1998).

Haggard, Mary, *Understanding Web Publishing* (Strategic Technologies), Microsoft Press (1998).

Hamel, Gary, and C. K. Prahalad. *Competing for the Future: Breakthrough Strategies for Seizing Control of Your Industry and Creating the Markets of Tomorrow,* Harvard Business School Press (1994).

Hance, Olivier and Suzanne Dionne Balz, *Business & Law on the Internet,* McGraw-Hill (1997).

Hardesty, David E., *Electronic Commerce: Taxation and Planning,* Warren Gorham & Lamont (1999).

Harold, Elliotte Rusty, *XML: Extensible Markup Language,* IDG Books Worldwide (1998).

Harris, Wayne, *Cybertools for Business,* Warner Books (1997).

Hartman, Amir, John Kador and John Sifonis, *Net Ready,* McGraw-Hill (1999).

Haylock, Christina Ford, Len Muscarella and Steve Case, *Net Success: 24 Leaders in Web Commerce Show You How to Put the Web to Work for Your Business,* Adams Media Corporation (1999).

Haynes, Ted, *Electronic Commerce Dictionary: The Definitive Terms for Doing Business on the Information Superhighway,* Robleda Co. (1995).

Hinchcliffe, Dion and Paul Evitts, *UML Pattern Language: Patterns of Form, Usage and Style,* MacMillan (1999).

Hinkelman, Edward G and Molly, Thurmond, *A Short Course in International Payments: How to Use Letters of Credit, D/P and D/A Terms, Prepayment, Credit and Cyberpayments in International Transactions,* World Trade Press (1998).

Holder, Greg, Frank, Catalano and Bud E. Smith, *Online Business Kit for Dummies* With CDROM, IDG Books Worldwide (1999).

Holden, Greg, *Small Business Internet for Dummies,* IDG Books Worldwide (1998).

Holden, Greg, *Starting an Online Business for Dummies,* IDG Books (1999).

Hoque, Reaz and Tarun Sharma, *Programming Web Components,* McGraw-Hill (1998).

Horstmann, Cay S., and Gary Cornell, *Core Java 2, Volume 1: Fundamentals, 4/e,* Prentice Hall (1999).

Horton, Ivor, *Beginning Java 2,* Wrox Press (1999).

Hoskin, Jim and Vincent Lupiano, *Exploring IBM's Bold Internet Strategy,* Maximum Press (1997).

Howard, Robert, *Site Server 3.0 Personalization and Membership,* Wrox Press Inc (1999).

Hunter, Jason, William Crawford, Paula Ferguson, *Java Servlet Programming,* O'Reilly & Associates (1998).

IBM Object-Oriented Technology Center, Foreword by Kennith Rubin. *Developing Object-Oriented Software: An Experience-Based Approach.* Prentice Hall (1997).

Inc. Micro Modeling Associates, *Microsoft Commerce Solutions Web Technology,* Microsoft Press (1999).

Jacobson, Ivar, Grady Booch and Jim Rumbaugh, *The Unified Software Development Process*, Addison-Wesley (1999).

Jacobson, Ivar, Martin Griss and Patrik Jonsson, *Software Reuse: Architecture, Process and Organization for Business Success*, Addison-Wesley (1997).

Jacobson, Ivar, P. Jonsson and G. Overgaard, *Object-Oriented Software Engineering*, Addison-Wesley (1992).

James, Geoffrey, *Business Wisdom of the Electronic Elite: 34 Winning Management Strategies from CEOs at Microsoft, Compaq, Sun, Hewlett-Packard, and Other Top Companies*, Random House (1996).

Jamison, Brian, Josh, Gold and Warren, Jamison, *Electronic Selling : Twenty-Three Steps to E-Selling Profits*, McGraw-Hill (1997).

Jardin, Cary A., *Java Electronic Commerce Sourcebook: All the Software and Expert Advice You Need to Open Your Own Virtual Store*, Wiley (1997).

Javed, Naseem, *Domain Wars*, Linkbridge Publications (1999).

Jell, Thomas. *Component-Based Software Engineering.* Cambridge University Press (1998).

Jenkins, Glenn P., *Information Technology and Innovation in Tax Administration* (Law and Electronic Commerce, V. 2), Kluwer Law International (1996).

Jezequel, Jean-Marc, Michel Train and Christine Mingins. *Design Patterns with Contracts*, Addison-Wesley (1999).

Jia, Xiaoping, *Object-Oriented Software Development in Java: Styles, Patterns, and Frameworks*, Addison-Wesley (1999).

Jilovec, Nahid, *The A to Z of EDI: And Its Role in E-Commerce*, Duke Communications (1998).

Jones, Caper, *Applied Software Measurement: Assuring Productivity and Quality.* McGraw-Hill (1996).

Jones, John W., Ph.D., *The Virtual Entrepreneur: Electronic Commerce in the 21st Century* (Virtual Management, Vol. 1), Business Psychology Research Inst. (1999).

Jubin, Henri, Jurgen Friedrichs and Jalapeno Team, *Enterprise JavaBeans by Example,* Prentice Hall (1999).

Judson, Bruce and Kate Kelly, *Hyperwars: Eleven Rules for Surviving & Profiting in the Age of On-LineBusiness,* Scribner (1999).

Kalakota, Ravi and Andrew B. Whinston, *Electronic Commerce : A Manager's Guide,* Addison-Wesley Pub Co (1996).

Kalakota, Ravi and Andrew B. Whinston, *Frontiers of Electronic Commerce,* Addison-Wesley Pub Co. (1996).

Kalakota, Ravi and Marcia, Robinson, *E-Business; Roadmap for Success,* Addison-Wesley (1999).

Kalakota, Ravi and Andrew, B. Whinston, *Readings in Electronic Commerce,* Addison-Wesley (1996).

Keen, Peter G. W. and Craigg Ballance, *On-Line Profits: A Manager's Guide to Electronic Commerce,* Harvard Business School Press (1997).

Kelly, Kevin, *New Rules for the New Economy: 10 Radical Strategies for a Connected World,* Viking Press (1998).

Kelly, Kevin. *Out of Control: The Rise of Neo-biological Civilization,* Addison-Wesley (1994).

Kent, Peter and Tara, Calishain, *Poor Richard's Internet Marketing and Promotions: How to Promote Yourself, Your Business, Your Ideas Online,* Top Floor (1999).

Kilmer, William E., *Getting Your Business Wired: Using Computer Networking and the Internet to Grow Your Business,* AMACOM (1999).

Kilov, Haim (Editor) and William Harvey. *Object-Oriented Behavioral Specifications.* Kluwer Academic Pub., (1996).

Kilov, Haim and J. Ross, *Information Modeling: An Object-Oriented Approach.* Prentice Hall (1994).

King, Janice M., Paul Knight and James H. Mason, *Web Marketing Cookbook,* John Wiley & Sons (1997).

Klusch, Matthias and Gerhard Weiss, *Cooperative Information Agents II: Learning, Mobility, and Electronic Commerce for Information Discovery on the Internet:* Second International works by CIA '9, Springer Verlag (1998).

Konopka, Ray, and Jeff, Duntemann, *Developing Custom Delphi 3 Components*, The Coriolis Group (1997).

Kosiur, David R., *Understanding Electronic Commerce,* Microsoft Press (1997).

Kruchten, Philippe. *Rational Unified Process.* Addison-Wesley (1998).

Ladd, Eric and Jim O'Donnell, *Using HTML 4, XML, and Java 1.2,* MacMillan Publishing Company (1998).

Lamersdorf, Winfried, Michael Merz and J. Hartmanis, *Trends in Distributed Systems for Electronic Commerce,* Springer Verlag (1998).

Larsson, Mats and David Lundberg, *The Transparent Market: Management Challenges in the Electronic Age,* St Martins Press (1998).

Lea, Doug, *Concurrent Programming in Java: Design Principles and Patterns,* Addison-Wesley (2000).

Leebaert, Derek, *The Future of the Electronic Marketplace,* MIT Press (1998).

Lemay, Laura and Charles L. Perkins, *Teach Yourself Java 1.1 in 21 Days.* Sams (1996).

Lessard, Bill and Steve Bald, *Net Slaves: Tales of Working the Web,* McGraw-Hill (1999).

Leventhal, Michael, David Lewis and Matthew Fuchs, *Designing XML Internet Applications* (Charles F. Goldfarb Series), Prentice Hall (1998).

Lewis, Ted, *Object-Oriented Application Frameworks,* Prentice Hall (1996).

Light, Richard, and Tim Bray, *Presenting XML,* Sams (1997).

Lim, Wayne C., *Managing Software Reuse: A Comprehensive Guide to Strategically Reengineering the Organization for Reusable Components,* Prentice Hall (1998).

Litan, Robert and William A. Niskanen, *Going Digital: A Guide to Policy in the Digital Age,* Brookings Inst. (1998).

Litan, Robert E. and Peter P. Swire, *None of Your Business: World Data Flows, Electronic Commerce, & the European Privacy Directive,* Brookings Institute (1998).

Loeb, Larry, *Secure Electronic Transactions: Introduction and Technical Reference,* Artech House (1998).

Lomas, Mark, *Security Protocols: International Workshop, Cambridge, United Kingdom April 10-12, 1996: Proceedings,* Springer Verlag (1997).

Loshin, Pete and Paul Murphy, *Electronic Commerce: On-Line Ordering and Digital Money,* Charles River Media (1997).

Lowery, Joseph, *Buying Online for Dummies,* IDG Books (1998).

Lundquist, Heeter Leslie, *Selling Online for Dummies,* IDG Books Worldwide (1998).

Lynch, Daniel C and Leslie Heeter Lundquist, *Digital Money: The New Era of Internet Commerce,* John Wiley & Sons (1995).

Maddox, Kate, and Dana Blankenhorn, *Web Commerce: Building a Digital Business,* Wiley & Sons (1998).

Markman, Jon D, *Online Investing (Independent),* Microsoft Press (1999).

Marks, Steven, *EDI Purchasing: The Electronic Gateway to the Future* (Purchasing Excellence Series), Pt Pubns (1997).

Marshall, Chris, *Software Components for the Enterprise: Building Business Objects with UML, Java, and XML,* Addison-Wesley Pub Co (1999).

Marshall, Donis, *Activex/OLE Programming: Building Stable Components With Microsoft Foundation Class,* R&D Books (1998).

Martin, Chuck, *Net Future: The 7 Cybertrends That Will Drive Your Business, Create New Wealth, and Define Your Future,* McGraw-Hill (1998).

Martin, James, *The Great Transition: Using the Seven Disciplines of Enterprise Engineering to Align People, Technology, and Strartegy,* AMACOM (1995).

Martin, James and James Odell, *Object-Oriented Methods: Pragmatic Considerations.* Prentice Hall (1996).

Martin, James and James Odell, *Object-Oriented Methods: A Foundation,* 2ed, UML Edition. Prentice Hall (1998).

Martin, James, *Cybercorp: The New Business Revolution,* Amacom Book Division (1996).

Martin, Teresa A, *Project Cool Guide to XML for Web Designer,* John Wiley & Sons(1999).

Maruyama, Hiroshi, Kent Tamure and Naohiko Uramoto, *XML and Java: Developing Web Applications*, Addison-Wesley (1999).

Mathiesen, Michael, Jan Zimmerman and Jerry Yang, *Marketing on the Internet: A Proven 12-Step Plan for Selling Your Products and Services to Millions over the Information Superhighway,* Maximum Press (1998).

Matthijssen, Luuk, *Interfacing Between Lawyers and Computers: An Architecture for Knowledge-Based Interfaces to Legal Databases*, Kluwer Academic Pub. (1999).

McComb, Gordon, *Web Commerce Cookbook,* John Wiley & Sons (1997).

McGrath, Sean, *XML by Example: Building E-Commerce Applications,* Prentice Hall (1998).

McKenna, Regis, *Relationship Marketing: Successful Strategies for the Age of the Customer,* Addison-Wesley (1993).

McKenna, Regis, *Real Time: Preparing for the Age of the Never Satisfied Customer,* Harvard Business School Press (1997).

McKeown, Patrick G. and Richard T. Watson, *Metamorphosis : A Guide to the World Wide Web & Electronic Commerce:* Version 2.0, John Wiley & Sons (1997).

Megginson, David, *Structuring XML Documents,* Prentice Hall (1998).

Merkow, Mark S. and Ken L. Wheeler, *Building SET Applications for Secure Transactions,* John Wiley & Sons (1998).

Meyer, Bertrand, *Object-Oriented Software Construction,* 2/e Prentice Hall (1988).

Micro Modeling Associates, *Microsoft Commerce Solutions,* Microsoft Press (1999).

Microsoft, *eCommerce Development With CDROM,* Microsoft Press (1999).

Minik, Phyllis Davis, *EDI QuickStart ebook,* Advanced EDI and Barcoding Corp. (1999).

Minoli, Daniel and Emma Minoli, *Web Commerce Technology Handbook,* McGraw-Hill (1997).

Mitrakas, Andreas, *Open EDI and Law in Europe: A Regulatory Framework,* Kluwer Law Intl. (1997).

Mitter, Swasti and Maria Ines Bastos, *Europe and Developing Countries in the Globalised Information Economy: Employment and Distance Education* (Unu/Intech Studies in New Technology), Routledge (1999).

Mohr, Stephen F, *Designing Distributed Applications With XML: ASP IE5 LDAP and MSMQ,* Wrox Press (1999).

Monson-Haefel, Richard and Mike Loukides, *Enterprise JavaBeans,* O'Reilly & Associates (1999).

Moore, Geoffrey A., *Inside the Tornado: Marketing Strategies from Silicon Valley's Cutting Edge,* HarperBusiness (1995).

Moore, James F *The Death of Competition: Leadership and Strategy in the Age of Business Ecosystems,* HarperBusiness (1996).

Mougayar, Walid, *Opening Digital Markets: Battle Plans and Business Strategies for Internet Commerce,* McGraw-Hill (1997).

Mowbray, Thomas J. and William A. Ruh, *Inside Corba: Distributed Object Standards and Applications.* Addison-Wesley (1997).

Moynihan, James J. and Marcia L. McLure, *EDI: A Guide to Electronic Data Interchange and Electronic Commerce Applications in the Healthcare Industry,* Irwin Professional (1996).

Multer, Kent, *The Official Miva Web-Scripting Book; Shopping Carts, Feedback Forms, Guestbooks, and More,* Top Floor Publishing (1999).

Nagel, Karl D. and Glen Gray, *2000 Miller Electronic Commerce Assurance Services,* Harcourt Brace (1999).

Nash, Tom and the Institute of Directors, *E Commerce.* Kogan Page Ltd. (1999).

Naughton, Patrick, *The Java Handbook,* McGraw-Hill (1996).

Nemzow, Martin, *Building Cyberstores: Installation, Transaction Processing, and Management.* McGraw-Hill (1997).

Newcombe, Tod, *Electronic Commerce: A Guide for Public Officials,* Government Technology Press (1998).

Newell, Frederick, *The New Rules of Marketing: How to Use One-To-One Relationship Marketing to Be the Leader in Your Industry,* Irwin (1997).

Norman Donald A., *The Design of Everyday Things,* Currency/ Doubleday (1990).

North, Simon, Paul Hermans, Sams *Teach Yourself XML in 21 Days*, Sams (1999).

O'Dell, Susan M. and Joan A. Pajunen, *The Butterfly Customer: Capturing the Loyalty of Today's Elusive Consumer,* Wiley (1997).

OECD, *Electronic Commerce: Opportunities and Challenges for Government.* ISBN: 9264155120, OECD (1997).

OECD, *Gateways to the Global Market: Consumers and Electronic Commerce,* OECD (1998).

Olfman, Lorne, *Organizational Memory Systems: A Special Double Issue of the Journal of Organizational Computing and Electronic Commerce,* Lawrence Erlbaum Assoc (1999).

Orfali, Robert and Dan Harkey, *Client/Server Programming With Java and Corba 2/e.* Wiley (1998).

Orfali, Robert, and Dan Harkey, and Jeri Edwards. *Instant Corba.* John Wiley & Sons. 1997

Orfali, Robert, Dan Harkey and Jeri Edwards, *Essential Client Server Survival Guide,* 3rd Edition, Wiley (1999).

Orfali, Robert, Dan Harkey, and Jeri Edwards, *The Essential Distributed Objects Survival Guide,* Wiley (1995).

Pallot, Marc and Victor Sandoval, *Concurrent Enterprising: Toward the Concurrent Enterprise in the Era of the Internet and Electronic Commerce,* Kluwer International (1998)

Papows, Jeff and David Moschella, *Enterprise.Com: Market Leadership in the Information Age,* Perseus Books (1998).

Pardi, J. William, *XML in Action,* Microsoft Press (1999).

Partridge, Chris, *Business Objects: Re-Engineering for Re-Use.* Butterworth-Heinemann (1996).

Payne, Judith E., *A change of course: the importance to DOD of international standards for electronic commerce,* ASIN 0833011685.

Payne, Judith E., *Electronic Data Interchange (EDI: Using Electronic Commerce to Enhance Defense Logistics),* Rand Corporation (1991).

Peppers, Don and Martha Rogers, *Enterprise One to One: Tools for Competing in the Interactive Age.* Currency/Doubleday (1997).

Peppers, Don and Martha Rogers, *The One-To-One Future: Building Relationships One Customer at a Time,* Currency/Doubleday (1997).

Peters, Tom, *Liberation Management: Necessary Disorganization for the Nanosecond Nineties,* McMillan (1992).

Pew, John A., *Instant Java, 2nd Ed.,* Prentice Hall. (1997).

Phillips Publishing, *Phillips Who's Who in Electronic Commerce,* Phillips Publishing Company (1996).

Pine, B. Joseph and Stan Davis, *Mass Customization: The New Frontier in Business Competition,* Harvard Business School Press (1999).

Porter, Michael E, *Competitive Advantage: Creating and Sustaining Superior Performance,* Free Press (1998).

Porter, Michael E., *On Competition,* Harvard Business School Press (1998).

Potts, Anthony and David Friedel, *Java Programming Language Handbook: Programming Language Handbook,* Coriolis Group (1996).

Powers, Shelley and Ron Petrusha, *Developing ASP Components,* O'Reilly & Associates (1999).

Preiss Bruno R., *Data Structures and Algorithms With Object-Oriented Design Patterns in Java,* Wiley (1999).

Preiss, Bruno R., *Data Structures and Algorithms With Object-Oriented Design Patterns in Java,* Wiley (1999).

Preiss, Kenneth, Rogel N. Nagel and Steven L. Goldman, *Cooperate to Compete: Building Agile Business Relationships,* Wiley (1997).

Rechtin, Eberhardt, Systems Architecting: Creating and Building Complex Systems. Prentice Hall (1991).

Robert S. Kaplan and David P. Norton. *The Balanced Scorecard: Translating Strategy into Action,* Harvard Business School Press (1996).

Roberts, Simon, Philip Heller, and Michael Ernest, *Complete Java 2 Certification Study Guide,* Sybex (1999).

Roman, Ed, *Mastering Enterprise JavaBeans: Practical Methods for Building Enterprise Applications,* John Wiley & Sons (1999).

Romm, Celia T. and Fay Sudweeks, *Doing Business Electronically: A Global Perspective of Electronic Commerce* (Computer Supported Cooperative Work), Springer Verlag (1998).

Romm, Celia T. and Fay Sudweeks, *Doing Business on the Internet: Forms and Analysis.* Intellectual Property Series. Law Journal Seminars-Press. Springer Verlag (1997).

Romm, Celia T. and Fay Sudweeks, *Doing Business on the Internet; Opportunities and Pitfalls,* Springer-Verlag (1999).

Rosenfeld, Louis and Peter Morville, *Information Architecture for the World Wide Web,* O'Reilly & Associates, (1998).

Rosenoer, Jonathan and Douglas Armstrong, *The Clickable Corporation: Using Innovative Ideas to Profit from the Internet*, Free Press (1999).

Ross, Manning L., *businessplan.com: how to write a web-woven strategic business plan*, Oasis Press (1998).

Rounds, Michael F., *Fishin With a Net.* 5th Ed., C P M Systems (1998).

Sokol, Phyllis K., *From EDI to Electronic Commerce: A Business Initiative*, McGraw Hill Text (1995).

Royce, Walker, *Software Project Management: A Unified Framework*, Addison-Wesley (1998).

Rudy, Dale and Diane Rudy, *Antiqs4u, Inc. Buyers/Sellers Guide for eBay Auctions and More*, Antiqs4u, Inc. (1999).

Rumbaugh, Jim, Grady Booch and Ivar Jacobson, *The Unified Modeling Language Reference Manual.* Addison-Wesley (1999).

Sakaiya, Taichi, *The Knowledge-Value Revolution, or A History of the Future*, Kodabsha International (1991).

Sametinger, J., *Software Engineering With Reusable Components*, Springer Verlag (1997).

Savage, Charles M., *Fifth Generation Management: Co-Creating Through Virtual Enterprising, Dynamic Teaming, and Knowledge Networking*, Butterworth-Heinemann (1996).

Schiller, Dan, *Digital Capitalism: Networking the Global Market System*, MIT Press (1999).

Schmied, Gerhard E., *High Quality Messaging and Electronic Commerce: Technical Foundations, Standards, and Protocols*, Springer Verlag (1999).

Schwartz, Evan I., *Digital Darwinism: Seven Breakthrough Business Strategies for Surviving in the Cutthroat Web Economy*, Broadway Books (1999).

Schwartz, Evan I., *Webonomics: Nine Essential Principles for Growing Your Business on the World Wide Web*, Broadway Books (1997).

Schweighofer, Erich, *Legal Knowledge Representation: Automatic Text Analysis in Public International and European Law* (Law and Electronic Commerce, V. 7), (1999).

Selzer, Richard, *Shop Online the Lazy Way*, Macmillan General Reference (1999).

Senge, Peter M., *The Fifth Discipline: The Art and Practice of the Learning Organization*, Doubleday/Currency (1990).

Senge, Peter M., Art Kleiner, Charlotte Roberts, George Roth and Rick Ross (Editors), *The Dance of Change*, Doubleday (1999).

Sexton, Conor, *E Commerce and Security*, Butterworth-Heinemann (1999).

Seybold, Patricia B and Ronni T Marshak, *Customers.Com: How to Create a Profitable Business Strategy for the Internet and Beyond*, Times Books (1998).

Shaffer, Steven L., and Alan R. Simon, *Transitioning to Open Systems: Concepts, Methods, & Architecture*, Morgan Kaufman Publishers (1996).

Shakun, Melvin F., *Negotiation Processes: Modeling Frameworks and Information*, Kluwer Academic (1996).

Shapiro, Carl and Hal, R Varian, *Information Rules: A Strategic Guide to the Network Economy*, Harvard Business School Press (1998).

Shaw, M. and D. Garlan, *Software Architecture Perspectives on an Emerging Discipline*, Prentice Hall (1996).

Shurety, Samantha, *E-Business with Net Commerce*, Prentice Hall (1999).

Sickle Ted Van, Truman, T. Van Sickle, *Reusable Software Components: Object-Oriented Embedded Systems Programming in C*, Prentice Hall (1996).

Siebel, Thomas M., Pat House and Charles R. Schwab, *Cyber Rules: Strategies for Excelling at E-Business*, Doubleday (1999).

Siegel , David, *Futurize Your Enterprise: Business Strategy in the Age of the E-customer*, John Wiley & Sons (1999).

Silverstein, Barry, *Business-To-Business Internet Marketing,* Maximum Press (1998).

Simensky, Melvin, Neil J. Wilkof and Lanning G. Bryer, *Intellectual Property in the International Marketplace: Valuation, Protection, Exploitation, and Electronic Commerce,* John Wiley & Sons (1999).

Simpson, John E., *Just XML,* Prentice Hall (1998).

Sims, Oliver and Peter Eeles, *Building Business Objects,* John Wiley & Sons (1998).

Smith, Bud E. and Frank Catalano, *Marketing Online for Dummies,* IDG Books Worldwide (1998).

Smith, Norman E., *Practical Guide to SGML/XML Filters,* Wordware Publishing (1998).

Spewak, Steven H. and Steven C. Hill, *Enterprise Architecture Planning: Developing a Blueprint for Data, Applications and Technology,* John Wiley & Sons (1993).

Spooner, Nick, *The Wizard of E; Notes from the Digital Warzone,* Capstone (1999).

St. Laurent, Simon and Ethan Cerami, *Building XML Applications,* Osborne McGraw-Hill (1999).

St. Laurent, Simon, and Robert, J. Bigger, *Inside XML DTD's Scientific and Technical,* McGraw-Hill (1999).

Standing Committee on Procurement and Federal Facilities Council, *Electronic Commerce for the Procurement of Construction and Architect-Engineer Services: Implementing the Federal Acquisition Streamlining Act,* National Academy Press (1997).

Stearns and Stearns, *Programming Microsoft Office 2000 Web Components,* Microsoft Press (1999).

Sterne, Jim, *Advertising on The Web,* Que (1997).

Sterne, Jim, *Customer Service on the Internet: Building Relationships, Increasing Loyalty, and Staying Competitive,* Wiley (1996).

Sterne, Jim, *World Wide Web Marketing: Integrating the Web into Your Marketing Strategy* (2nd Ed), Wiley (1998).

Stevens, Perdita, and R. J. Pooley, *Using UML: Software Engineering With Objects and Components,* Addison-Wesley (1999).

Strauss, Judy and Raymond D. Frost, *Marketing on the Internet: Principles of Online Marketing,* Prentice Hall College Division (1999).

Sudweeks, Fay and Celia T. Romm, *Doing Business on the Internet: Opportunities and Pitfalls* (Computer Supported Cooperative Work), Springer-Verlag (1999).

Sullivan, Robert L., *Electronic Commerce with EDI,* Twain, Inc (1998).

Szuprowicz, Bohdan O., *E-Commerce: Implementing Global Marketing Strategies,* Computer Technology Research Corporation (1999).

Szuprowicz, Bohdan O., *Extranets and Intranets: E-Commerce Business Strategies for the Future,* Computer Technology Research Corporation, (1998).

Szuprowicz, Bohdan O., *Webcasting Strategies: Effective Push Technologies for Intranets and Extranets,* Computer Technology Research Corporation (1998).

Szyperski, Clemens. *Component Software: Beyond Object-Oriented Programming.* Addison-Wesley. 1998. ISBN:0201178885.

Tan, Felix B., Scott P., Corbett and Yuk-Yong Wong, *Information Technology Diffusion in the Asia Pacific: Perspectives on Policy, Electronic Commerce and Education,* Idea Group Publishing (1998).

Tapscott, Don, *The Digital Economy: Promise and Peril in the Age of Networked Intelligence.* McGraw-Hill (1995).

Tapscott, Don, et al. *Blueprint to the Digital Economy: Wealth Creation in the Era of E-Business.* McGraw-Hill (1998).

Tapscott, Don (Editor), *Creating Value in the Network Economy,* Harvard Business School Press (1999).

Targowski, Andrew S., *Global Information Infrastructure: The Birth, Vision, and Architecture,* Idea Group (1996).

Taylor, Jim, Watts Wacker and Howard Means. *The 500-Year Delta: What Happens After What Comes Next*, HarperBusiness (1977).

Testerman, Joshua O., *Web Advertising and Marketing*, Prima Publishing (1998).

Thurow, Lester C., *The Future of Capitalism: How Today's Economic Forces Shape Tomorrow's World*, William Morrow (1996).

Torok, Gabriel , Troy Downing and Paul M. Tyma. *Java Primer Plus: Supercharging Web Applications With the Java Programming Language*, Waite Group (1996).

Treese, Winfield G and Lawrence C. Stewart, *Designing Systems for Internet Commerce*, Addison-Wesley (1998).

Troy, Carol, *Understanding Electronic Day Trading*, McGraw-Hill (1999).

Turban, Efraim, Jae Kyu Lee and David King, *Electronic Commerce: A Global Perspective*, Prentice Hall (1999).

U.S. House of Representatives, *Electronic commerce and interoperability in the national information infrastructure: hearing before the Subcommittee on Technology, Environment, and Aviation of the Committee on Science, Space, and Technology, U.S. House of Representatives, One Hundred Third Congress, second session*, ASIN: 0160459087, (1994).

Valesky, Tom, *Enterprise Javabeans: Developing Component-Based Distributed Applications*, Addison-Wesley (1999).

Van der Linden, Peter, *Just Java 2* (Java Series), Prentice Hall (1999).

Van Der Linden, Peter. *Just Java*. Prentice Hall (1997).

Van Der Linden, Peter. *Not Just Java*, Prentice Hall (1997).

Vartanian, Thomas, H., Robert Ledig and Thoman P. Ledig and Lynn Bruneau, *21st Century Money, Banking & Commerce*, Fried, Frank, Harris, Shriver & Jacobson(1998).

Vassos, Tom, *Strategic Internet Marketing*, Que (1996).

Vogel, Andreas, and Madhavan Rangarao, *Programming with Enterprise JavaBeans, JTS, and OTS*, John Wiley & Sons (1999).

Wadman, Barry, *The Microsoft Merchant Server Book,* Ventana Press (1996).

Ware, James, Judith, Gebauer, Amir Hartman and Malu Roldan, *Search for Digital Excellence,* McGraw-Hill (1998).

Warmer, Jos B. and Anneke G. Kleppe, *The Object Constraint Language: Precise Modeling With UML,* Addison-Wesley (1999).

Watson, Mark, *Intelligent Java Applications for the Internet and Intranets,* Morgan Kaufman (1997).

Watson, Mark, Java *Programming for Windows: Using Microsoft AFC, WFC, and XML,* Academic Press-Morgan Kaufmann (1998).

Wayland, Robert E and Paul Michael Cole, *Customer Connections: New Strategies for Growth,* Harvard Business School Press (1997).

Wayner, Peter, *Digital Cash: Commerce on the Net,* Ap Professional (1997).

Weinzimer, Philip, *Getting It Right!: Creating Customer Value for Market Leadership,* Wiley (1998).

Westland, J. Christopher and Theodore, H. K. Clark, *Global Electronic Commerce: Theory and Cases,* MIT Press (1999).

Whinston, Andrew B., Dale O. Stahl and Soon-Yong Choi, *The Economics of Electronic Commerce,* Macmillan Technical Publishing (1997).

Whitmire, Scott A., *Object-Oriented Design Measurement,* Wiley (1997).

Wieringa, Roel J., *Requirements Engineering: Frameworks for Understanding,* Wiley (1996).

Williams, Al and Woody Leonhard, *Steal This Code!: Create Reusable Software Components for Windows 95 and Windows NT*/Book and Disk, Addison-Wesley (1996).

Wirfs-Brock, Rebecca, B. Wilkerson and Lauren Wiener, *Designing Object-Oriented Software,* Prentice Hall (1990).

Wright, Benjamin and Jane, K Winn, *The Law of Electronic Commerce,* Aspen Publishers Inc (1998).

Wright, Benjamin, *Law of Electronic Commerce EDI, Fax, and E-Mail: Technology, Proof, and Liability,* Aspen Publishers Inc. (1994).

Wyckoff, Richard D., Andrew Wyckoff and Alessandra Colecchia, *Economic and Social Impacts of Electronic Commerce,* OECD (1999).

Yannopoulos, Georgios N., *Modeling the Legal Decision Process for Information Technology Applications in Law* (Law and Electronic Commerce, Vol. 4), Kluwer Law International (1998).

Yesil, Magdalena, *Creating the Virtual Store: Taking Your Web Site from Browsing to Buying,* John Wiley & Sons (1996).

Zahavi, Ron, *Application Integration with CORBA: Enterprise Solutions Using Components and the Web,* John Wiley (1999).

Zahavi, Ron, *Systems Integration With Corba,* John Wiley (1999).

Zeff, Robbin and Brad Aronson, *Advertising on the Internet,* Lee, John Wiley (1999).

Index

About the Authors

Peter Fingar is one of the industry's noted experts in component-based electronic commerce and an internationally recognized author. He is Technology Advocate for EC Cubed where he provides leadership, technology direction and liaison with industry standards organizations and strategic technology and business partners. He has held technical and management positions with GTE Data Services, the Arabian American Oil Company, American Software and Computer Services, and Perot Systems' Technical Resource Connection. He served as Director of Information Technology for the University of Tampa and as an object technology consultant for IBM Global Services. Peter has written six books on computing, presented conference papers worldwide, and published numerous professional articles in *CIO Magazine, Component Strategies, Object Magazine, Sun World Online* and *Datamation*. He taught graduate and undergraduate university computing studies in the United States and Saudi Arabia. As a practitioner, his systems development experience was gained in diverse industries and spans technology generations from unit-record to Web Object Computing. He has played an active role in promoting the commercial applications of object-oriented and intelligent agent technology for competitive advantage. Peter is a long standing member of the IEEE Computer Society and the Association of Computing Machinery (ACM), and assists the Object Management Group with its representation in the Middle East.

Harsha Kumar is co-founder of EC Cubed and serves as the Director, Product Strategy. His current responsibilities include driving technology strategy and alliances, as well as product roadmap for EC Cubed. He is a frequent speaker at professional conferences relating to e-Commerce technology. Harsha was responsible for crystallizing EC Cubed's vision of "application components" into the ecWorks™ suite by driving and leading the product specification, design and development functions. Mr. Kumar also worked with clients including GE Capital Vendor Financial Services, TransAmerica Leasing and the GartnerGroup on their e-Commerce strategies and implementations. He plays an advisory role in the CommerceNet Catalog Inter-Operability Pilot project. While at GE Capital, Mr. Kumar was a Lead Architect on the industry's first B-to-G.com, "SourceOnline". He has worked in several R&D organizations including Bellcore and the HCI Lab at the

University of Maryland. While at Bellcore, Mr. Kumar developed supply chain applications for inventory planning and replenishment for the Bell companies. His work with Prof. Ben Shneiderman on hierarchical visualizations has been published in international journals. Mr. Kumar received a Bachelor of Technology degree from the Indian Institute of Technology, New Delhi, and an MS in Systems Engineering from the University of Maryland.

Tarun Sharma is co-founder of EC Cubed and serves as Director, Product Management. His current responsibilities include evolution of the ecWorks™ product line and evangelism of component-based computing architectures for e-Commerce. Mr. Sharma is an authority on component technologies and has been published widely in professional magazines. He has co-authored another book, *Programming Web Components*, published by McGraw-Hill (1997). Tarun is a popular speaker at industry conferences on e-Commerce and related technologies. He also represents EC Cubed at the Object Management Group. At EC Cubed, he has led client projects ranging from strategy, to implementation and rollout for several large-scale business-to-business initiatives. These include the GE-TPNRegister content aggregation portal, MasterCard's Commercial Card Gateway and American Express' @Work customer self-service portal. Prior to EC Cubed, Tarun developed portions of GE Capital's "SourceOnline," the industry's first B-to-G.com. While at ICL, Tarun developed financial applications for companies including the National Commercial Bank (Jamaica) and the Caribbean Development Bank (Barbados). Earlier, he taught Computer Science courses at NIIT and worked as a researcher on Artificial Intelligence-based Natural Language Processing at C-DAC, Pune, India. Mr. Sharma received his Bachelor of Engineering degree in Computer Science from the Pune Institute of Computer Technology.